Format Friction

NEW MATERIAL HISTORIES *of* MUSIC

A series edited by James Q. Davies *and* Nicholas Mathew

ALSO PUBLISHED IN THE SERIES:

Sex, Death, and Minuets: Anna Magdalena Bach and Her Musical Notebooks
David Yearsley

The Voice as Something More: Essays toward Materiality
Edited by Martha Feldman and Judith T. Zeitlin

Listening to China: Sound and the Sino-Western Encounter, 1770–1839
Thomas Irvine

The Search for Medieval Music in Africa and Germany, 1891–1961: Scholars, Singers, Missionaries
Anna Maria Busse Berger

An Unnatural Attitude: Phenomenology in Weimar Musical Thought
Benjamin Steege

Mozart and the Mediation of Childhood
Adeline Mueller

Musical Migration and Imperial New York: Early Cold War Scenes
Brigid Cohen

The Haydn Economy: Music, Aesthetics, and Commerce in the Late Eighteenth Century
Nicholas Mathew

Tuning the World: The Rise of 440 Hertz in Music, Science, and Politics, 1859–1955
Fanny Gribenski

Music in the Flesh: An Early Modern Musical Physiology
Bettina Varwig

Creatures of the Air: Music, Atlantic Spirits, Breath, 1817–1913
J. Q. Davies

Sounding Human: Music and Machines, 1740/2020
Deirdre Loughridge

Format Friction

Perspectives on the Shellac Disc

GAVIN WILLIAMS

THE UNIVERSITY OF CHICAGO PRESS
CHICAGO AND LONDON

The University of Chicago Press, Chicago 60637
The University of Chicago Press, Ltd., London

Published 2024
Printed in the United States of America

33 32 31 30 29 28 27 26 25 24 1 2 3 4 5

ISBN-13: 978-0-226-83324-8 (cloth)
ISBN-13: 978-0-226-83326-2 (paper)
ISBN-13: 978-0-226-83325-5 (e-book)
DOI: https://doi.org/10.7208/chicago/9780226833255.001.0001

Library of Congress Cataloging-in-Publication Data

Names: Williams, Gavin, author.
Title: Format friction : perspectives on the shellac disc / Gavin Williams.
Other titles: New material histories of music.
Description: Chicago : The University of Chicago Press, 2024. | Series: New material histories of music | Includes bibliographical references and index.
Identifiers: LCCN 2023044870 | ISBN 9780226833248 (cloth) | ISBN 9780226833262 (paperback) | ISBN 9780226833255 (ebook)
Subjects: LCSH: Sound recordings—History.
Classification: LCC ML1055 .W44 2024
LC record available at https://lccn.loc.gov/2023044870

⊚ This paper meets the requirements of ANSI/NISO Z39.48-1992 (Permanence of Paper).

Contents

INTRODUCTION

Friction into Format

Around 1900, dozens of Western record companies were in busy competition over the emerging gramophone market. Flat circular discs, and the hand-wound, clock-sprung machines needed to play them, established a rival sonic format to the phonograph cylinder and had already begun to flourish.[1] Spun at seventy-eight revolutions per minute, the shellac disc had become an industrial standard even while the gramophone itself remained a novelty. With its flared metal horns yet to be submerged in plush wooden cabinets, the instrument remained conspicuous in wealthy homes; in public spaces such as churches and restaurants, it was still worthy of ironic comment.[2] On the cusp of becoming an established musical format, disc technology was, however, already a global undertaking. From the start, record companies recruited vocal artists, musicians, and comedians from home and abroad. Sound studios were set up in US and European urban centers, while elaborate recording expeditions were undertaken, reaching Western colonies and beyond.[3] These tentative musical infrastructures, which drew on well-established colonial networks for transport and trade, were created to capture sounds that might sell among different linguistic and ethnic groups. Such were the political and economic conditions in which the shellac disc, as a format, emerged: within an acoustic hall of mirrors, assembled and motored by imperial capital, which strove to mediate localities on a global scale.

Yet the recording of sounds was only one element in the making of a global format. Along with the sounds captured, this book addresses the environments plundered, the materials seized, the ears entangled. It interrogates the gendered international divisions of labor and knowledge involved in such activities as studio recordings, factory work, disc circulation, and ultimately listening itself. It examines from a global perspective, and in a selective way, the objects and agents animated by an historical form of listening, homing in on an elaborately controlled encounter between needles and discs.[4] In other words, it presents a necessarily messy portrait of the dominant sound format of the first half of the twentieth century. Individual chapters will go on to examine aspects of the format's materiality (shellac), political economy (empire), earliest transnational celebrity (Caruso), regional coverage (in South Wales) and metaphysics (existentialism).[5] Across these areas, a returning theme will be the shellac disc's modes of multiplying relations between listeners and sounds.

I will be concerned with the years between 1900 and 1950, as the format peaked in terms of global dominance.[6] But I should say at the outset that I do not offer or aspire to a synoptic view. Instead, my aim is to rekindle historical perspectives on the shellac disc through a set of local encounters. I want, in other words, to reanimate a "dead" format: one that, in terms of cultural memory, has been buried beneath thick seams of vinyl, magnetic tape, compact discs, and, more recently, streaming.[7] Nowadays, shellac discs are remembered almost exclusively by self-appointed experts: a coterie of music scholars, sound archivists, and record collectors. Through these experts' connections with powerful museums, certain discs have come to stand for the sonic heritage of countries and nations, as well as ethnic groups across diaspora, even while the disc itself has become an object of curiosity when presented to a wider public. For this last reason especially, the shellac disc presents a challenge to historians.[8] Forgotten by the many, yet familiar to the point of second nature to experts, it has become hard to think about—beyond loose analogy with later sound formats, with their better-remembered patterns of distribution and listening habits—as a once-living format, with sprawling, messy, and uneven histories.

Not everyone has forgotten the format, though, even as firsthand memories become ever rarer as the years go by. The following passage comes from the oral history of Tan Tong Seng (陈仲生, b. 1929) conducted at Singapore's National Archive in 2004. Tan worked for Radio Malaya after the Second World War, and as a distinguished broadcaster, he was invited to recall his life on record in his mid-Seventies. Sound reproduction technology came up in his recalling of his childhood in Singapore:

> At that time there were already cassettes, something called . . . not [like] our cassettes, you know? In the past, there was this kind of rotating cylinder, very old, a cylinder cassette made from coils. But it was not for the general public's use; mostly family-run workshops were using it for commercial purposes, or for military purposes. But they used to use this [cassette] to get [the songs] and then put them on records, or something else, [so that the songs could be] imported into [Singapore]. Some people who knew music would also transcribe them into scores; well, then it would spread out. Very quickly you would get hold of these songs (*laughter*). This "Yellow River Chorus," I hadn't yet graduated from the elementary school,

> probably the fourth grade, [and] I already knew how to sing it. How old was [I] then? [. . .]
>
> Before the war my mother was a housewife, so my father was working, leaving home early in the morning and coming back late at night. Then she was [alone] with us kids. She was really bored, you know? My father knew this, [so he] bought a gramophone, the kind of gramophone that needed to be wound up manually, for her to listen to. But [we] had no money to buy records, [so] every day or two, there were people on tricycles who came with a lot of records to be rented, to rent out [the records]. It was like, per record, [I] can't remember, one or two cents each? You went and [took one home to let it] sing, finished singing it, then took it back [to the tricycle], switched [to some other records and then] took them home again. So at that time, I used to listen to Zhou Xuan's songs a lot; [I] also [listened] to these anti-Japanese songs thoroughly; [the records] were all 78 rpms, all were listened to using the gramophone. Wow, at that time, most of the anti-Japanese songs had already been recorded on those 78 rpm discs. Before the war there were already 78 rpms, issued by EMI.[9]

Recalled across more than half a century, Tan's memories of both wax cylinders and shellac discs are wonderfully detailed (see the interlude in this book for more on the topic)—and I'm grateful to Min-Erh Wang for listening to this passage, along with several others from oral history interviews conducted in Mandarin, and to Xiaoyan Tan for the above translation.

Tan conjures the phonograph for a twenty-first-century interviewer in the shape of a "cylinder cassette": a master record imported into Singapore from China, which could then be converted into to shellac discs by clandestine means. Tan goes on to say that both cylinders and discs were expensive—that they were beyond the means of ordinary people, such as his family, even while ownership of gramophone machines was more prevalent. This cost barrier (a decisive aspect of the shellac disc throughout its career as a format, as we will see) could be overcome in creative ways. Local arrangements for the renting of discs sprang up in Singapore, as Tan notes, together with the practice of copying lyrics and transcribing music into notation by hand. Noteworthy, too, is the way in which fast-changing political regimes crowd Tan's memories of sound reproduction. He makes passing reference to British censorship of Chinese political songs, and notes anti-Japanese songs that circulated on disc during the 1942–45 Occupation. While particular, of course, to Singapore's history, the close connection between sound on record and geopolitics turns out to be a constant feature of gramophone memories.

Tan's recollections are typical of the ways in which gramophones and phonographs were remembered by those for whom the format had once been part of everyday life: as frictional encounters. "Bored" housewives and rental systems, cost barriers and censorship—these were some of the many different forms of productive resistance to listening in the heyday of the shellac disc. In the passage above, the scratching of pencils in the transcription of songs hints at handwriting as a generative component in the circulation of song-on-disc (a notion borne out by other oral histories I will examine later, in this book's interlude). Such details highlight something easily overlooked in comparing shellac discs with subsequent formats like LPs and CDs, and can illuminate them in turn: the frangible practical and economic conditions under which shellac discs were accessed. For example, a dominant fantasy of digital music streaming is that of unlimited access on demand; but for the vast majority, such freedom of access is often troubled by mobile phone costs, incompatible devices, patchy internet connections, and endless ads, to say nothing of access to the electrical grid.

Materials

Another place to begin thinking about shellac discs historically, alongside oral history, is their materiality. In this section, I want to begin by recalling some basic characteristics. Shellac discs are spiral-grooved flat plates, usually tinted black, weighing around two hundred grams (half a pound) each. They comprise a uniform mixture of mashed minerals and powdered rocks—most commonly slate, limestone, barytes, and lampblack—melded together with clay, gum copal, and shellac—that is, "natural" plastics.[10] The background hiss that accompanies the playback of 78s (what Theodor Adorno called the *Hörstreife*, the acoustic stripe) has a distinctly stony, granular quality: it sounds like a brush sweeping over a rock. Shellac discs were widely produced in two sizes, ten and twelve inches in diameter, which played for roughly three or five minutes each side (almost all discs made after around 1905 were double-sided, or duplex; before that, they were mainly single-sided). As has often been pointed out, this time limit structured gramophone listening in important ways; some have even suggested that it set the mold for the length of the average pop song.[11]

Another aspect of the shellac disc's materiality, no less decisive if less often rhapsodized, was the precision-drilled central hole, which allowed discs to sit on the gramophone turntable without wobbling. It "centered" listening in a literal way, allowing for playback that unfolded smoothly and predictably. Around this hole was pasted a circular paper label showing the disc's catalog number and basic information: details of performers, song titles, musical genres, and so on.[12] The paper labels displaced an earlier practice, once common on both shellac discs and wax cylinders, of having an announcer speak the metadata, telling the listener who was performing, at the beginning or end of a recording. In an age before liner notes, paper labels provided a minimal textual supplement. This textual minimalism opened wide vistas of imagination between recording and playback, context and sound—opening spaces for imagination between listeners and music.

How did the disc come to take a round, flat form? Here I must heed the format's inventor, Emile Berliner. He claimed that the shape—though not the material composition, which was the product of trial and error—was conceived in a flash of discovery. Around ten years after Edison invented the cylinder-playing phonograph, Berliner conceived an alternative projection of a grooved coil: on a flat plate. He demonstrated proof of this concept before an audience of scientists at the Franklin Institute in Philadelphia on 16 May 1888 in a lecture-cum-performance consisting of "songs, recitations, and instrumental solos."[13] These sounds were projected from metal plates, initially named phonautograms, which Berliner famously predicted would find applications in the teaching of languages and elocution, in relaying political speeches, and, most importantly, in allowing "singers, speakers or performers" to derive an income from royalties.[14]

Berliner's story is well known, not least because he often told it himself in interviews and public demonstrations. What is more, as Jonathan Sterne has shown, Berliner's narrative was a typical North American inventor's tale of "male birth," which presented the technology as the brainchild of an especially fertile late-Victorian genius.[15] Still, it is worth noting details of Berliner's story that cut against the grain. In contrast to later tellings of the disc's invention, which stressed the advantages of discs over cylinders for mass reproduction (discs could be stamped, cylinders could not), in this early version Berliner presented discs—to differentiate them from wax cylinders—as a means of fixing the human voice more securely, in a harder medium, to render it more enduring and profitable as intellectual property.[16] As he put it, "Addresses—congratulatory, political or otherwise—can be delivered by proxy *so loudly* that the audience will be almost as if conscious of the speaker's presence."[17] It was promise of volume, then, rather the idea of mass reproduction, that inspired the creation of the disc format. (This detail is significant because histories of sound reproduction technology—which narrate the phonograph ceding to the stampable, "mass"-reproducible disc—are structured as quasi-evolutionary stories, the trimmer format outlasting the bulkier one.[18] Berliner's comment suggests, by contrast, that there was nothing obvious or inevitable about such a development.)

An increase in volume required, among other things, an increase in friction between needle and groove. This points to the central dilemma, and a major engineering problem, for the disc as a format under construction. After all, more friction implies more wear; yet Berliner wanted gramophone records to be durable, ideally even permanent engravings of sounds. After his demonstration of metal plates, he went on to experiment with celluloid and vulcanized rubber: plastic materials that could aspire to these at-odds values of volume and durability. In a previous career at the Bell Telephone Company, he had overseen a change from hard rubber to shellac in the making of telephone handsets.[19] Recalling this episode, he commissioned (from a factory that made electrical fixtures) the pressing of a disc from a nickel matrix and was encouraged by the result: "Because the material was harder than hard rubber, the reproduced sound was louder and more crisp."[20] The shellac mixture "proved at once a great success," and the rest was history—or so he claimed in 1913, on the twenty-fifth anniversary of his invention, when he was invited to return to the Franklin Institute to reminisce.[21]

Even as the shellac disc took on a standard shape and shellac became the standard source of their plasticity, shellac mixtures were never stable.[22] An ideal balance of plastics and mashed minerals to resist the immense pressure exerted by needles in the groove remained elusive:

> Few people have a conception of the untiring efforts which have been made year after year, and still continue, in order to obtain a composition which will answer all the requirements necessary for resisting the wear of the needle or prevent the latter from being ground blunt too fast. If the material is too hard and gritty it will wear the point of the needle, so that before the end of the record is reached the reproduction becomes weak and blurred. If the material is too soft the record groove will quickly wear rough and the record reproduction become scratchy.[23]

Neither too hard nor too soft, the Goldilocks mix was never found, despite endless tinkering with "mineral and fibrous" adulterants by "experts who do nothing else all the year around but test substances and the mixing processes which are employed for producing record material."[24] To put this another way, the regulation of friction was not the kind of problem that could be solved once and for all, but remained open-ended; it gave rise to an entire field of industrial research.

Format

Beneath a consistent appearance, the shellac disc was always changing. This observation takes us to the heart of recent conversations about the nature of formats, sonic and otherwise. As Marek Janovic, Axel Volmar, and Alexandra Schneider point out in a recent edited volume, formats exist in the spaces between infrastructures of industrial production and those of consumption.[25] At once concepts and practices, formats emerge in the interstices "between the content and material constraints of media, the local and the translocal, individuals and collectives, intended and unintended use."[26] While the concept of format has roots in nineteenth-century art history (Jacob Burkhardt, for example, once described how the canvas as a format prevented painting from "dissolving into endlessness"), it has more recently become a more widespread category of scholarly interest, together with the proliferation of formats in digital life—formats that comprise the busy interface between society and capitalism in the twenty-first century.[27] As Sterne observes in a book on MP3, format shapes user experiences more profoundly than does media technology, since it is format that encodes the rules as to what may and may not travel between different devices—and where travel is possible, in what ways (streaming, downloading, editing rights, and so on).[28] At the same time, formats serve business interests in extending ownership over content across virtual spaces. Inspired by Sterne's work on .mp3, Janovic, Volmar, and Schneider argue more broadly that formats are always "sites of condensed power, power struggles, and valuable commodities" in their own right.[29]

Developed for the study of digital culture, format theory embraces older formats as well. The film scholar Erika Balsom has demonstrated how format theory can be "tremendously useful for the study of analog media, as it entails adopting a more granular level of analysis than is conventional."[30] In a study of Polavision, an instant home movie system, Balsom shows how format theory invites us to break down clunky assemblages—such as "photochemical film," often discussed as if it were one thing—"to reveal the varied technologies encompassed by this category and the diverse experiences and ecologies to which they give rise."[31] I will be taking a kindred approach to shellac in chapter 1, which takes an assemblage apart and puts it back together again, as an historical method to explore how listening experiences and political environments are mutually constructed. Following Janovic, Volmar, Schneider, and Sterne, I will be examining the overlapping levels, particularly "the local and translocal," through which the shellac disc became a "site of condensed power"—a nexus where sounds congealed into vehicles of multinational capitalism, an ascendant force globally around 1900, and also a means of challenging political and cultural authority.

Through my focus on the shellac disc, I hope to suggest fresh ways of thinking about formats more generally. I want to suggest that, because it hails from well before the digital present, the shellac disc can help probe the limits of format theory—in particular, the field's tendency to isolate individual formats by way of the standards and rules they bring into effect. Given the illusory weightlessness of digital formats, this tendency is understandable and has a clear purpose: to expose the heavy, dirty material interests that lie embedded within them. Format theory aspires to unmask formats, which acquire a "sheen of ontology" that hides their true natures as cultural constructions.[32] This approach makes good sense when it comes to .mp4, .docx, and so on, which are composed of computer scripts and shot through with power relations, and whose inner workings are opaque to most users.[33] At the same time, however, analog formats encourage us think over larger spans of time. For in the long run, the standardization of 78-rpms benefited consumers—that is, people who could afford to buy them—who could play discs from multiple companies on a single machine. Such "interoperability" increased within the gramophone industry as the twentieth century went on, as power was consolidated in the hands of well-to-do listeners.[34]

More broadly, the shellac disc highlights an area of format theory indicated by Janovic, Volmar, and Schneider that so far remains largely unexplored: the cultures of use through which formats are made and remade. Alongside standards and rules—and in tandem with attempts to shape and monetize consumer desires—there is the roiling sedimentation of practices that co-shape formats in turn. To get traction on this aspect, friction can be useful on multiple levels. Not only was friction an open-ended problem within the gramophone industry, as previously discussed; it also defined the experience of shellac discs for listeners, who were obliged to replace needles constantly as they became blunt. No mere annoyance, something that might ideally be factored out from the experience of disc listening, friction was the very basis of sound production in early sound reproduction technologies. If Berliner strove to improve on the phonograph in creating a louder and yet more durable format, then diverse practices of using shellac discs involved new ways of engaging with sound as friction.

In taking friction as a point of focus—an elemental materiality of sound shaped through cultural practice—sound reproduction technology takes on different historical aspects. On the one hand, a friction-based perspective helps to further undermine well-known stories of triumphal newness, which likes to tell the history of sound reproduction technology as a series of vaunted North American inventions. Instead, friction calls attention to the primal source of sound production, which has no clear beginning: it encourages us to think of gramophones and discs, together with phonographs and cylinders, as friction-handling devices among others such as violins, kazoos, and turkey callers.[35] On the other hand, and more narrowly, friction can invite a change of perspective on sound reproduction itself. It is worth noting in this connection that gramophones and phonographs were often regarded as musical instruments in the early twentieth century, and that the people who played them were cast as performers (see chapter 2), even prototype DJs. Here, the significance of sound reproduction consisted not only in the copy's relation to the original—in the notion of *re*producing sounds—but also and more fundamentally in the copy's relation to the copy. From this angle, the historical importance of shellac discs and wax cylinders may be understood to lie in having inaugurated a new form of social control over sound-as-friction by making it possible to summon a series of sounds that could be multiply repeated: a cascade of copies.

It might be worth taking a moment to consider how a frictional perspective might also inflect ways in which sound reproduction has come to be understood in recent decades, in the age of sound studies. In *The Audible Past* (2003), Sterne importantly showed how clunky devices such as phonographs and telephones relied on an illusion of reproducing "original" sounds.[36] As he argued, such originals did not precede their copies, but were retroactively constructed through an emergent discourse of sound reproduction. In calling attention to the original/copy binary, Sterne highlighted technology as a target of deconstruction (though, as mentioned above, his work has since moved away from a critique of media devices, leading the way in the study of formats). By contrast, friction helps foreground the many ways in which sounds on disc or on cylinder were handled: played, repeated, dubbed, pirated, rerecorded, worn out, replaced, thrown away, or more respectfully retired.[37]

My interest in cascades of copies finds a parallel in my home field of music studies, which has undergone a similar shift of attitude in regard to sound reproduction. Nearly thirty years ago, Steven Feld examined "pygmy POP" as the severing of sounds from their sources and as a political technique of domination, according to which Western pop musicians expropriated and monetized musics of the Fourth World.[38] Feld importantly redefined sound reproduction as "schizophonic mimesis"—that is, a way of instrumentalizing the separation between copy and original to entrench neocolonial power. Since Feld's article, ethnomusicologists have largely abandoned schizophonia as a framework for interpreting the politics of sound media.[39] As Benjamin Piekut and Jason Stanyek have pointed out, the splitting of sound from source is not specific to sound reproduction technology but a property of all sonic experience.[40] They have proposed "rhizophonia" as a term better suited to technologies like the gramophone, where the decisive factor lies in the unpredictable proliferation of copies themselves.[41]

Along similar lines, Michael Denning has underscored the unpredictable spread of shellac discs in his book *Noise Uprising*.[42] Homing in on the decade between 1925 and 1935—a period that saw the introduction of electrical microphones in recording studios and a step change in the vividness of sounds reproduced—Denning has shown how a revolutionary consciousness was stimulated by the gramophone, as port cities became newly audible to each other through the movement of shellac discs along global shipping routes. These novel paths created an "archipelago of colonial ports," which circumvented imperial metropoles and allowed for a new kind of vernacular popular music.[43] By speaking and singing in common tongues—endlessly plural, yet united through their difference from official European languages, and loosely connected through musical gestures and sounds, such as the steel guitar—this recorded popular music established a worldwide political culture. Denning argues that the shellac disc brought about the "decolonization of the ear" and the dancing body, prefiguring, in aesthetics, the waves of political decolonization that followed the Second World War.

Denning highlights a moment of synergy between musical creativity and an emerging technology of mass production, given new life by the carbon mic. In contrast to much work in musicology and sound studies, which often stresses the negative aspects of capitalism at play in the recording industry—such as Feld's article, discussed above, which emphasized the expropriation of local music by multinational record companies—Denning has shown how sound-on-disc could give rise to novel forms of expression and anticolonial resistance. He cites Jacques Attali as a forebear in his approach to the sociology of music, and indeed, Attali's sometimes problematic influence is apparent when Denning stresses the music-technological underpinnings of political revolution.[44] However, there is another—and, for music scholars, more generative—category of interest in *Noise Uprising*, in the political geography of listening. Alongside his interest in singers and composers and the changing means of (sound) production, Denning calls attention to playing, listening, and dancing to discs. By focusing on patterns of use, he reveals colonial ports as nodes in an imperial network, showing how the practice of sound reproduction bears a close and at times oppositional relation to political power.

Second Natures

My interest in this book in sideways relations between copies—the shapes and patterns through which reproductions spread—also stems from changing priorities within sound studies, as infrastructures of listening have risen up the agenda in recent years. It has become pressing, for example, to identify the ways in which sounds draw from deep wells of labor and natural resources, while impacting and transforming broader political environments. As Alexandrine Boudreault-Fournier and Kyle Devine propose, "natural resources and infrastructural developments are tied to music as an aesthetic practice," and there are "very real environmental costs to music making and listening, including the aggregate effects of data streaming, music production and concert touring"—to name some of the more conspicuous examples.[45] Within this scholarly context, and as the Anthropocene exerts pressures all around, the goals of sound studies shift, even move in reverse. After attempts to reveal the cultural scripts that form the DNA of technologies and formats, the central issue now becomes to understand how cultural scripts harden into second natures and so take on wider political and environmental significance.

In this spirit, I return to the gramophone, long a key object of analysis in sound studies, to ask what shellac discs can tell us about the congealing (second) natures of sound and listening.[46] My suggestion will be that discs impinge directly on nature/culture distinctions because, as a format, they highlight a zone of overlap in which those distinctions were made and remade. In other words, discs were emblematic of exchange and use, at once embodying and enabling specific transformations between energy and sound. As architectures of friction, discs marked the tipping point between infrastructures of listening and sensory experience. For this reason, I will endeavor to approach discs—if not always grammatically, then conceptually—in the plural, as formatted objects that repeated, multiplied, and interpolated social relationships in countless ways.

Another brief word on method may be helpful. This book comprises a series of investigations, each chapter offering a detachable perspective on format. Rather than engage the heroic fiction of the scholar who expends their energies focusing on a single, well-defined topic, I want to allow a complex object to fracture forms of scholarly attention and modes of analysis. The modular construction that results corresponds to an historical method and set of assumptions. Notably, I will be taking it as read that the most interesting moments in the life of the shellac disc as a format lie in the middle, and I will try to take slices from across this history, rather than try to narrate its origins and endings. To put this more abstractly, my assumption is that formats are the products of non-dialectical synthesis, as assemblages of materials and ideas that come into relation in ways that are complex and changing, yet specific and nonreducible.[47] Here I borrow terms from Deleuze's early writings, which offer a set of ideas with which to redescribe hardening ontologies as multiplicities.[48] In these terms, formats can be thought of not as things but as complex relations between things and ideas—with the implication that that a format, like any hardening ontology, cannot be adequately grasped from any one perspective, but is better understood through the switches in perspective it makes possible.

The claims I am advancing about formats may sound familiar to musicologists from another area of music research. For example, Ana María Ochoa Gautier has argued that the legacies of structuralism in anthropology and ethnomusicology should be revisited in the current ecological crisis—not to denounce the environmental impact of musical consumption, significant and destructive as it often is, but to reanimate foundational questions about the nature of sound itself.[49] Ochoa Gautier wanted to disarm a dominant politics that frames nature (in the singular) as a resource for, and the unchanging basis of, cultures (in the plural). Drawing on the writings of Eduardo Viveiros de Castro, she proposed that multinaturalism be contrasted with multiculturalism as a framework for ecomusicology and music studies more broadly, which needed to re-examine the acoustic assemblages within which aurality is enmeshed.[50] As though to counter-effect the climate emergency as it bears on the sonic disciplines—by insisting on the urgency of resisting urgency, and of taking time to think—Ochoa Gautier suggested a programmatic focus on the acoustic/aural as a liminal zone in which perspectives switch, and as a prime site where distinctions between nature and culture emerge and do political work.

More than a decade on, Ochoa Gautier's proposals remain provocative and, for the most part, undigested by music studies and sound studies alike. In calling on the writings of Viveiros de Castro—whose body of work itself is based on, yet of course is incommensurable with, a theoretical outlook inherent in indigenous cosmologies of the Amazon—the idea of acoustic multinaturalism remains hard, and likely impossible, to assimilate, so deeply ingrained are vibrational ontologies and epistemologies across the sonic disciplines.[51] Anticipating the scope of this challenge, Ochoa Gautier closed her 2010 article with the suggestion that indigenous cosmologies might be of particular interest to sound scholars who want to challenge dominant scientific descriptions of sound's nature(s)—even while she noted that it would be undesirable for sound students suddenly to "go native."

Alternative ontologies also nestle and roost within Western modernity, of course.[52] And this book singles out the shellac disc as a site of ontological difference, and thus as one place to investigate sound's nature. After all, the shellac disc has been a much-used tool for constructing sound's nature, not least in sound studies itself. As Andrea Bohlman and Peter McMurray point out, the interdiscipline of sound studies was erected over a "phonographic regime": one that has cohered around a set of cylinder- and disc-derived concepts including inscription, indexicality, storage, and preservation.[53] To topple this regime, Bohlman and McMurray explore alternative ideas—such as rewinding, overdubbing, and the fluidity of memory—that arise from a tape-centered epistemology. Their work evokes important connections between media and the sonic ontologies they sustain, and proposes switching the medium of sound theory to tape.[54] For similar reasons, but by different methods, this book instead returns to the gramophone in an attempt to decenter the phonographic regime from within.

I will be suggesting that friction was not only central to historical experiences of the format, but also an important alternative ontology of sound. As the twin of reproduction, friction underscored the energetic source of sound production, together with constant if microscopic transformation at the material level. Emerging as sound at the interface between needles and discs, machines and infrastructures, friction was also a catalyst of multiplicity: nonreducible relations between materials, listeners, and politics. In this sense, sound as friction pinpoints another way of hearing the gramophone—an aural switch from sound reproduction to production that might occur at any moment of listening—and suggests other possibilities for thinking about sound more broadly. On the one hand, to rethink sound through friction returns sonic inscriptions to their material forms and energetic sources.[55] On the other, friction provides the accompanying shadow of vibrational ontology, evoking the techniques and infrastructures of control through which sounds achieve political ends.

Friction

There is yet another way in which friction might productively decenter sound theory; and here this book's case study of the shellac disc opens out onto matters of broader scholarly interest. As Anna Tsing showed in a famous ethnography of deforestation, friction has particular affordances and holds certain advantages for thinking about entangled histories and cultures.[56] As a metaphor, it invokes the generative tension between universalist projects, such as capitalism, rationality, and freedom, and local cultures as they coproduce political realities in collision. In Tsing's often-cited words, friction points to the "awkward, unequal, unstable, and creative qualities of interconnection across difference" as an ongoing process within global cultures.[57] Such thinking has special force when directed toward sounds. As both metaphor and material practice—the results and causes of different kinds of friction—sounds create and enact moments of interconnection across difference. Paying attention to friction as an acoustic ontology, even and perhaps especially where it goes unremarked, gives grist to sound theory writ large.

To illustrate this last point, consider the following statement, which opens a justly celebrated handbook of sound studies: "Sound is vibration that is perceived or becomes known through its materiality. Metaphors for sound construct perceptual conditions of hearing and shape the territories and boundaries of social life."[58] The authors, David Novak and Matt Sakakeeney, make their intervention clear: sound is culturally inflected vibration, hovering at the boundary between nature and culture. What is more, they interpose metaphor and materiality as key domains that structure listening and, more broadly, all modalities (such as touch) by which vibrations come to be perceived as sounds. However, there is an acceleration from the first sentence to the second: between the identification of sound with vibration and the ushering of sounds into the realm of perception. It is as though the second sentence rushes to contain the implications of the first—as if, after hovering at the sticky edges between nature and culture, it is necessary to contain sound once more in the world of social life.

What if sound not only belongs to the world but creates other worlds? Novak and Sakakeeney gesture towards this possibility when they write that "metaphors of sound" can "shape territories and boundaries." Latent here is the potential that our aim as sound scholars should go beyond explaining how vibrations and listening connect under the umbrella of social life, to consider how sounds may make other worlds. No doubt there are many ways of doing this, but I want to suggest that friction as a scholarly epistemology—one conveniently installed within dominant scientific descriptions of sound's nature as vibration—might, after Tsing, call attention to this generative aspect of sounds as the products and results of collision.

This is of course not the place to explore the many and various ways in which friction, as a material and metaphor, might be of use to music and sound studies. I hope that in mentioning it here, I will allow readers of this book to understand my approach to the shellac disc as a case study for basic questions of more general interest. But I cannot resist gesturing toward another moment in the long history of sonic theorizing that might be productively revisited in this vein. I refer to a tract by the scientist-philosopher Charles Babbage: "On the Permanent Impression of Our Words and Actions on the Globe We Inhabit" (1837). Babbage put forward the case for understanding the cosmos as a palimpsest of "words and actions," remaining forever retrievable, if only by divine ears:

> The pulsations of the air, once set in motion by the human voice, cease not to exist with the sounds to which they give rise. Strong and audible as they may be in the immediate neighborhood of the speaker, and at the immediate moment of their utterance, their quickly attenuated force soon becomes inaudible to human ears.[59]

Babbage went on to imagine a vibration circling the earth, returning to its point of origin in, he calculated, twenty hours. Like a pebble thrown into a lake, vocal sounds ripple outward with a decaying half-life, even while the wave itself is never fully extinguished, but lingers on in a quivering atmospheric archive: "The air itself is one vast library, on whose pages is for ever written all that man has ever said or even whispered."[60] In words prescient of the digital twenty-first century, or even—if we allow undying sounds to stand for carbon molecules—climate breakdown, Babbage remarked, "What a strange chaos is this wide atmosphere we breathe!"[61]

Together with his 1854 campaign against street nuisances—a notorious rant against the Italian organ grinders and German brass bands who toured his neighborhood in London's Manchester Square—"On the Permanent Impression of Words and Actions on the Globe We Inhabit" comprises Babbage's enduring gift to sound studies. John Picker, for one, has read Babbage's insistent materialization of sound as characteristic of the broader Victorian soundscape in its twin drives toward control over and preservation of voices and other sounds, and as a pre-reverberation of the sound reproduction technology to come later in the century.[62] But of course there was also a strongly mystical side to Babbage's planetary vision. He wanted to use sound to re-enchant a world fallen prey to scientific calculation—of the kind that he himself pioneered.[63] More particularly, he sought to respond to Charles Lyell's calculations of the weight and epochs of the earth, by presenting a materialist cosmos invested with spirit, one that could reconcile geological thinking with Christian theology.

The result of Babbage's synthesis was the hope of a frictionless world. He took to extremes, and to the point of parody, the assumptions of vibrational ontology in summoning sounds that could fade but never die.

According to his imagination, the universe became the unfailing amanuensis of all that humans (and indeed nonhumans) ever did or uttered. Babbage even went so far as to claim that augmentations of human listening should lead to moral cleansing. In a typically idiosyncratic contribution to romantic sensibility, he held that access to a wider field of amplitudes would inevitably attune the soul, which surely could never stand the injury of wicked sounds slowly fading upon its ears. As esoteric as all this might seem, it might nevertheless ring a bell in terms of broader argumentative strategy. With a sleight of hand that music scholars will likely recognize, sound provides for flight into an ideal world, a world without friction—a world much harder to access, even imaginatively, in sound's absence.

In this connection it is worth comparing the passage from Babbage's *Ninth Bridgewater Treatise*, quoted above, with another, taken from his "On the Elevation of Beaches by Tides":

> If the earth were a spheroid of perfect revolution, covered by one uniform ocean, two great tidal waves would follow each other round the globe at a distance of twelve hours. Suppose several high strips of land were now to encircle the globe, passing through opposite poles, and dividing the earth into several great unequal oceans, a separate tide would be raised in each. When the tidal wave had reached the farthest shore of one of them, conceive the causes that produce it to cease; then the wave thus raised would recede to the opposite shore, and continue to oscillate until destroyed by the friction of its bed.[64]

With water in place of sound, and ridges of land in place of open air, the influence of friction becomes unavoidable, even in this abstract mental exercise. A shift (merely?) in the imagination, it is a shift that the present book pursues in sound itself. Through sustained reflection on the disc rather than on Babbage's tidal sphere, I hope to evoke a more general reorientation in sonic thought toward the productive, if ever-exhaustible, frictions of the material encounter.[65]

Histories of Listening

The chapters that follow aim to use and apply friction, to put pressure on the role of discs in the history of listening. Each in a different way strives to slow down discs, to render them available for detailed inspection at various stages in the course of their manufacture, recording, playback, listening, storage, and disposal, and in their recollection later in the twentieth and twenty-first centuries. My hope is to find strange new places for recorded sounds in histories of listening: to show how sound reproduction technology not so much transformed listening but multiplied spaces between listeners and sounds. While the book spins out in different directions, the following chapter summaries outline a common thread in exploring the many kinds of "interconnection across difference" (to recall Tsing's words) that friction brought about through the formatting of sounds.

Chapter 1 puts the brakes on shellac itself. It shows how lac—the resinous encrustation of an insect as well as a technique for preserving things over time, widely cultivated by Adivasis and other rural groups in central and northeastern India—became shellac, a global commodity, in the age of European empire, and went on to aid the development of the gramophone industry. Tracking the activities of British colonial forest officers, entomologists, and biochemists, it circles in on a scientific bureaucracy that promoted the study of the lac insect during the gramophone's 1920s heyday, and shows how musical demand intensified a system of migrant, indentured, and technical labor involved in processing lac into shellac. At the same time, it underscores the limits of British colonial intervention in Indian forests, suggesting that lac continued to rely heavily on rural and indigenous knowledge even while shellac was the product of entangled knowledge systems (industrial, scientific, political, and musical).

While the first chapter explores interconnection across difference between listeners and shellac producers, chapter 2 examines the friction-filled gaps between recording and playback. Within a larger network of recorded sound that was still under construction, it homes in on a tentative connection between the London-based Gramophone Company and a department store in Singapore. In this context, it considers the activities of the famed recording experts Frederick Gaisberg and George Dillnutt in their parallel function as traveling corporate executives, striving to establish the shellac disc as a multicultural and quasi-universal form of sonic exchange. It argues that roving recording experts embodied forces of multinational capitalism in the period around 1900. At the same time, the materiality of sound recording productively resisted their efforts: wax masters routinely became degraded by mold during their transit across the oceans, arriving at disc-pressing plants across Europe and in India in unusable condition. What is more, it proved difficult to attract Singapore's Chinese, Indian, and Malay customers even as Singapore's relatively tiny British and European colonial class became enthusiastic consumers of sounds imported from their home countries.

Chapter 3 interrogates a well-known gramophone tale: that of the famous opera singer Enrico Caruso, who was the first recording artist to draw listeners to the medium in mass numbers. By focusing on format rather than medium, and on friction rather than vocal magnetism, it asks after what made Caruso a reproducible person. On the one hand, it reveals Caruso as a singer deeply invested in his own celebrity across the media of caricature, sculpture, film, and opera house, and, in this sense, as someone who exerted considerable agency over his own reproduction. On the other, it explores how such reproductive investment resonated with interlocking networks of opera fans and the Italian diaspora in New York. As I show, it was only in death—and through the writing of history—that Caruso's voice came to assume its dominance in stories of early recorded sound, as tales of his body (and of the powerful association with the Italian diaspora it had once represented) faded from memory.

Chapter 4 considers the bumpy interface between the working classes and shellac discs in South Wales during the late 1920s, a time of crisis and depressed wages in the coal industry that gave rise to an historic nine-day, UK-wide general strike in May 1926, which continued for several months in coal-mining regions. With many men and women suddenly thrown out of work, protests and carnivals became widespread in South Wales, together with an explosion of so-called "jazz bands" playing "gazookas." These musical instruments, kazoos with horns, functioned as gramophones manqués: a low-tech, low-cost means of reproducing sounds in a time of extreme hardship. By examining local newspapers alongside fictional works by Gwyn Thomas, a novelist from the Rhondda valley who lived through the Miners' Lockout as a child, I go on to consider the place of the gramophone in the later 1930s, a period of economic recovery brought about by the politics of rearmament, together with the tentative connections between working-class listeners and shellac discs that emerged at this later moment.

Chapter 5 zooms in on the connection between a famous disc and a notorious listener: Antoine Roquetin, alter ego of Jean-Paul Sartre in his debut novel *Nausea* (1938). Taking the form of a series of diary entries, this novel tracks Roquetin's growing obsession with "Some of These Days," a jazz record he discovers in a local café—a disc that provides him with a remedy against a series of progressively worsening attacks of psychotic dizziness that render him unable to distinguish between people, objects, and sense impressions. By contrast, the shellac disc represents predictable temporal succession, in bearing witness to the immortal event of a performance that Roquetin imagines and vividly hallucinates, but can never grasp. In his fervid imagination, he infamously mistakes the race and ethnicity of both singer and composer—evoking endemic ambiguities of listening across difference in the shellac network.

As this scatterplot summary of the chapters can suggest, they shuttle between many different perspectives, alternately emphasizing what shellac discs were and what people made of and with them during the first half of the twentieth century. In other words, there will be busy traffic between material and metaphorical kinds of friction in the pages that follow. Rather than accidents of scholarly slippage, I hope this movement will suggest a more deliberate strategy, which tries to derive concepts from historical discourse and material practice. Such friction-based traffic is clearly illustrated in chapter 5, which examines how a particular shellac disc was interwoven with claims about the nature of reality. However, a close interplay between the physical and metaphysical emerges in other chapters, each of which investigates how infrastructures and practices gave rise to political frictions of different kinds. Whether in the plans of corporate executives, in the cult of an opera singer, or in the mouths and ears of the South Wales proletariat, friction signals the many ways in which sound was managed, channeled, and put to unexpected use.

CHAPTER 1

Shellac as Musical Plastic

Around 1920, an early silent film about the making of gramophone discs was released. Plainly entitled *Making a Record*, it was an industrial documentary avant la lettre, offering a series of novel views on an everyday-sounding object.[1] An establishing shot twenty-one seconds into the film reveals the inside of a recording studio. We see a female singer accompanied by a violinist, a clarinetist, a flutist, and trumpet players who are all crammed around a horn suspended in midair, funneling musical vibrations toward a rotating wax disc.[2] These performers are accompanied by a sound technician, centrally located, who holds the horn from below while looking at the singer's mouth. The singer, who goes unnamed in the film, stares back at him, adjusting her tone in response to his facial cues. Everyone looks a bit on edge. Perhaps the nerves were due to the presence of the film camera and crew, together with the jitters commonly reported in early experiences of the recording studio.[3]

Having shown the performers and technicians, *Making a Record* goes on to track the outcome of their collaborations in the wax impression, which is "graphited and placed in a special bath," to quote from the intertitles. A man brushes a blackened comb over the wax, then dunks the wax in the bath, where it builds up a metal coat that eventually forms into a hard shell, later to be peeled away, releasing the negative impression: the master record. This master is then reinforced with a steel back in preparation for stage three, the pressing of the records themselves. Several shots show men in flat caps feeding large clumps of a molten mixture—"shellac, lampblack and clay," to quote again from the intertitles—through huge motor-driven mangles, flattening the material into sheets. The purpose is to render the material pliable, ready to be pressed out. The molten mixture is encased, together with the master and a paper disc label, within a steel pocket, and then is sealed and compressed under hydraulic pressure. A closing shot shows a record slowly rotated before the camera by a faceless worker.

With this display of the final product, *Making a Record* comes to an end. It has guided us along a chain of industrial processes and material encounters, from musical input to manufacture, culminating in the widely known, if less widely owned and used, sonic commodity. The gramophone record turns out to be both familiar and full of mysteries—mysteries that this new kind of industrial film can both outline and pleasurably solve.[4] But of course, *Making a Record* inevitably leaves much out. By tracing the disc back to the moment of performance, it omits the labor that made studio recording possible (at one end, the musical composition and rehearsals; at the other, the heating of the wax and readying of the turntables). In its overriding interest in factory work, metals, and mold making, the film also elides the infrastructures on which such work relied: the international, gendered division of labor involved in stamping records, along with the larger colonial networks of resource extraction needed to supply the disc's materials.

This chapter tells a new story about the making of records, one that ventures beyond the industrial frame of *Making a Record* and other documentaries, a frame shared by pioneering work in the field of sound studies.[5] Rather than looking again at Western science, engineering, and musical performance, I home in on an often overlooked aspect of the disc's materiality: specifically, those black clumps of molten mixture fed through the industrial rollers glimpsed in the film. Among other things, that mixture could contain crushed limestone, slate, barytes, and other mashed rocky minerals; lampblack collected from industrial smokestacks; and a resinous sap called gum copal.[6] All these materials invoked global supply chains, and each gave discs certain physical traits. The ground rocks were sourced from countless locations, providing frictional resistance against the pressure of gramophone needles.[7] Lampblack—also known as carbon black, a fine soot—could be gathered wherever fossil fuels were consumed. It blackened discs and gave them a consistent appearance, helping to create the impression of a uniform commodity, despite widespread variability in their material composition.[8] Gum copal is derived from the accretion, over the course of centuries, of sap from the *Daniellia* tree of West and Central Africa, and became a global commodity with the rise of the Indian Ocean slave trade in the nineteenth century; it worked as an adhesive in the heterogeneous ensemble of disc materials.[9]

I have left until last the component of the mixture that will be my focus in this chapter. This is shellac, the chief binding agent within gramophone discs and across the gramophone industry's colonial architecture. While never the main disc material in terms of physical mass, shellac became essential for their making; it could not be readily substituted, and when supplies dwindled, the industry faltered. This industrial dependence had fundamentally to do with shellac's plasticity, a physical property that was itself the result of elaborate manufacture, enabling the material to take the shape of sounds, holding and preserving them over time. As a varnish, shellac had been produced for centuries if not millennia; it originated in forests around the Indian Ocean, and derived from the resinous secretion of the lac insect that inhabits those forests.[10] First as a luxury commodity, then as a run-of-the-mill component in the nineteenth-century paint industry, shellac changed over time to become increasingly thermoplastic in response to musical and electrical industries that demanded precision molds. It was an important component in the making of gramophone discs, and the history of its manufacture reveals yet again the crucial role of non-Western environments and knowledge systems in so much Western industry.[11]

Environment, Empire, Friction

Despite the historical centrality of shellac, it has become a topic of interest only recently through the rise of ecocritical approaches to sound media.[12] Jacob Smith presents shellac as an environmentally friendly material, drawing a comparison with the more polluting formats that were to follow, such as vinyl, CDs, and digital streaming.[13] While agreeing that shellac is indeed biodegradable and thus in some ways preferable to synthetic plastics, Kyle Devine has instead underscored the material's human and environmental costs: the systems of colonial extraction by which countless workers, insects, and trees were expended in the name of musical consumption.[14] What is more, shellac established a long-standing pattern of musical consumerism, one that relied on disposable materials and people, and resulted in the endless buildup of media waste. Elodie Roy explores this afterlife of shellac as "vibrant matter" embedded in larger socionatural cycles of renewal and decay.[15] She puts forth infrastructural thinking about shellac—the processes through which the material is assembled and constantly reassembled in light of the present—in order to "excavate and *recirculate* repressed or buried issues, most notably the colonial question."[16]

Guided by these explorations, this chapter interrogates shellac's history as a musical commodity, further investigating the labor conditions on which mediated listening experiences depended. I intend, however, to make new spaces in shellac's history for the agency of workers, both as the bearers of technical knowledge and as political actors. And it is here that this book's interest in friction resonates most powerfully: in the grinding of cogs between knowledge systems—scientific and Adivasi, and those of colonists and laborers, listeners and makers.[17] By the 1920s, the gramophone industry accounted for 30 to 40 percent of global shellac yields, creating a dynamic bond between users of musical media and mostly Indian shellac workers—Adivasi cultivators of lac, other rural workers in a widely distributed shellac cottage industry, and shellac factory laborers mainly in Calcutta.[18] While lac cultivators remained insulated to a significant extent from global market forces, rural and urban factory-based shellac workers were largely indentured to their employers and thus were more dangerously enmeshed in the circuit of imperial capital. These exploitative labor practices were typical of colonial economies, and constitute an important vector of the material's history—but were not the only ones. Shellac work also involved far-reaching technical knowledge, and could be a means of resistance to capitalist and colonial forms of authority.

Writing ahead of a wave of newer materialisms, Arjun Appadurai famously proposed a focus on commodities and the politics of knowledge they enfold, as a way to interrogate potentially global cultures. Rather than privileging local meanings of exchange, Appadurai advocated allowing the forms, uses, and trajectories of things to illuminate relations within and between societies.[19] This approach has come in for some criticism, in particular from ethnomusicologists, because commodified things—as nonhuman actants that create human societies through their exchange—may paradoxically be overlooked in terms of their material effects and forms of nonhuman agency.[20] Appadurai nevertheless highlighted a dimension of materiality that has faded from more recent scholarly turns to the post- and nonhuman. By stressing the "complex forms and social distributions of knowledge" involved in commodities, he famously expanded their remit beyond Western industrial society.[21] He called fresh attention to the processes that things—often luxury articles such as museum artifacts, tourist art, and fashion—underwent as they moved in and out of the commodity state, as a way to highlight the politics inscribed across swaths of economic, physical, cultural, and epistemological distance.

As a global commodity, shellac was embodied and embedded in both industries and environments; it thus points to the epistemological entanglement of the gramophone as a sound reproduction technology. To put this another way, shellac was the material in which one set of techniques—those for making plastic—interfaced with and sharply switched into another—those for musical listening.[22] While this second set of techniques is more or less familiar to musicologists and sound students, the former is perhaps less so.[23] Yet cultural techniques of production, however distant, mundane, or even uninteresting they may sometimes be, are nevertheless central to musical materiality. The production of shellac for the purpose of gramophone records, for example, overloads even the most inclusive or expansive definition of "musicking" as a social activity (to name one of the more celebrated accounts of musical ontology presently in circulation).[24] Instead, it can suggest a more disjunctive material conception of music as worldly thing: one produced in friction between knowledge systems and along complex global supply chains.[25]

Along similar lines, global historians of science have recently stressed the need to find and acknowledge the multiple objects and sites of knowledge production.[26] This is a pressing issue for historians of the nineteenth and twentieth centuries in the wide orbits of European empire, where one-sided accounts stemming from the archives of colonial science preponderate.[27] Kapil Raj, for example, has urged historians to note the constant implication of bodily practices in knowledge systems of all kinds, which coproduce scientific knowledge through "the encounter and interaction between heterogeneous specialist communities of diverse origins."[28] In a musical register, shellac can be understood in this way: the material itself is more than a colonial archive. Its familiar presence in disc collections around the world constitutes a dispersed latter-day monument to the knowledge practices and patterns of circulation that underpinned the gramophone industry during the first half of the twentieth century.

The global dispersal of shellac as a commodity across wide-ranging musical archives (past and present, domestic and official) also speaks more pointedly to frictions between knowledge systems—to the abrupt switch between the sets of cultural techniques of production and listening adumbrated above. After all, gramophone discs most often did not circle back to shellac workers and makers; musical consumption was in this sense a terminal stage in the material's commodity journey.[29] In the pages that follow, I track this path and the switch to musical use, which has broad implications for thinking about shellac, the gramophone, and sound reproduction technology writ large.

Varnish into Plastic

Shellac's journey must begin in the middle of things. Its very name embeds another material: lac, the resinous encrustation produced by the lac insect, a substance cultivated mainly in South and Southeast Asia. The word "lac" derives from the Sanskrit *lakṣa*, the number one hundred thousand—an etymology that seems to refer to the material's genesis in the insect multitudes that swarm twice yearly on certain trees.[30] But "lac" also denotes a product of human labor, one that has to be harvested, removed from the trees on which the encrustation develops.[31] Shellac is a material derived from lac; it can more easily be measured, bought, and sold. These two words, "lac" and "shellac," mark interconnecting histories that unfold over different timescales. By far the more ancient word, "lac" occurs in the Sanskrit epic the *Mahābhārata*, in a tale about a house specially designed to go up in flames and kill its inhabitants.[32] More than two thousand years later, lac appears in a more familiar guise in a lengthy account of Akbar's court, as a building material for varnishing wood and in the name of a category of workers who "varnish reeds etc. with lac" in the Mughal Empire.[33]

"Shellac" (an English condensation of the French *lacque en écailles*, or lacquer in shells) is a much more recent coinage: it and its cognates are first found across early modern Europe. Shellac is mentioned, for example, in Daniel Defoe's *A New Voyage around the World by a Course Never Sailed Before* (1725). A story inspired by contemporary narratives of global circumnavigation—and designed to enthuse British readers about establishing a new East India Company—this work listed shellac among the "solid Goods" worth "spending Money for" in India: "The necessary or useful Things are Pepper, salt Peter, dying Woods and dying Earths, Drugs, Lacks, such as Shel-lack, Stick-lack, etc., Diamonds, and some Pearl, and raw Silk."[34] As a species of commodity, "shel-lack" was born of global trade; and, as the context in which Defoe's novel was written demonstrates, the word emerged through Western colonial multinationalism.[35] In Defoe's list, shellac appeared among other commonly desired Indian commodities, and in ready contrast to "stick-lack" (lac still attached to the twigs on which the lac insect feeds). "Shel-lack" specified the flakes or shells, the result of removing and refining the insect's hard encrustation—of grinding, washing, melting, purifying, stretching, and shattering lac. Neither lac nor shellac were natural products, then. Both are better described as "socio-natural commodities," to borrow the environmental scholar Nancy Peluso's term; neither had any "significant use or exchange value unless . . . industrially treated."[36] Shellac, however, passed through a greater number of industrial processes, and thus concentrated a greater quantity of human labor.

Lac continues to be traded to this day, but the rise of shellac in the seventeenth and eighteenth centuries highlighted an important historical shift. Whereas Mughal lac could be a varnish used as a building material in the land of its origin, shellac was an Indian commodity sought after by European colonial powers. In other words, it rebranded lac as a material for export, processed and awaiting future use, sometimes far from the places in which it was made. Early accounts mention shellac as a material used in conjunction with wax to seal letters, and as an ingredient in japanning (European lacquer work) and French polish.[37] It was applied to wooden floors, furniture, and musical instruments such as guitars, violins, and harpsichords.[38] In this way, shellac shaped both the acoustics of various musical instruments and, much more broadly, the way elite spaces sounded and felt. A luxury commodity applied—and, as it wore down, intermittently reapplied—to other luxury commodities, "vernice indiana" (Indian varnish) mediated the touch of tables and chairs, the way footsteps rebounded on wooden floors.[39]

By the nineteenth century, both lac and shellac were consumed at scale. In India, Pakistan, and elsewhere, age-old traditions of lac-turnery—a technique by which shellac is applied through friction against a rapidly rotating object—flourished, supporting a growing industry in jewelry and wooden toys.[40] Around 1850, however, shellac (some processed from lac in India, some in European factories) also took on global importance in the paint industry. For this purpose, the material was newly traded in "Standard T. N. bags" and "Standard T. N. cases," where "T. N." signified "Truly Native," a trademark and colonial brand referring to the material's Indian origins.[41] Shellac continued to fulfill many older purposes—for example, it remained key in the hat industry in stiffening wool and fur to make felt—but toward the end of the century, it was also applied in Western electronics industries where precision molds were needed. In particular, shellac became the major binding agent within a class of "hot molded organic materials" for the making of switches, handles, telephone handsets, and gramophone records.[42] Within a fast-changing industry of protoplastic mold making, it was widely deployed to impart qualities of flexibility and resistance.[43]

The word "plastic" entered the discourse on shellac in the early twentieth century, concurrently with the rise of synthetic resins. Key in this regard was US experimentation with celluloid as an industrial substitute—in the making of clothes, combs, and dental plates—where "natural" materials such as rubber and shellac were in short supply.[44] Celluloid, in spite of its origins in camphor laurels and pine trees, was widely understood as being more artificial than the materials it was meant to replace, largely on account of the conspicuous role of chemical research in its manufacture.[45] As Wiebe E. Bijker has shown, celluloid supplied nascent research into plastics with a "technological frame"—a set of concepts shared by a community of scientists and industrial engineers, together with the series of interactions and exchanges between them.[46] This technological frame defined materials research around 1900, and created the paradigm within which synthetic plastics developed.

But celluloid also reshaped the uses of and expectations regarding older materials such as shellac. Once understood mainly as a varnish, it could now be reinterpreted as natural plastic. Through comparison with celluloid, shellac was reimagined as a product of nature's laboratory, while the lac insect itself came to be understood as a kind of chemical factory productive of diverse commodities. In a passage attached to a hand-drawn sketch of a 1920s biplane, shellac was presented as "essential in aeroplanes, electrical appliances, insulating materials, and in the manufacture of phonograph records. It is also used in the manufacture of buttons, grinding wheels, oil-cloth, dominoes, poker chips, linoleum, imitation ivory, mica products, shoe polishes, sealing wax, stiffening for hats."[47] This typical passage comes from Elizabeth Brownell Crandall's *Shellac: A Story of Yesterday, Today and Tomorrow* (1924). Traveling through past, present, and future, Crandall presented a romanticized view of the material and its uses, calling attention to shellac's South Asian origins while underscoring its pervasiveness in everyday life in the West. She doubly recast shellac as an ancient, exotic varnish and as a hypermodern plastic. The above passage enacted this transition and expansion from varnish into plastic; the listed items shapeshift—grinding wheels into oil cloth into dominoes, and so on—as if to invoke shellac's plasticity and fire enthusiasm for untapped potential.[48]

In the parade of shellacked objects in Crandall's list, phonograph records came next to airplanes, electronics, and electrically insulating materials, musical use providing a link between older and more futuristic applications. By the middle of the twentieth century, however, records had become, for the most part, a historical concern within this discourse. In a manual written in the 1950s, the shellac promoter and engineer Edward Hicks outlined the ebb and flow of the record business, with the production of shellac tethered to its changing fortunes: rising at the birth of the gramophone industry in the early twentieth century, falling at the advent of radio, rising again in the 1930s with the "rebirth of the phonograph record business" following the Wall Street Crash, but then falling off once again with the interruption of shellac supplies during the Second World War. Wartime shortages had long-term effects and shellac continued to be prohibitively expensive, permitting "great inroads by synthetic resins such as vinylite, ethyl cellulose and polyvinyl compounds," which ultimately enabled the production of LP records.[49]

Looking back at a historical industry, and alert to the synthetic plastics that displaced shellac for musical use, Hicks offered an archaeological account of how gramophone discs were made that highlighted shellac's plasticity. Largely technical in scope, his manual homed in on the kind of shellac required: it had high fluidity, long life under heat, a low wax content, and a low content of insoluble matter—qualities found only in high-grade shellac.[50] Like Bakelite, high-grade shellac was prized for its capacity to become malleable and then quickly solid without significantly changing shape as its temperature rose and fell—while only gradually wearing down the metal stamper that gave it shape.[51] Hicks located shellac retrospectively as a moment within a longer history, describing its value for the gramophone industry in terms of its protean thermoplasticity.

Insect Narratives

As musical use of high-grade shellac increased in the first half of the twentieth century, the material demanded a greater quantity and intensity of Indian labor, with important consequences for the industries and environments in which both lac and shellac were made. The testimony of botanists and entomologists—who tried and often failed to increase yields—can illustrate some of these changes. Shellac researchers have left behind an extensive paper trail, a typically one-sided colonial and scientific archive in which the interests of British imperialists largely, though never entirely, eclipsed Indian knowledge and labor.[52]

A comparison of a number of encyclopedia entries published around the turn of the century—the first set around 1890, the second in 1908—can illustrate this displacement of knowledge within the colonial archive. All were edited by Sir George Watt, the official reporter on economic botany in British India, and they present contrasting snapshots of lac and shellac, before and after the emergence of the gramophone as a musical medium around 1900. Watt's interest in the material was long-standing: he curated an enormous display for the Economic Chamber of the 1883 Calcutta International Exhibition, including a large section on gums and resins.[53] He went on to compile a monumental six-volume *Dictionary of the Economic Products of India* (1889–93), in which he included a long entry on lac and a shorter one on the insect, "Coccus lacca."[54] Watt synthesized current science on the insect and its parasites and pests, the distribution of lac across India and Burma, lac's chemical properties, and its manufacture and manifold uses. It is worth keeping his rubrics in mind; they recurred throughout his enormous *Dictionary* and were familiar categories in economic and colonial botany, helping to shape an enduring narrative about lac and shellac, one that flowed from nature to culture.[55]

Beginning with the insect and its forest habitat, Watt's 1890 *Dictionary* entry on lac moved on to discuss biology, industry, and finally human purposes, culminating in a lengthy, quasiethnographic discussion of Indian traditions of lac-turnery.[56] Along an arc from nonhuman nature to human users, human *producers* of lac did appear in the entry, but only briefly, as though squeezed in among botanic categories. For example, in a section on lac's distribution, in a subsection dedicated to the Central Provinces, he observed that

> large quantities of lac are found in all the districts of these Provinces, but particularly the Eastern parts. It has been stated that the Central Provinces could readily supply some 25,000 tons of stick-lac annually. A considerable amount is consumed locally for the manufacture of bracelets and other articles, but most districts also export to a greater or less [*sic*] extent. The incrustation is collected by jungle-tribes—Bahelyas, Rajhors, Bhirijas, Kurkus, Dhanuks, Nahils, Bhois, and some classes of Muhammadans—who sell the produce in small quantities to Patwas, who again retail it in larger quantities to the regular dealers.[57]

This passage constitutes one of the earliest descriptions of the many people involved in cultivating lac. Yet fewer than twenty years later, in Watt's *The Commercial Products of India* (1908), the names of different groups were replaced by a simple head count: he cited a census counting "2,592 persons" involved in "collecting" and "selling" lac in the Central Provinces.[58] Watt also commented that in living memory, lac had been transformed from a domestic into an export market in which "only a small quantity was retained for local use," even while the quantity of exported lac fluctuated markedly.[59]

At the same time as this shift to an export market, an important change in the epistemology of lac can be charted by comparing Watt's accounts across these decades, as it was increasingly understood less as a botanical resource and more as an insect product available for scientific intervention. Whereas Watt's *Dictionary* contained a long entry on lac and a supplementary one on the insect, by 1908 the insect—now given as "*Tachardia lacca*," the latest taxonomy—became the dominant category.[60] Updating and significantly lengthening former entries, this later article reorganized knowledge of lac around the insect. Cultivators were now mentioned in a subsection ("Central Provinces") of a subsection ("Distribution") within an article on the insect. At the same time, they became lac "sellers" and "collectors." Yet such categorization was significantly misleading, since lac could only be "collected" once it had been cultivated—for example, by tying bundles of twigs on living branches at certain times of the year, in such a way that the bundles could be untied at the time of collection.[61] Watt did not say so, but a wealth of techniques were involved in cultivating both trees and insects to make the encrustation develop on these detachable bundles, together with a depth of environmental knowledge informing where and when such cultivation took place.

A parallel story can be reconstructed for the workers who refined lac into shellac. Watt's *Dictionary* included a great deal of information on the complex activities involved in making shellac—but did so in a short supplementary article about the insect. His summary was written up largely in the passive voice: "Twigs are removed" from the trees; "the resinous crust is broken from the twigs"; "it is beaten with a wooden pestle or trodden under foot."[62] Matter-of-fact though his account was, Watt offered a degree of detail that might suggest direct observation. The granules were washed, purified, dried, and placed in bags ("10 feet long and 3–4 inches in diameter")—bags that were stretched across charcoal fires to melt, and then twisted and drained into specially constructed troughs. The molten yield was then forced through a cloth mesh, spread into sheets and dried again, and finally broken into shellac flakes. In all this, Watt described a formidable division of labor, but only indirectly gestured to the accumulation of knowledge it entailed.

Watt offered a similarly unpeopled account of shellac manufacture in 1908, one that was even more tightly focused on the insect. As formerly, he included hefty sections on the insect's life history, and on the distribution, chemistry, manufacture, and human uses of lac. But now the narrative led from the forest to the factory, introducing, among other things, the chemicals recently developed in modern methods of production.[63] This new emphasis gave Watt's article a prognostic bent, as though anticipating increased use of machinery in shellac manufacture—even though traditional methods were still the dominant modes of production and would remain so for decades to come. This 1908 article also included two new categories of entomological knowledge: a comprehensive account of the lac insect's appearance in human history, and an executive summary of international trade. Marking the rising value of shellac as a colonial export, these new sections bookended and significantly reframed older botanical ones, as Watt freshly mined Sanskrit and ancient Greek records of the lac insect to promote the consumption of shellac in millinery, lithographic ink, and, above all, gramophone records.[64]

As Watt's later writing reveals, the lac insect emerged as the protagonist within scientific accounts of lac and shellac at the turn of the century, as the many people involved in their production, only tentatively acknowledged within the frame of earlier economic botany, were reduced to the status of mere laboring bodies. Around 1900, men and women were routinely shown at work in drawings and photographs representing the division of labor. Figure 1.1, for example, which shows the skilled work of the lac stretcher (sometimes referred to as a Bhilwaya), comes from the extensive 1921 *Report on Lac and Shellac* compiled by two British scientists, Harlow and Lindsay, who were also colonial forest officers.[65] In

Figure 1.1 A diagram from Harlow and Lindsay's *Report on Lac and Shellac* (1921), showing the process of stretching lac.

their commentary on the image, these scientists constantly sought to distinguish between skilled and unskilled labor: "The chief operator in the firing room is the roaster or Karigar, a skilled and highly paid workman. He is assisted by the shellac stretcher or Bhilwaya, also skilled, and the bag twister or Phirwaya, an unskilled worker."[66] The purpose of such interest in skill was to illustrate the cost of the labor expended in the making of shellac. More bluntly, such science was a form of market research conducted in the service of Western capital.

Yet in giving an account of the skilled work of the lac stretcher, British scientists nevertheless recorded important connections between knowledge and labor—connections that pointed well beyond knowledge of the insect that the *Report on Lac and Shellac* more broadly advanced. For example, Harlow and Lindsay itemized the tools associated with the Bhilwaya—a "glazed porcelain cylinder 10 inches in diameter and 2 ft 6 inches long, full of warm water," a piece of cloth, and a strip of palm leaf. They also documented how each tool was used: "The Bhilwaya spreads out [the glutinous mass] on the cylinder with his palm frond, polishes it with the cloth, and then removes the sheet carefully from the cylinder. Seizing it with hands and feet and mouth, he stretches it from its original size of about 2 ft by 1.5 ft to about 4 ft or 5 ft by 3 ft or 4 ft, warming it in front of the fire every now and then to soften and anneal it."[67] Plain though this description is, it nevertheless retains a trace of the act of observation: of the heat. To be stretched, lac had to be melted over fires and molded over heated porcelain. In rural shellac manufacture, which took place in countless small factories known as *bhattas* (ovens), shellac was unavoidably hot work: lac could be stretched only within a limited window of time before cooling and hardening into sheets, which were then to be shattered into shellac flakes.

A thermal view of figure 1.1 might stress the entanglement of observer and observed in the production of knowledge. As a scientific diagram, it conveys the embodied knowledge required to convert lac into shellac—both the dexterity needed to smooth out the material and a capacity to withstand heat. At the same time, the image signals the dangers of heat and unhealthy working conditions that were not yet widely discussed, but which would become so in the decades that followed. Just after the Second World War, the government economist Bhalchandra Pundlik Adarkar published his wide-ranging *Report on Labour Conditions in the Shellac Industry*. Proceeding by region, Adarkar built up a picture of a "medium-scale, unorganized cottage industry" consisting of a widely distributed network of around five thousand bhattas worked by a fluctuating population of roughly twenty-five to thirty thousand men, women, and children—of whom he noted that the "overwhelmingly large majority of the workers were found to be indebted."[68] Additionally, there were roughly 360 shellac factories, mostly concentrated in urban centers, in which working conditions were perhaps only marginally better: while legislation to protect workers' rights existed, Adarkar concluded that "no labour law is properly respected in this industry."[69] Drawing a grim comparison between conditions in more prevalent rural bhattas and urban factories, Adarkar wrote,

> Environments of city life coupled with the din and dust of factory work are injurious to the health of the industrial worker, but the large-scale factories are subject more often than not (barring inadequate enforcement of labour laws) to severe restrictions, while in the case of the small-scale cottage industries, even if village or small-town life is in some ways more congenial to health and welfare, there is a greater element of sweating, of underpayment, of arbitrary dealing, and of general insecurity of work and rights.[70]

Adarkar noted that major strikes had taken place in one of Calcutta's largest factories, Angelo Brothers, in 1929 (lasting five weeks) and 1936 (lasting five months), while riots sometimes broke out at other factories. Yet the system of bhattas remained the dominant mode of production in 1945, sustaining a migrant workforce that moved between regions according to unpredictable lac harvests.

As for the cultivators of lac, it was not until the 1980s that an official account established the conditions of largely rural and Adivasi working practices. Titled *Dependence and Dominance: Political Economy of a*

Tribal Commodity, this report was the outcome of months of sociological fieldwork at a major center of lac cultivation in Jharkhand (what was then South Bihar) by another economist, Kamal Nayan Kabra. Kabra found that just under half of the people involved in gathering lac were Mundas, Kurukhs, and other scheduled tribes—the rest being nontribal (both Hindu and Muslim) rural groups. He also noted the involvement of women and children.[71] Acknowledging that lac had always been a secondary source of income for Adivasi and other rural cultivators, granting them a significant degree of autonomy from market forces, he nonetheless voiced a forceful critique of the political economy of lac: colonial and postcolonial governments had routinely sought to empower lac cultivators through technocratic intervention, consistently failing to interrogate the imperative of foreign demand that encouraged rural dependence on distant metropoles. Lac had come to be thought of as something made to be sent to the bhattas and then transformed into shellac for export abroad.

Both Kabra (in relation to lac) and Adarkar (in relation to shellac), though writing decades apart, made the same recommendation: Since India held a "virtual monopoly" over the material, owing to the insect's geophysical distribution, there was a pressing need to end dependence on foreign markets by reinvigorating local demand.[72] Alongside many other commodities, lac and shellac entered into a larger project of anticolonial and nationalist economic critique in which hitherto ignored cultivators and producers became newly important.[73] Lac insects, in other words, would lose some of their imaginative power in the postwar period, as discourses of rural development and labor practices became newly widespread. However, developmental proposals inspired by anticolonial critique often overlooked an important theme of the history of lac and shellac, since the colonial ideal of "manufacturing dependence" was only ever partly achieved. Whether due to parasites, pests, or political resistance, the shellac industry was beset by delays caused by bad harvests and deliberately neglected harvests, as well as by riots and strikes.

Colonial Knowledge and Its Limits

Urged on by wildly fluctuating prices back in London—in 1914 the price of shellac per hundredweight was three pounds; by 1920 it had reached an all-time high of fifty pounds—the Government of India's Forestry Department commissioned a wide-ranging investigation. Written up in 1921 as *Report on Lac and Shellac* (the very report by Forest Officers Harlow and Lindsay mentioned above), the study linked an unpredictable supply of the material to a lack of knowledge about the insect.[74] Such compulsive focus on the insect as the primary agent of production will by now be familiar, as will the forest officers' approach to lac cultivators. Typically, nowhere in their report did cultivators appear as bearers of knowledge about lac, being viewed rather as an underdeveloped labor force:

> When the price of lac is low trees may be neglected and production may fall off comparatively quickly; and production may be similarly affected through indolence of the cultivator if the agricultural season is good and he is obtaining full prices for his field crops. It thus happens that the margin of production in the case of lac is considerably wider and more elastic than is usual in the case of agricultural industries proper.[75]

Couched in the metaphors of liberal economics, this passage underscores the fact that lac cultivation was rarely a primary means of income for rural households, which depended more on wage labor and industrial agriculture; for rural cultivators, lac was a means of generating extra income in times of hardship, but could otherwise be ignored. After all, lac encrustations did not "go off," but might be left on trees to be harvested at some future moment.[76] What was needed, according to these British officers, was to create greater rural dependence on this forest product—a goal that, they believed, a more productive insect would inevitably bring about through supposedly universal laws of supply and demand. Scientific intervention in the reproduction of the lac insect would transform the forest environment, or so they anticipated, creating a surge in the activity of lac cultivation and harvesting, while increasing the dependence of cultivators on global market forces.

That was at least the plan. A few years later, on the report's recommendation, the Indian Lac Research Institute opened its doors. Its first director, the Manchester-born biochemist Dorothy Norris, assembled a team of research scientists consisting of four biochemists, four entomologists, and three physical chemists—each subject area headed by a British chief, but otherwise staffed by Indian scientists—along with three laboratory assistants, four fieldmen, an entomological photographer, a mechanic, five administrators, a librarian, and twenty-five "menial" staff.[77] Figure 1.2 shows a map included in Norris's book on the institute, which reveals that it occupied several laboratories, a staff club, a tennis court, a cook house and servants' quarters, a research library, experimental plantations, and a miniature lac factory.[78] This map provided a blueprint for colonial science, showing how political hierarchy—and entanglement—was built into the site's architecture. One of the oldest continuously running laboratories in India, the Lac Research Institute was established in Namkum, Ranchi (where it operates to this day as the

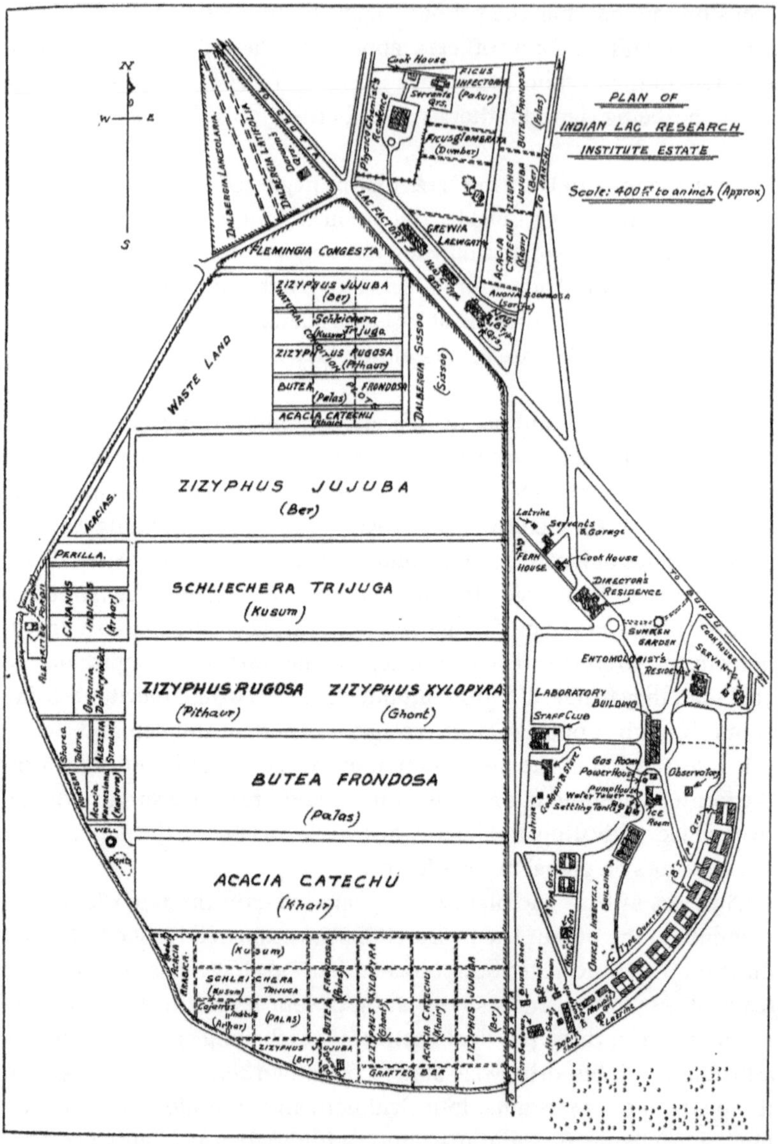

Figure 1.2 A map of the Indian Lac Research Institute showing experimental plantations, laboratories, residences, gardens, a staff club, a tennis court, a cook house and servants' quarters, a research library, and a miniature lac factory. In Dorothy Norris, *Lac and the Lac Research Institute* (Calcutta: Criterion, 1934), main stacks, TP939 N6, Doe Library, University of California, Berkeley.

Indian Institute of Natural Gums and Resins), taking advantage of its central position within the Chotanagpur forest plateau, at a midpoint between central and northeastern clusters of lac cultivation.[79] As the map of the grounds indicates, the institute was cordoned off from its surroundings by a high wall and security detail.

For the most part, the Indian Lac Research Institute did not engage lac cultivators, but focused on research into the physical, biological, and chemical nature of lac, and especially the lac insect's habitats, predators, and parasites. In 1934, ten years after the institute's founding, Norris reported on its activities: it had published more than eighty research articles and generated much new knowledge—notably the classification of multiple species of lac insects with complex, interlocking reproductive cycles. Old problems persisted, however. Recalling the reason for the institute's creation, Norris wrote that "crops are neglected when prices are low," cultivators still preferring to wait it out.[80] As before, parasites continued to feast on lac insects, who were themselves subject to the laws of an unpredictable climate.[81] To put all this more bluntly, colonial aspirations had mostly failed: a wealth of new scientific knowledge had neither incentivized cultivators nor much increased the yields of the forest.

In this sprawling colonial-scientific bureaucracy, the gramophone emerged as a central preoccupation and frequent cause of concern. By the 1930s, musical use had become the dominant motivating factor underpinning the scientific research; but it was also, in Norris's report, the occasion for anxious reflections on the future of shellac:

> The industries into which shellac enters are extremely numerous and diverse in character. The most important are the gramophone, electrical, and varnish trades and of these the first named now accounts for 30–40% of the annual lac output, but this amount is likely to decrease partly due to competition from substitutes and also to the introduction of new methods of sound recording. For high class gramophone records, those with a shellac base are still undoubtedly the best, but the production of these is likely to decrease for the reasons just stated.[82]

Norris projected corporate confidence in shellac's many uses, but felt that her institute was under threat from changing patterns of musical consumption. Anticipating the displacement of shellac by synthetic plastics coming largely from North America, Norris cast around for extramusical reasons to justify continued scientific research.[83]

This threat posed by the rise of synthetic plastics was more widely felt. The biochemist Motnahalli Sreenivasaya, of the Indian Institute of Science in Bangalore, predicted the imminent demise of the shellac industry as a whole.[84] In the journal *Current Science*, he sketched the bleak industrial outlook for 1932. Beginning, like Norris, by noting the violent fluctuations of the shellac market, he traced these back to the unpredictability of insect ecosystems.[85] He departed from Norris, however, in identifying human contributions to this situation. Rather than the "indolence" of cultivators, he attributed market fluctuations to the vagaries of foreign demand, and pointed to the gramophone consumer as a chief danger.[86]

The "ruinous crisis" Sreenivasaya predicted in the shellac industry, caused by a shift to plastics in the gramophone trade, did not come to pass until after the Second World War. But even in the 1930s, he clearly expressed a historical and political tendency in the material: its fateful co-option by foreign demand. As he put it, shellac had grown to be a major industry as the result of a broad and "greedy hunt for new raw materials from all parts of the globe" by Western colonial powers, leading to the neglect of local demand in recent times: "Bangle-making could have grown into the moulding trade, later developed in the West; the lacquer industry could have been built up . . . for metals and wood; but there existed neither the atmosphere nor the urge to elaborate industries based on the utilization of indigenous raw materials."[87] Sreenivasaya anticipated critiques of lac and shellac (outlined in subsequent decades by Adarkar and Kabra), and proposed a radical solution: "The remedy to this threatening situation is not in propaganda in foreign countries extolling the virtues of our raw material, but in building indigenous industries which will consume it in our own country."[88] Sreenivasaya's target here was perhaps none other than Norris's Lac Research Institute, which had recently established offices in London and New York to promote shellac and conduct market research in the major centers of consumption.[89] In opposition to such activities, he appealed to researchers to cease pandering to foreigners and to direct their efforts toward Indian markets as a matter of urgency "which bears heavily on the economic prosperity of the country."[90]

In calling for a change of scientific priorities from foreign to local demand—with a move away from a hungry gramophone industry—Sreenivasaya's writings are highly unusual within shellac's colonial archive. Not by chance, he showed a keen interest in the knowledge of cultivators, suggesting that scientists might learn from them. In a short article of 1935, he presented a quasi-ethnographic portrait of an unnamed village near Mysore (probably near Channapatna), aiming to distill local knowledge about lac, where "an adequate scientific explanation . . . cannot at present be given."[91] Such knowledge—for example, the ratio of top to root involved in pruning trees, and the insect's preferences for certain climates—was borne out by practice.[92] Yet Sreenivasaya also wrote about the customs followed by the men who spread lac insects on trees, noting that they were prohibited from taking oil baths and from shaving, in order to avoid "branches appearing clean shaven and besmeared with oil" on harvest day. On that day, milk was boiled beneath the tree in a new earthenware pot, and the vigor with which the milk boiled was taken as a sign of the future health of the host tree, a bubbling foam presaging the "white filaments characteristic of healthy and bumper crops."[93]

Sreenivasaya provided this rare glimpse of one set of local customs surrounding lac cultivation under the pretext of translating such traditional knowledge into modern science. His remark, for example, that the branches might appear "clean shaven and besmeared with oil" communicated a specific sense of unease that a tree might be lac-free on harvest day. Such words constituted an act of anthropological transcription, one that notated "superstitions" in the documentary mode required by a scientific journal.[94] Yet Sreenivasaya more fundamentally demonstrated the entanglement of scientific knowledge about lac (and hence shellac) in local beliefs, bodily practices, and on-the-ground observations.[95] He opened a window onto an epistemology in which "all lac-bearing plants" were haunted by evil spirits, and sacrifices of rams, goats, and chickens were practiced before solar and lunar eclipses—casting light on the conditions of lac cultivation at the height of the gramophone industry.[96] His description of animals laid to waste in the fields around Channapatna presents a complement to the scientific bureaucracy established in Namkum: he drew a contrast between, yet inadvertently sketched a continuity across, public research and appeasement of the evil spirits of plants. He did not venture to interpret the significance of animal sacrifice in this unnamed village, yet his act of observation pinpointed a moment of friction between knowledge systems—one brought about, in large part, by musical consumption.

Musical Plastic

Despite the energies and anxieties it stimulated among scientists and workers throughout the industry, lac rarely if ever appeared in the endless consumer discourse generated by the gramophone and discs. Here, "lac" was completely absorbed by "shellac." A short story published in 1930 can demonstrate this. Written by the little-known author Laurence Oliver, and entitled simply "Shellac," it was published in *Nash's Pall Mall Magazine*, a fashionable London-based women's journal, and lavishly illustrated.[97] It was a love story of sorts. Olive, raised in a small Devonshire town, has recently married George, an English shellac trader. Attracted by the colonial lifestyle, she moves with him to Calcutta, but soon becomes disenchanted with both man and city. The couple quarrel; the tropical heat is oppressive; a cook runs off with silverware. George becomes unable to fulfill orders from international clients because he is shortchanged by a Calcutta dealer who has control over supplies from the rural bhattas. He acts boldly, to save both business and marriage, by moving his business into the country—the first white man to do so, we are told—to a small town outside Ranchi.[98] Here George can trade face-to-face with shellac manufacturers.

Both the love story and its illustrations construct a particular view of shellac. In figure 1.3, the material enters George and Olive's bungalow against a forest backdrop, ready-processed and packaged in a burlap sack.[99] "Lac" never enters the picture. George is busy in conversation with traders; Olive watches the transaction and gazes into the forest beyond. Shellac is revealed to her—and to the reader—as a wondrous material, transforming her perception of George's work:

> Hitherto she had thought of shellac, if she had wasted thought on it at all, as a dull uninteresting commodity, rather like coke or cement or chicken food, just something musty that was bought and sold in sacks and used inexplicably in the manufacture of gramophone records; and she thought George had chosen a distinctly inferior plane for his activities, as unromantic as a corn merchant's. . . .
>
> But now she found that it was positively first-rate, thrilling and romantic. Shellac was almost on a place with the manna that fell in the wilderness. Thousands of minute scaly insects feeding upon certain trees of the acacia species and thereby creating a wonderful amber-like resinous matter, which, collected from the trees, ground and washed and filtered, became in due course the medium by which Kreisler, Backhaus, Melba and Sophie Tucker fed their music on plates to a hungry world, millions of plates of music for millions of greedy ears—could anything be more marvelous? And for George to be an intermediary in this thrilling achievement—it was simply too romantic for words. Minute insects provided by a generous and far reaching providence for the manufacture of gramophone records—it was little short of miraculous.[100]

Olive's thoughts circle back to lac insects, marvelous creatures that, in being noticed, recast George as a musical medium: previously a merchant, he becomes a "poet." But his business remains doomed, and the couple will shortly be driven from the village by angry locals. In a closing scene, Olive will face them down with a handgun.

If "Shellac" traded on colonial adventure and cliché to reignite a falter-

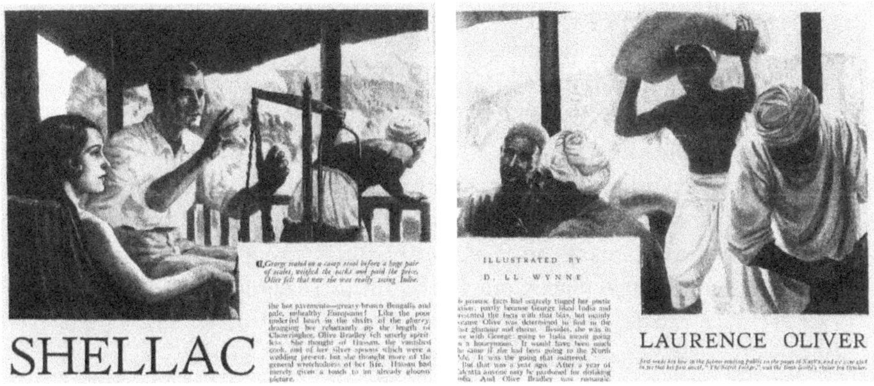

Figures 1.3a and 1.3b Illustrations by D. Lloyd Wynne for Laurence Oliver's short story "Shellac" (1930)

ing relationship (its teaser-tagline was "It's not all romance in India—all the time"), then the material became the means by which romance was restored. Beneath the veranda and before Olive's eyes, shellac changed from dull commodity into the substance from which the music of celebrities was made. Famous names in the classical world, alongside the well-known jazz singer Sophie Tucker, sprang to her mind; the male author conjured a chain of connections for a women's readership. Insects magically converted trees into plates to feed "greedy ears," by way of grinding, washing, and filtering—human dimensions within an imagined division of labor that were acknowledged, but only in passing, in a celebration of insects, wilderness, and George. Sitting next to her husband the shellac dealer, Olive projected a view of the material from the perspective of consumption in which human labor all but disappeared. Yet it was only in proximity to the realm of production that such labor appeared at all: as the above passage declares, under normal circumstances consumers did not "waste thought" on shellac.

When consumers did think about the material, music was the mode through which their thoughts were habitually channeled. In "Shellac," the author depicted a dawning consciousness of shellac as a musical good, representing the act of consumption in overtly gendered terms.[101] This dynamic of musical recognition was a broader feature of discourse on the material, as gramophone audiences throughout the 1920s and '30s routinely claimed to be surprised that discs were made from shellac. In 1922 an editor for the magazine *The Talking Machine World* reported that North American consumers had until recently been "completely unaware that shellac is the principal ingredient in the manufacture of disc records"; only as record prices spiked around 1920 did they begin to wonder "what shellac had to do with" the gramophone industry, many believing that discs, "with their beautifully polished surfaces, were made of vulcanite."[102] An industrial material derived from rubber, vulcanite was a product often used in place of, or together with, shellac in making "hot molded organic materials."[103] And so, while North Americans may have been (or at least claimed to be) largely unaware that discs were made of shellac, their first guess was pretty close, betokening an awareness of the industrial and colonial genesis of thermoplastic products.

A similar scenario played out in the United Kingdom whenever listeners were moved to reflect on the materiality of discs. Price hikes were often the cause of plastics becoming a topic of discussion. In *The Gramophone*—the long-running journal launched in 1923 to proselytize for classical music, and the earliest such publication marketed at consumers, rather than traders, of music on record—shellac became a new measure of music's value, as the material that simultaneously increased the price of discs while enhancing the listener's musical knowledge. An editorial of 1924 is typical of this approach. After discussing the need to increase consumption in order to drive disc prices down, the anonymous writer addressed the reader as amateur listener: "As to lifting the level of appreciation, lots, I think, can be done; and with the lifting also a lot of broadening. As to the resultant standard of reproduction, again, much; for as a realist I insist upon the objective Edisonian test, as far as the limitations will allow. Heifitz in the flesh, so! Heifitz via the shellac, so! (or 'not so' as it mostly is)."[104] The editorial went on to say that such aural comparisons—for which amateur gramophone clubs were the proposed venue—were indispensable for a true appreciation of classical music. At the same time, the author disclosed a set of contemporary meanings for shellac as the currency through which an amateur might stockpile a musical education. Shellac appeared in the act of making amateur aural comparisons between the recorded and the "live," providing the imaginary counterpart to, and extension of, the performer's body.

This materialization of shellacked performers and performances was common in *The Gramophone* magazine in the 1920s. The inaugural issue, for example, contained an article by Compton Mackenzie, the journal's founding editor, titled "Good Singing," in which shellac was said to permit only the finest singers to shine through:

> [It is] only the first-rate that can hold its own on the gramophone. The perfectly placed voice is a mystic thing that floats on the breath like a celluloid ball on a jet of water. It is neither in the throat nor in the nose, but outside the lips, where it remains immovable. . . . Strong dramatic songs

> seldom come off on the gramophone. It is almost impossible to convey drama through a soundbox. A brilliant exception is, of course, Chaliapine in Boris, but his stupendous personality and sense of the stage would penetrate more than mere wax, vulcanite and shellac.[105]

The record Mackenzie had in mind was Feodor Chaliapin's 1922 "Farewell of Boris," a record that began at the opera's climax with the line "Proshchai, moi syn, umiraiu!" (Farewell, my son, I am dying!). Chaliapin sang these words in blunt, truncated phrases; as the monologue continued, his voice gradually swelled, carrying an auditory focus across deep pauses. But for Mackenzie it was not so much Chaliapin's voice as his aura that erupted from the sound box, through contact between needle and plastic. Shellac emerged in Mackenzie's prose as he reached for a material carrying presence: the plastic medium in which living bodies, as the mirror of the voices they emitted, were held as though in suspense.

And yet . . . it bears repeating that shellac more often than not went unmentioned in discussions of musical listening. Only in the broader realms of the consumer imagination—such as in an occasional work of fiction expressly dedicated to the substance—did the musical connection more fully emerge.[106] Musical journalists and gramophone enthusiasts largely directed their attention to the effable contents of listening experiences, rather than to their plastic containers. When the shellac material came up, its naming was inspired by mundane circumstances: consternation at the rising costs of discs, or the banal needs of gramophone journalists in completing a sentence ("Heifitz in the shellac, so!" or "more than mere wax, vulcanite and shellac"). Not so much a pressing concern of gramophone promoters, it might be fairer to say that the material more gently occupied the mental landscape of consumers, and of those who mused about sounds-on-record on their behalf.

Shellac could, if only occasionally, be recalled in musical experiences. And this marked one endpoint in the commodity's journeys. As it entered into combination with other disc materials, as one commodity converted into another, its travels were effaced. In giving plastic shape to gramophone discs, shellac faded into the background of global musical markets—into the very background that it supplied. The material's neutrality was in this sense an inescapable condition of sound reproduction technology and the new kind of musical globalization it facilitated. Shellac needed to stay invisible and inaudible for the gramophone to channel sounds, and for a musical medium to function as such: its aesthetic transparency was closely bound up with the political conditions of its international availability, together with the cultural and epistemological distances traversed in the process of colonial exchange.

Acoustic Stripes

Around 1940, exiled in New York, Theodor Adorno observed:

> When you place the needle upon a revolving phonograph record, first a noise appears; as soon as the music begins, the noise recedes into the background, but constantly accompanies the musical event. . . . The slight, continual noise is a sort of acoustic stripe.[107]

Could this acoustic stripe be the sound of shellac? Jacob Smith has argued along these lines that the noises of gramophone discs "be heard not simply as noise to be eliminated but as an eco-positive attribute of shellac, giving voice to the kusum trees and reddish insects that provide a material base for the voices of Gilbert Girard or Enrico Caruso."[108] In other words, when listening to these celebrated human voices, we behold the labor of insects, along with the work of the nonhuman nature that those insects more broadly represent. Less redemptive, and more attuned to the politics of such an ecology, Kyle Devine has invited us to hear instead a "constant reminder of the ways that this format enfolds and indexes frictions such as exploited resources and workers, traumas of war and waste."[109] The acoustic stripe is, on this reading, the result of a huge and clamorous ensemble of materials, actors, and agents, elaborately organized around the frictional encounter between needle and shellacked groove.

These are some of the stakes for ecocritical listening to media formats, which hearkens well beyond familiar sites of musical performance and listening. In this respect, the "acoustic stripe"—the very sound of mediation itself—proves to be an almost irresistible object of interpretation: giving voice to insects, on the one hand, or serving as the index of colonial violence, on the other. And yet, while listeners may and perhaps should listen to shellac discs in these ways now, it is worth pondering why such noises were rarely heard in the gramophone's heyday—or why they were able to recede as the musical event began. What Adorno described from the listener's perspective as a sudden conversion of noise into music, even as the noise persisted beneath the emerging sonic signal, can also be understood from the perspective of production: as a moment of transformation in which techniques of production swiftly turn into techniques for listening. As the plastic material connecting heterogeneous knowledge systems and bodily practices, shellac held a multiplicity in tension. Unbeknownst to Adorno as to many others, the ability to ignore the acoustic stripe and to have access to mediated sound was, in other words, contingent on the knowledge required to manipulate the insect and to stretch lac across the body.[110] Shellac, as a plastic, embedded lac stretching (among other skills) as a bodily technique—one that could be later deployed elsewhere to harmonize multiple disc ingredients, while providing the material condition for their audible transformation into more than the sum of their parts.

A focus on this moment of transformation—a material switch into musical listening—can evoke an ecocritical priority not only for shellac but also for other media materials. It invites us to ponder a widespread infrastructural mystery by which plastics exert their presence only to vanish in the process of listening. Notably, Michael Silvers has outlined political-ecological links between Brazil's phonograph industry and cylinder wax, which involved intimate knowledge of the drought-resistant carnauba palm and large quantities of skilled and badly paid labor.[111] Carnauba wax holds significant parallels with shellac as a plastic, in which knowledge of the environment and patterns of resource extraction were remade into listening practices in which carnauba palms were almost entirely, if never completely, effaced.

Shellac also bears comparison with more recent uses of plastic in musical media, whose acoustic stripes may be less conspicuous or even completely silent. After all, shellac for discs was prized for its inaudibility: its value as a musical commodity lay in its relative transparency to the senses. This affordance of shellac—as a plastic able to carry objects, such as sounds, and yet go largely undetected and unremarked—illuminates both its historical role and its musical and technological purpose. It also suggests the larger ecological and political effects of constructing absences for the senses, both in disc media and in larger musical infrastructures that are held together by plastic means. Other plastics (Bakelite, vinyl, PET, ABS) could tell different stories about sound reproduction technology and the political and environmental structures that enable those very materials to withdraw and be mercilessly consumed—a larger issue that connects music to the overwhelming environmental hazards of plastic use throughout the twentieth and twenty-first centuries.[112] An ecocritical approach to media should be able to account not only for these human and environmental costs, but also for the way in which the many different things implicated by mediated sounds recede from them.

The history of shellac shows one way this could happen: through colonial modes of fabrication that facilitated the plastic's production and musical effacement. In other words, the frictions that brought shellac-for-music into being also constructed a one-way mirror: a hiss that became all but inaudible to the distant listener, and which sustained a predictable production of reproduced sounds. As I have tried to show, the production of lac/shellac was shot through with knowledge, but also with gaps: first and foremost, those between makers of lac and of shellac. On the one hand, lac was the outcome of rural labor and Adivasi knowledge of the forests in which colonial officers and scientists struggled to manufacture dependence.[113] On the other, shellac was the product of migrant and indentured labor, involving highly specialized techniques and appalling working conditions, which invited rioting and strikes. These inglorious conditions, and workers' resistance to them, rose to their peak as a musical medium grew.

Against the rickety canvas presented by plastic materials and their histories, our views of sound reproduction may begin to shift away from their cultural origins toward the hybrid realms of global commodity exchange.[114] No longer only a host of technologies for detaching sounds from their sources, or a range of social techniques for coordinating copies and originals, sound reproduction is also, and perhaps always, a series of political and environmental relations between knowledge systems that allow sounds to be molded, carried, and more or less inaudibly sustained. Shellac puts such a decentered history of sound reproduction in perspective by illustrating the politics of knowledge that gather in complex patterns around plastic commodities as they become musically essential: as things urgently needed in the making of sonic things, both required and demanded, if only to be overlooked and underheard.

CHAPTER 2

Sound Capital

SALE OF HOUSEHOLD FURNITURE, ETC.

The property of J. A. Hansen, Esq.
To be sold by auction at No. 3 Victoria Street
On Saturday, 15th June, 1901, at 2pm.

The undersigned have been instructed to sell by auction a Cottage piano by Gustav Haesler (in good order), Europe-made Chiffonier with marble top and mirror back, ebony whatnot side table, bentwood rocking chair, bentwood settee, spring-seated and upholstered standard Chairs, teak occasional table, gramophone, zon-o-phoke, Europe-made wardrobe, hard wood almeirahs with mirror doors, iron double bedstead, American standard chairs, seriah sideboard, Singer's sewing machine, lady's bicycle &c. Crockery, glassware and plated ware &c. Also 2 well grown cloths-of-gold and 1 bridal rose trees.

The above auction notice appeared in the *Straits Times*, Singapore's leading English-language newspaper.[1] It lands us in the middle of lots of things. First, the piano—probably the most valuable item in the list—followed by a cupboard, tables, chairs, a settee, a gramophone, and a Zon-o-Phone (another kind of gramophone, the brand name misspelled in the ad). This rounds out materials from the receiving rooms. Next comes the bedroom furniture: wardrobe, bedstead, more chairs, more cupboards. Finally, after the hardwood items, the list finishes with various odds and ends, gendered female: the sewing machine, lady's bicycle, crockery, and decorative plants.

Who lived in a house like this? In the *Singapore and Straits Directory*, a comprehensive guide to who was whom in business and society, J. A. Hansen identified himself as a "professor of music, piano tuner and repairer."[2] "Esquire" outs him as British and an imperial subject, which means that he and his partner likely belonged to the European colonial elite. By contrast, the overwhelming majority of Singapore's population were, of course, Chinese, Malay, Indian, Peranakan, and Eurasian.[3] The small fraction of Europeans were largely military types or clerks, recruited by mainly British firms engaged in typically colonial ventures such as rubber plantations, pineapple farms, and tin mines. Singapore, together with the other port cities (Penang, Malacca, Dinding) that made up the Straits Settlement, had been administered as a Crown colony since 1867, under the umbrella of British Malaya.[4] Well-connected Brits sailed to Southeast Asia in search of their fortunes.[5] For example, in addition to being a music teacher, Hansen founded a private company, Hansen & Co., which bought and sold generic commodities, while also dabbling in "news and advertising."[6]

For present purposes, my interest in Hansen lies in his ownership of gramophones. Having two in one home was unusual if not eccentric, perhaps reflecting his professional interests. Elsewhere in early-twentieth-century Singapore, piano tuners sometimes moonlighted as gramophone repairmen, which might begin to explain how these instruments came into his home.[7] A popular brand, which made cheap discs along with low-cost machines, Zon-o-Phone (later Zonophone) began operations in the United States in 1899.[8] Its catalogues offered standard gramophone fare—music hall hits, minstrelsy, popular operatic numbers, comic talk—but did so more cheaply than was usual, aiming to ply the gramophone trade more deeply among the North American middle classes. Only two years later, then, this US novelty could be found on the other side of the world. A music professor-cum-wheeler-dealer provided one conduit for such rapid cultural transfer. And, if an auction notice can be read as a snapshot onto a domestic lifeworld, gramophones were already securely lodged in well-to-do Malayan homes. In the above list, gramophones nestle happily among the hardwood items—rather than, say, next to the sewing machine and bicycle as yet another mechanical contraption.

This chapter enquires into the gramophone's ready adoption among Southeast Asia's elites, in particular its European colonial class, and scrutinizes the early spread of the gramophone industry along imperial channels. I home in on the Gramophone Company's efforts and failures to expand in Southeast Asia, by way of Singapore, during the first decade or so of the twentieth century. My suggestion will be that this case study shows what went on more broadly, as US sound technologies became global media by finding new ways of tapping into the political and economic networks of European empire. This transformation from technology into medium took place through novel business practices that were characteristic of multinational capitalism. While "multinationals" such as Cadbury, Nestlé, and Yamaha have by now become all too familiar, the Gramophone Company represents an early, protean example of a genre.[9] I will be particularly interested in the role of sound in this connection, and will be suggesting that the movements of sounds along imperial networks, embodied and encased in shellac discs—a sonic format, a medium of exchange—helped birth a new kind of capital.

By focusing on discs, I want also to reanimate a basic question about early recorded sound: How did gramophones become "global" at the turn of the twentieth century?[10] Later moments in the history of sound media are better understood and have been intensively studied. In a recent book, Michael Denning argues that shipping routes provided the political infrastructure of sound on records—a global network along which music, in the shape of discs, could travel.[11] He conjures up the flood of vernacular popular musics in the decade between 1925 and 1935: an "archipelago of colonial ports" placed in fresh contact with each other, for the most part without the mediation or censorship of the imperial metropoles. He terms this new aural connection the "decolonization of the ear," sound on records seeding transcolonial consciousness among an imperial underclass and, in the process, reinventing the senses. What is more, the movement of sounds paved the way for the decolonization armies and legislatures, eventually resulting in the creation of Third World nations in the period after the Second World War.

These are impressive claims, but similar points have been made before by others, albeit using different methods and with more fine-tuned results.[12] Tan Sooi Beng has notably shown the ways in which the gramophone became an instrument of pan-Asian cosmopolitanism in British Malaya, and a means of talking and singing back to British colonial power.[13] Her study guides and motivates the present chapter's investigation of the gramophone's emergence as a medium a few decades earlier, as I track the ways in which the ear was first "colonized" by sound on record—significantly, through the ears of the European colonial class itself.[14] I also draw on pioneering work by Vibodh Parthasarathi, who has shown how colonialism was a precondition of the gramophone's emergence and provided the template for sound-on-record's multilayered extraction of financial, symbolic, and material resources.[15] But how did this work in practice? This chapter explores one avenue of explanation. By first sketching out the emerging gramophone networks between London and Singapore—long-range connections between recorded sound, European imperialism, and Anglo-American capital—it gradually homes in on the frictional formatting of the colonial ear.[16]

London Calling

The Gramophone Company was born in 1898; it was the British progeny of Emile Berliner's New York-based National Gramophone Company, which in 1901 would become the Victor Talking Machine Company. The UK organization was a copy of the American firm moved to a new context, to expand the industry beyond already intense competition for market share in the United States. In 1897, one of Berliner's board members, William Barry Owen, steamed to London.[17] His mission was to set up new headquarters at the heart of the British gramophone market, and, more importantly, to establish a base from which to launch future expansions into Europe and the British Empire.[18] As Berliner's envoy, Owen was tasked with recruiting a British investor who could stake capital in the business and so anchor it more firmly in the United Kingdom. He identified such an investor in Edmund Trevor Lloyd Williams, a forty-year-old Welsh lawyer and financier. In February 1898, Williams invested five thousand pounds—the equivalent of roughly a million US dollars today—into the establishment of a Gramophone Company in London, installing Owen as its general manager.[19]

Under an agreement between Williams, Owen, Berliner, and Eldridge Johnson—the last once the chief engineer in Berliner's lab, and now his business partner as the holder of several key gramophone patents—the Gramophone Company was to buy all machines for retail in the United Kingdom directly from the US parent company, and was forbidden from making its own hardware.[20] Nor was the London firm initially permitted to manufacture any discs, which were to be imported either directly from the United States or printed and sent from a pressing plant in Hanover.[21] In other words, the Gramophone Company agreed to restrict its activities to generation of sonic content suitable for European audiences. Accordingly, Owen's first task as general manager was to establish recording premises. He chose a site in London's theatre district on the Strand, near established venues for popular singers, musicians, comics, and other entertainers. He would soon replicate this model in several other European cities, setting up branches in Paris, Milan, and Berlin. This last office was particularly successful, allowing the German company to establish its own subsidiaries in Austria and Russia (which soon became the company's most important market outside the UK) before the end of the nineteenth century.[22]

Even though it manufactured nothing, the London-based business made a fortune under Williams and Owen. The Gramophone Company creamed off the larger production networks established and maintained by the Victor Talking Machine Company, at least in the early years. But in 1904, when Owen retired to run a chicken farm in Kentucky, the situation suddenly changed, as the company came under the direction of Theodor Birnbaum, former manager of the all-important German and Russian branches. As the historian Peter Martland has shown, Birnbaum strove to consolidate power in London, much to the consternation of his American partners.[23] For one thing, he brought European branches under his direct control; for another, he immediately pushed for manufacturing powers. In 1907, three Gramophone Company disc-pressing plants were opened in Barcelona, Calcutta (Dum Dum), and London (Hayes)—in addition to existing facilities in Hanover and Riga—massively increasing the company's disc-making resources. Even worse from Victor's perspective, Birnbaum went on to cancel the company's gramophone order from the United States, announcing plans to open the company's own machine-making factory in London. This prompted an angry transatlantic visit from Victor's CEO, and resulted in Birnbaum's resignation during a boardroom meeting.[24]

Birnbaum's successor, Alfred Clark, was a US citizen who reaffirmed the Gramophone Company's allegiance to Victor, its North American "parent" (now the preferred metaphor for relations between the companies). Yet Clark benefited from and advanced Birnbaum's independence-oriented reforms. He proceeded to build a London gramophone assembly plant, even as executives on both sides of the Atlantic came to realize that machines were no longer as important as they once were. More critical now were the discs, and in this sense Birnbaum's creation of pressing plants proved farsighted. With the company's expansion, it became ever more impractical to post every wax-master recording back to Hanover and later Riga (when Victor acquired Zonophone and its pressing plant there in 1903), to be stamped out in shellac discs and then mailed back to an increasing number of locations around the world. For the sake of growth, infrastructural developments were required: the creation of quicker regional discmaking circuits.

Capital in Person

Ranging far beyond London HQ, though in constant communication with it, "recording experts" were key figures in this expansion of the business. The Gramophone Company's most well-known recording expert was Washington-born Frederick Gaisberg, sent by Berliner to London on its founding in 1898 to build up musical stock. In April 1902, Gaisberg persuaded the up-and-coming Neapolitan tenor Enrico Caruso to record at a deluxe hotel in Milan (a topic to be explored in chapter 3). Before the year was over, he recruited another regional celebrity, this time in Calcutta, making a series of recordings (again in an upscale hotel room) of Gauhar Jaan, a dancer and singer from Uttar Pradesh.[25] The continuation of Gaisberg's travels into 1903 saw him record hundreds more musicians, clocking up thousands of wax masters in Tokyo, Shanghai, Hong Kong, Singapore, Bangkok, and Rangoon. Across these different locations, Gaisberg's strategy remained constant: to indigenize the company's disc offerings, recording local sounds that might appeal to new audiences and markets.

Before 1914, the Gramophone Company employed at any given moment only eight or nine recording experts around the world.[26] Traveling alone, or sometimes in pairs, these (exclusively male) experts circled vast territories with heavy recording equipment in tow. They were, to borrow a phrase from Parthasarathi, "techno-theocrats," wandering sahibs of colonial lore, who aimed to build confidence in the new industry.[27] Rather than wielding political, administrative, or even intellectual power, these emissaries were endowed with a new form of capital power.[28] They knew little, at least at first, about the languages, musics, and cultures in which they moved. For example, William Sinkler Darby, a native of South Carolina, was for several years responsible for generating sonic content for the whole of Russia and Eastern Europe, without prior knowledge of Slavic languages. Similarly, George Dillnutt—born to a working-class family in South London, and accompanying Gaisberg on a famous "Eastern" expedition of 1902–3—was the main and sometimes sole recording agent for South and Southeast Asia until after the First World War. These recording experts were retained on multiyear salaried contracts, with additional funds for travel expenses; they were required to update London HQ on their movements and activities, and to log every recording they made in a company inventory.[29] They behaved like executives at large: as representatives of the company embedded in regional markets, and as spies keeping close watch on rival gramophone firms.

Such incipient corporate behavior can be observed in events surrounding Gaisberg and Dillnutt's first recording session in Singapore. Ahead of their arrival in May 1903, a representative of Robinson & Co.—one of Singapore's oldest department stores and an important vendor of pianos and other musical instruments to the archipelago—lined up a roster of Javanese, Malay, and Dutch musicians. Given such preparation, Gaisberg and Dillnutt were able to make more than two hundred recordings (wax masters) in less than a month. Before leaving Singapore, the pair also carried out essential business, persuading Robinson to enter into a new kind of contract with an all-important, and historically recent, "noncompetition" clause. To summarize the terms: Robinson agreed not to sell the phonographic equipment of any other firm, so long as the Gramophone Company supplied their discs and machines exclusively to Robinson, among all retailers in the Straits Settlement and Federated Malay States.[30]

Wax Molds

Exclusive contracts of this kind were intrinsic to the early gramophone trade, which promoted the construction of regional monopolies. In "opening up" new markets and trying to attract new audiences, the Gramophone Company aimed to secure relationships with dealers through which recordings might be sold. But there were also subtler technological pressures toward monopoly, resulting from the yawning interval between the recording of wax masters and their return as shellac discs many months later. On one end, recording experts were unable to listen back to the recordings they made without risking injury to the wax masters. On the other, the wait to learn how a recording had turned out could take six months or more—plenty of time for partners such as Robinson to lose interest in selling the resulting discs. This lengthy delay was an inescapable feature of the gramophone's global spread in the early years. After being heated up for recording, wax masters were cooled and carefully packaged for long-haul transport; they were then sent back to Hanover and Riga, where they were converted, through electroplating, into metal stampers—negative impressions that could be subsequently pressed out in hundreds or thousands of shellac discs.[31]

Several other pitfalls were built into the early gramophone network. For example, board members in London and factory managers in Hanover and Riga were poorly placed to judge which discs might appeal in places physically distant and culturally remote from Europe. Another major hazard arose from posting wax masters over large distances, resulting in a high rate of attrition, only a fraction surviving the long journeys intact. After recording sessions in Singapore, wax masters routinely arrived in London—and Calcutta, after 1907, when a nearer disc-pressing factory was opened there, albeit one still more than four thousand miles away—covered in and degraded by mold. In short, wax molds molded, constituting a deathly friction within the early shellac network.

A corporate memo from 1909, based on advice from Gaisberg and Dillnutt, outlined this problem of wax-master mortality, while also proposing an original solution:

> Instead of allowing the delicate original, which is subject to climate changes and breakage, to take a long trip either to Calcutta or home, the matrices could be made immediately and then the shell shipped either to Calcutta or England, without any danger. I think from my own experience in this direction, and together with Fred [Gaisberg]'s and Dillnutt's, we will find sufficient business in the Dutch Indies, together with Singapore, Siam and also Ceylon, to have a small plating plant erected in Singapore.[32]

Circulated ahead of a boardroom meeting in London, this report advocated for an electroplating plant in Singapore: a small works capable of converting the wax master into a metal matrix (a "shell"). The rest of the manufacturing process—the creation of stampers, and so on—could then be carried out (whether immediately or at some point in the future) at the nearest large-scale pressing plant.

Although the Singapore electroplating plant was never built, it is worth entertaining Gaisberg and Dillnutt's proposed technological fix, along with the redistribution of labor across South and Southeast Asia that it would have implied. They envisaged Singapore as a regional recording/electroplating hub, producing "stampers" which could then be pressed out in Calcutta, with the whole process under the remote control of London HQ. Moreover, the memo quoted above presented the new electroplating plant as part of a global strategy to reach new listeners around the world:

> The big markets of Europe are too closely competed for us to expect big profits. It is the small countries in Central Asia, Malay Straits, Persian Gulf, North African countries, Dutch Indies, Siam, Caspian and Black Seas [to which we should look]. These countries *in their own native way are extremely musical and pleasure-loving*, and if the recording is carefully watched it means business with a profit. The visits of experts for recording should be timed to a certain schedule twice a year, so as to show our dealers in these countries our serious intentions of supporting them in pushing our goods.[33]

In the corporate jargon of its period, this document highlights the regions in which the company wanted to expand, with a focus on the procedures for recording and selling discs. It also (if inadvertently) signaled the company's limits, slightly over a decade after its founding. After all, the territories listed were places that had so far resisted the company's advances—despite, in the case of Malaya, several previous attempts to record and sell local music.

Catalog Arias

Even as the problem of molding wax remained unresolved, Singapore became a recording center for the Gramophone Company in Southeast Asia, as Gaisberg and Dillnutt had hoped.[34] Just as significantly, it also became—as a result of the monopoly deal struck between Robinson and the Gramophone Company—the center for disc distribution throughout British Malaya. In this respect, a key technology was the mail-order shopping catalog.[35] Regional booklets, made in collaboration with local department stores, focused on the needs of clients in "remote" places. From 1907 onward, in partnership with Robinson's in Singapore, the Gramophone Company maintained an edition of their by now enormous back catalog tilted toward the needs of customers in British Malaya. As the inside cover of the 1909 edition explains:

> This catalogue is issued for the convenience of our valued customers who *do not reside* in Singapore, and represents our stock to-day. [. . .] Our Post Order Department is under the supervision of experienced assistants, and every attention is paid to all orders entrusted to us, which are dispatched by the quickest and cheapest route, the greatest care being taken in packing so that goods may reach their destination in perfect condition.[36]

Addressed to customers on the periphery of Singapore—since residents might go directly to Robinson's department store—this customer guarantee identifies the port city as a center for disc consumption, as well as the base of a mail delivery operation.

The contents of the 1909 Singapore catalog provide a snapshot of an evolving epistemology of sound on record. In table 2.1, I summarize the contents of the first 126 pages but simply reproduce the original rubrics from page 127 on to give the reader a sense of the categories invented and applied to non-Western musics by the gramophone industry. Turkish selections were presented in Arabic, addressing Muslim elites of the archipelago, while Chinese records were advertised in Mandarin ("duplex" refers to double-sided discs). Javanese songs and Indian selections were given in roman script; disc labels, by contrast, were printed in Arabic, Jawi, Chinese, and Indic scripts. Unlike the largely European selections in the first 126 pages, which were arranged largely by genre (bands, dance, songs, opera), the final twenty pages were organized by language and ethnicity, and then gender, and finally musical genre.

To what extent can this catalog be said to represent the tastes of early gramophone consumers in British Malaya? On the one hand, the prevalence of European and to a lesser extent South Asian music reproduced strengths in the Gramophone Company's holdings, and so cannot be read as a straightforward reflection of regional listening habits. On the other hand, the sheer availability of foreign music in Malaya mirrored a broader reality in the confluence of consumer choice and imperial power. The catalog's structure replicated a colonial logic separating the West from the non-West while cordoning different ethnicities off from each other.[37] This was a broader feature of colonial governance in Singapore, of course, where Europeans lived in "suburbs" imagined along the

Table 2.1. Outline of an early mail-order shopping catalogue, *The Singapore and Straits Directory* (Singapore: Kelly & Walsh, 1909). The contents of pp. 1–126 are summarized in the right-hand column, while for pp. 127–45 the original rubrics are reproduced.

Pages	*Contents*
1–8	Advertisements for gramophones, including spare parts
9–18	Military bands from Europe (English, German, etc.)
18–28	Dance music and instrumental numbers
28–85	European vocal music
28	Opera excerpts, organized by singer
42	Opera ensembles: duets, trios, quartets; sea shanties
46	Gilbert and Sullivan excerpts
50	Oratorios, anthems
57	Comic songs by men and women, minstrelsy
69	Gregorian chant
70	German records (opera, yodeling)
78	Zonophone (descriptive and novelty records)
113–26	Opera celebrities (Patti, Tetrazzini, Caruso, Tamagno)
127–30	"Turkish Bands, Songs, Vocal, Clarionet"
131	"Javanese Songs"
132–34	"Duplex Chinese Records"
135	"Tamil Band, Instrumental: Violin, Female Songs, Male Songs, Recitations"
136	"Canarese Female Songs"
	"Sanskrit Female Songs"
137–39	"Telegu Instrumental: Violin, Female Songs, Male Songs"
140–45	"Hindustani Records: Bands, Male Songs, Female Songs, Duets, Chorus, Instrumental, Comic Talk"

lines of nineteenth-century UK garden cities, while the majority of Malay and Chinese groups were administered through ethnically discrete kampongs.[38] The catalog's presentation of genres might, in this sense, be understood as a matrix of elite listening permutated by political economy. Through this transformation, European elites were abundantly catered for, while Malay and Chinese music, predominant throughout Malaya, was least represented.

It might be possible to unscramble this matrix, to readjust the proportions of the catalog's ethnic hierarchies and arrive at a more inclusive picture of gramophone listening in British Malaya. The challenges are formidable, however. As Tan Sooi Beng has pointed out, hundreds of locally made discs released in Singapore in 1903 entirely disappeared from the company's catalog a few years later—either because they did not sell or because they could not find listeners at this early moment.[39] By contrast, it was possible to order a tremendous variety of European music by mail in early-twentieth-century Singapore. The military brass band was particularly well represented. To list only some of the bands represented in early catalogs: the Coldstream Guards, the Guards Cuirassiers Regiment, the Niederschlesisches Infantry Regiment, the Ostpreuss Infantry Regiment, the Garder Husar Regiment Musikkorps, the Kaiser Alexander Garde Grenadier Regiment, the Kaiser Franze Garde Grenadier Regiment, Her Majesty's Royal Artillery Band, and the Royal Military Band. Copiously represented in Singapore's catalogs, more so than in London, the multiple species of European military band are conspicuous.[40]

Another notable bulge is a thirty-five-page insert dedicated to the records of Zonophone, the US company acquired by Victor in 1903 which subsequently became crucial to the Gramophone Company's success in Europe and elsewhere. Retaining its original name, Zonophone served as a foil to the Gramophone Company's brand association with luxury and expense, offering novelty records at cheaper prices. To give an example typical of the many Zonophone records that could be bought from Robison's Post Order Department, there was a "Football Match" between Newcastle and Manchester City, and a "Lancashire Lad's Trip Round London (assisted by Brass Band and Bell Effects)."[41] Next to these UK soundscapes, it was also possible to find discs simulating British dog racing and the selling of a piano in a London auction house, as well as dozens of "English vocal records"—mainly traditional, sentimental songs.[42]

Imperial Elites

So far in this chapter I have been exploring the disc through its rising importance, discursively and financially, within the Gramophone Company, together with the tentative infrastructures of its recording, pressing, and distribution. But when it comes to how those discs were used, the trail runs cold. First-hand accounts of gramophone discs are near-impossible to recover in the period before the First World War, in Malaya as else-

Table 2.2. First half of a concert program performed in 1901, as reproduced in the *Straits Times*, 13 April 1901, p. 8.

Pianoforte Solo	"Dances from Henry VIII"	Mrs. Merewether
Song	"There's a Land"	Mr. Bell
Song	"Only Once More"	Miss Westerhout
Violin Solo	"Le Myosotis"	Mr. A. Westerhout
Song	"Who Carries the Gun"	Hon. E. M. Merewether
Gramophone	"Lulu" & "Laughing Song"	Mr. McClelland
Plantation Song	"De Ole Banjo"	Misses Westerhout & Webster, Messers. Howell & A. Westerhout

where.[43] And yet, references to gramophones and phonographs were widely (if thinly) scattered throughout early-twentieth-century newspapers, providing clues as to where and when gramophones were played. In British Malaya ca. 1900, the preeminent English-language newspaper was, as previously noted, the *Straits Times*. Addressing a broad constituency of Europeans and Anglophone Asians, it reported on minute details of daily life—including regular updates from correspondents throughout Malaya—while also reprinting stories from the wider world. Items mentioning phonographs and gramophones follow this scheme, placing the machines in both local and global contexts.[44] An amateur concert recalled in the *Straits Times* in 1901, for example, revealed the gramophone's place in the first half of a musical program (table 2.2).[45] This concert, mounted at a high school in Malacca, followed a football match between a local team of Europeans and group of officers of the Royal Navy, stationed on the *Algerine*, a nearby warship. The second half of the program was much the same as the first, minus the gramophone, but again culminated in a closing plantation song calling on US minstrelsy.[46]

As the foregoing numbers might suggest, the program was anchored within the imaginative coordinates of little England. The first item comes from *Henry VIII*, a comic opera by Edward German featuring faux-medieval modal melodies, that debuted in London in 1892. The second, "There's a Land," was a hymn and popular song in turn-of-the-century Britain, and was more commonly known as the "Sweet By and By." Subsequent contributions by the Westerhout family—one of the oldest Dutch families in Malacca, who made their fortunes in gold and tin mining, and whose patriarch was for many decades Malacca's sheriff—gently departed from the all-British theme with a violin arrangement of the piano work "Le Myosotis," by the German composer Friedrich Baumfelder.[47] However, "Who Carries the Gun"—a setting of a ballad by Arthur Conan Doyle, set to music by the Irish composer Alicia Adélaide Needham—performed by E. M. Merewether, Malacca's recently retired justice of the peace, swiftly returned to the concert's dominant sensibility in a song that famously imagined "lads" from across the British Isles taking up arms to build the empire.[48]

After a brief report of the football match (the *Algerine* beat Malacca 4–0), the newspaper's Malacca correspondent went on to describe musical festivities. He noted the "tasteful" decoration of the school, while abundantly praising the concert's organizers. It was a "smoking concert," where tobacco and alcohol liberally mingled. A recognized format in European colonial contexts, "smokers" often included women, both as performers and attendees. The reporter summarized proceedings as follows:

> Where all the items were good it is somewhat invidious to draw distinction, but the palm of the evening must certainly be awarded to Mr. R. McClelland whose screamingly funny songs simply convulsed the audience. In fact, one of the *Algerine* officers who laughed long and loud was apparently afraid of laughing too long and too loud and so had to use his 'kerchief as a gag. I think this is a sufficient compliment to our friend "Mac" and so will not further eulogise him.[49]

In short, the gramophone stole the show. Appearing alongside a pianist, a violinist, and several singers, McClelland was credited as a performer in the program, and as the commentary described, the songs he played were considered his own. Of course, "Lulu" and the "Laughing Song" were originally US records: the latter was composed and first sung on wax cylinder by George Washington Johnson, an African American, but was rapidly appropriated, modified, and recorded by numerous white singers in the United States, the United Kingdom, and elsewhere.[50]

Given the account above, it may be tempting to imagine that the hilarity provoked by the gramophone was caused not only by the song but by the incongruity of the machine and machinist among "live" performers. And yet, consider this account of another concert—another "smoker"—that took place a couple of years later:

> A very enjoyable "smoker" was held at the smelting works Club house at Pulau Brani last night. Mr. S. B. Archdeacon, the President, in a few well-chosen words, explained that the concert was the outcome of a recent billiard handicap and it was his pleasant duty to present the prizes won at the tournament. The hall was prettily decorated and the "smoker"

> judged a huge success by everyone present. Recitations were well given by Messrs. Kemble and Brough and some excellent songs were very creditably rendered by Messrs. Bruyers, Doughtry, Raebrun, Lee and Bartlett, while some very pretty guitar and violin duets were played by Messrs. Kemble and Wilkie. Mr. James Carroll helped to enliven the proceedings with some excellent selections from his huge gramophone, which were greatly appreciated. The gathering dispersed some time this morning.[51]

Rushed into print for the *Straits Times*, this short article lavished journalistic attention on what was of course a relatively minor event: the lifeblood of local news.

Gramophones were more often interspersed within "smokers" and other amateur concert programs that comprised mainly "live" music, as gramophone owners and players were routinely credited as performers, something like latter-day DJs. It was also common for journalists to note the enormous size of the gramophone in question. Consider a final example, which relates events at the Singapore Chinese Weekly Entertainment Club on a Saturday evening in November 1908. Known colloquially as the Millionaire's Club, it represented a new kind of society founded by Chinese and Eurasian businessmen in the Straits, and was then celebrating the thirtieth anniversary of its founding. In attendance were "300 European and Chinese guests"—the majority prominent Chinese men, including several "presidents and secretaries of various Chinese clubs in Singapore."[52] Following a lengthy roll call of attendees, the *Straits Times* recounted the show:

> Mr. Dreyfus delighted those present with his popular cinematographic show, which was greatly appreciated by the guests. The Regimental band of the Madras Infantry discoursed sweet music, and a huge gramophone worked by electricity was a pleasure to all present. There will be a Chinese wayang to-day, and on Wednesday night the club will give another "at home" for ladies only.[53]

Fernand Dreyfus was an exhibitor for French Pathé who traveled extensively in South and Southeast Asia, although cinema had been a fixture of urban life in Singapore and Penang, with countless cinemas and outdoor screenings taking place from 1900 onward.[54] Featured alongside film screenings, gramophones were a standard component of early cinemagoing, with sound on records serving to accompany pictures and mitigate the noise of the projector.[55]

As in the "smoker" at Malacca, but here on a larger scale, mechanical entertainments mingled with "live" performances that referenced

Singapore in intimate ways. Both wayang and film exhibition were common features of the cityscape, while some of the earliest Chinese music on record—whether recorded locally or imported from the Chinese mainland—took selections from street operas.[56] As an index of the city, the Madras Infantry Band was also apt. It was the oldest and most prominent marching band in Singapore at the turn of the twentieth century, routinely featured as part of official ceremonies and festivals.[57] Trained at barracks in British India, this band was fluent in the repertory of the European military band.[58] A popular entertainment outfit—which routinely performed at Singapore's botanical gardens, among other places—the band also provided a none-too-covert advertisement for imperial power, since the Madras Infantry formed part of the British empire's military presence in Malaya.

To put all this in another way, there was a zone of indistinction between recorded and live entertainments in the early history of the gramophone—one that in the Straits Settlement took on political significance. On the one hand, the gramophone quickly came to belong to public urban landscapes, helping the transition between different musical worlds in the city. It alternated within heterodox programs consisting of films and bands at the Chinese Recreation Club, providing links between them—and was itself a kind of performance, much as in the smaller and more informal smoking concerts. On the other hand, the sheer presence of the machine came preloaded with political meaning. Like the Madras band, which called attention to British power in another way, it represented the power to move people, things, and sounds through space.

Multinational Gaps

As in many other places in the world, well-to-do homes were an important site for sound on record in the first decade of the twentieth century. But in this chapter I have instead highlighted elite clubs and amateur concerts, for two reasons. First, public or semipublic occasions underscore an important dimension of the early gramophone: as an instrument of performance. Second, such performances themselves hint at broader meanings of sound on record within an extractive colonial economy, in which a small minority of Europeans dominated a multiethnic majority. Unlike in settler colonial contexts, where Europeans established their presence in large numbers, British power in Malaya lay in the hands of the tiny few and their capacity to puppeteer labor and resources from elsewhere, whether through exploiting recent arrivals from the Chinese mainland or by raising colonial troops in British India to be deployed overseas.[59] In this political context, performances of recorded sound presented a homology with colonial power itself in exhibiting Anglo-American control over flows of sound.[60]

In making a case for the politics of the gramophone as a format, I take my coordinates from *Audible Empire*, an edited volume that explores ways in which empire becomes—and sometimes fails to become—present to the senses, across the twentieth and twenty-first centuries.[61] *Audible Empire* showcases the many ways in which music can be rich with political implication, both imperial and anticolonial. Yet more provoking still are the parts of the book that lay stress not so much on the soundtracks and counterpoints of empire, but on the various structures that condition audibility in imperial contexts.[62] For example, Gavin Steingo shows how the production and distribution of South African kwaito—rather than the sound of kwaito itself—promotes economic virtues of communication, creativity, and intellectual property, which have come to be prized in the context of hegemonic multinational capitalism. He concludes that while empire in its present-day corporate guise may not be audible as such in kwaito's songs, it configures "the relations through which kwaito becomes audible in the first place. . . . Most intriguingly, those relations are musical or artistic in themselves, or at least exhibit certain *qualities* (in the Hardt sense) of artistic labor."[63]

With the emergence of the gramophone industry, and at an early moment in the history of multinationalism, a similar interplay between structures of listening and prevailing political and economic conditions can be found at work. This might be no surprise. As recounted above, the Gramophone Company was itself an early multinational corporation established by the transplantation of North American technological capital into London, with the intention of creating further nodes throughout the British Empire. From there, it branched out to, among many other places, Malaya via Singapore, in part through the actions of roving English and US recording experts acting as executives at large.[64] The uneven trickle of "local" music these recording experts recorded, and the business arrangements they contrived, were subject to definite frictions: the slowness with which wax masters were converted into shellac discs, and the waste produced through the molding of wax in transit. Meanwhile, there was also the abundance of foreign discs from recording centers far away: India and China, and, above all, the United States and the United Kingdom.

Through these prevailing conditions of audibility, a new kind of listening came into being: a colonial ear, freshly attuned to both the strong and the weak points in a broader network. The disc, as the least unit created by and moving within this network, evokes both the strengths and the weaknesses: it was a form of mass production that could be applied across an international division of labor and endlessly adapted to local uses; yet it was also a slow format, vulnerable to delay and destruction at several moments in its life cycle, from recording to delivery by mail. On the one hand, sounds on discs could furnish a seemingly endless supply of European music, but with significant demand from only a minority of elites. On the other, recording experts made countless discs locally in the hope of attracting larger audiences, yet struggled to stimulate demand.[65] Both of these economic models—a form of cultural imperialism versus a crude multiculturalism—were simultaneously at play within early record companies. As the early history of the Gramophone Company—a company that, contrary to its name, made discs rather than gramophones—bears out, the contradictory impetuses to push previously recorded materials and to indigenize sonic content were there from the very start. With unlimited access to US catalogs, the London firm set out to create local discs for diverse European audiences; the same logic was then swiftly applied to ethnic communities across and even beyond European imperial circuits.[66]

Not reducible to colonialism, yet inseparable from it, the Gramophone Company typified the rise of multinational firms during the nineteenth and twentieth centuries. This new kind of economic entity implied, at minimum, the investment of a company (based in some "host" economy) in one or more foreign economies—often, though not always, through setting up subsidiaries.[67] In the long history of multinationals, the Gramophone Company more specifically represented an early example of North American capital flowing into the British Empire, much like Ford and Singer, well-known brands of cars and sewing machines.[68] As though to stand in for the United States' supposed and notorious lack of formal empire, corporate arrangements with European firms inside existing empires allowed for the rapid expansion of North American technological commodities.[69] In the absence of international intellectual property law around the turn of the twentieth century, the right to sell such articles could then be channeled through ghost companies and gentlemanly compacts, or what would later come to be known as "noncompetition agreements."

The longer-term consequences of multinationalism are everywhere apparent today, particularly when it comes to US media technologies. Notoriously difficult to pin down or even to define, twenty-first-century multinationals continually mutate in response to the attempts of their critics to pin them down, even while their rapacious behaviors—in their treatment of laborers and environments—are plain to behold.[70] And it is in this ongoing history that the rise of the disc in the early twentieth century most powerfully signifies. As a cluster of ideas, business strategies, and material processes, the shellac disc came into being in the intervals between mold-prone wax, electroplate, and shellac impression. Within these intervals and in the frictions between them lie the roots of a multinational past. Long dead though the format may be, it provides an historical anchor within the spiraling multinational present.

INTERLUDE

Remembering 78s in Singapore

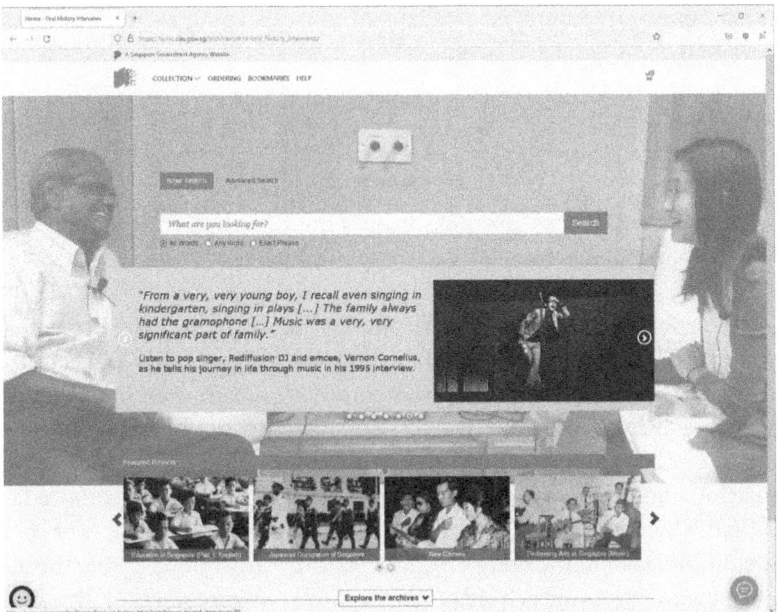

Figure int.1 The homepage of the Oral History Centre, National Archives of Singapore. The Oral History Centre, founded in 1979, produces and administers most of Singapore's national oral history collection. The collection has about 5,900 interviews, most of which are publicly available through the Centre's online database. Courtesy of the Oral History Centre, National Archives of Singapore, nas.gov.sg/archivesonline/oral_history_interviews/.

What are you looking for? The question is greyed out, waiting to be typed over. A cursor blinks in an input field, behind which a background wash shows a young interviewer and an elderly interviewee in a happy illustration of an oral history interview (figure int.1). But what am I looking for? What can I hope to find? The cursor blinks more slowly.

Finding it hard to break a research habit, I type "gramophone" and hit return. Milliseconds later, the results appear: twenty per page, going on for several pages. Each can be clicked, linking to the moment in a reel, within an oral history interview, around which the word was spoken three or four decades ago:

> You know what a gramophone is? The one that you wind first before you put a record on and play it. . . .[1]

> Gramophone records, for us, we can hardly afford to buy. I remember I had a rich, very rich relative. . . .[2]

> Oil lamps and handheld punkahs or fans, listening to gramophones wound up by hand and so on. . . .[3]

> We had, you know, the kind of gramophone that you had to wind up [*laughter*]. . . .[4]

> Radio we didn't know anything about it until much later. So we had this wind-up kind of gramophone. . . .[5]

These snippets provide a sample of what you might find, and the words you might hear, if you repeated the exercise described above.[6] Of course, these phrases have been temporarily removed from their contexts: of speakers' lives, of the interview scenario, of a broader political environment, even of a finished utterance. I will go on to sketch some of these missing contexts in what follows. But before performing this more familiar scholarly gesture of contextualization, I want to pause over this first impression of the search results—in this case, to linger over the almost meaningless speech that is the starting point for users of digitized oral history archives. Almost meaningless, but not quite—after all, there is some meaning here. The auditory snapshots underscore the gramophone's materiality: the expense of discs, the ownership over and presence of devices, the contrast with radio. A key action begins to emerge: to turn, to wind up.

I want to begin by lengthening the first quotation, with the reproduced snippet placed in italics for ease of comparison:

> I better mention something people today don't know. When you had a gramophone . . . *you know what a gramophone is? The one you wind first before you put a record on and play it*. . . . Those who had a gramophone, especially the box almost standing one side . . . that was regarded as a well-to-do man's object. Today you can own anything, people don't say anything at all. Everybody has the same things nowadays. . . .[7]

These words were spoken by Abu Bakar Ali in 1996, then in his late sixties, in the course of a life history interview at Singapore's Oral History Archive. He recalled his childhood on Pulau Brani, an island on the southern tip of Singapore: a maritime hub since time immemorial, and one of the busiest ports in British Malaya during the 1930s. Pulau Brani was where Abu Bakar was born and spent most of his adult life, first as a laborer in the British Army and then as a lighthouse technician. The quotation comes from a section on his childhood, in which he shared memories of his daily routine: going to Malay school during the day and selling cakes at night at a hawker center, to "supplement your spending every day, because you need something to subsist your parents' earnings."[8] Following this last comment, Abu Bakar interrupts his story ("I better mention something . . ."), breaking off to tell the interviewer about the gramophone. His audience, though, was not necessarily the interviewer herself—Stella Ng, an oral historian who had worked at Singapore's National Archive for many years at this point—but the youngsters of today, and beyond them, all those who might listen to the interview later. He wanted to let these unknowable listeners of the future know both what the gramophone is, a wind-up device for playing records, and what it was, "a well-to-do man's object."

A more sustained reflection on the gramophone occurs in a life history interview of Mrs. Chia Kim Teng, née Patricia Choo Neo Oh, conducted at the same place in 1995 (and represented by the second snippet in the sample above). As an upper-secondary pupil at the Geylang Methodist Girls' School in the late 1930s, she recalled playing gramophone records of film songs while making handwritten copies of the lyrics in order to "exchange songs" with other students in the school. She remembers being "crazy over those film stars like Errol Flynn, Nelson Eddy, and Jeanette MacDonald," all famous Hollywood actors of the time. She explains:

> Somebody somehow or other will get a piece, type one, I think from the source or what, and then we all would pass round and we would all . . . waaa . . . what you call that, what's the word we used, "vigorously" copy and copy. All those love songs, you know [*laughter*]. . . . Those days, like "In the Still of the Night," you know, Nelson Eddy, you know, then Jeanette MacDonald, you know. Then those, what, "One Day When We Were Young," you know. All those oldies, lah, you can easily, you can . . . "The Rose in Her Hair," Dick Powell sang, I still remember.[9]

She goes on to explain that these songs, which came from the cinema, were learned via the gramophone. But even though her family owned a gramophone, they could not afford to buy discs; they loaned them from an adopted sister who had married into a rich family.

> So happy every time I borrowed records from them. I don't think I could afford. I never bought any records except sometimes, I think, my uncle bought [and] gave me. Other than that, I personally couldn't afford to buy, couldn't afford to buy.[10]

Her Chinese father had no interest music. It was her Malay mother who insisted on acquiring the gramophone, together with a select few Malay records. She remembers her mother listening to "one named Momo" (probably Momo Latiff, a well-known singer), together with another singer from Sarawak (the Malaysian state on Borneo). There are long pauses as she tries to remember the names of other Malay singers before giving up: "Can't remember." As though to recover her thread, she launches into an anecdote about the recorded origins of "Terang Bulan" (Bright Moon), the popular song that supplied the melody for the Malaysian national anthem, "Negaraku." Then she briefly sings another song, "Gitar Berbunyi" (The Guitar Sounds, a hit by Puteh Ramlee).[11] Before leaving the topic of gramophones behind, to reminisce about the excitement of Chinese New Year, she reflects: "Should have kept it, would have become. . . ."

Perhaps the earliest mention of a gramophone being "wound up" in Singapore's oral history archive comes from an interview with Douglas Hiorns, a UK citizen who grew up in Malaya and went on to become a real estate tycoon.[12] Recollecting his childhood on his father's rubber plantation, he said (in 1984):

> The planters would go there in the evenings [to the club] to drink, listen to the gramophone. . . . All of course by our modern-day standards were under very primitive conditions, with oil lamps and handheld punkahs or fans, listening to gramophones wound up by hand and so on. In fact, the only sophisticated thing about it would be the endless supply of Johnny Walker whisky which would be available to them. . . .[13]

In this reminiscence, the gramophone manifests in a club, this one within the factory complex house on the plantation itself, frequented by the twenty or so "European assistants" who worked there. As we saw in chapter 2, it was in private clubs such as this that gramophones first became prominent in Malaya in the early twentieth century. In a scene that will by now be familiar, Hiorns presents the gramophone alongside drinking, here as a form of conviviality among his parents and their plantation-administering friends ("For every five hundred acres we would have a European expatriate assistant living in his bungalow," he estimates).[14] Yet beyond this context that Hiorns supplies, the instrument also performs a work of memory in this interview. He uses it as a period detail, alongside the punkah and oil lamp, to conjure up the 1930s. His description is a picture postcard of a far-off time in which the gramophone as a pre-electrical technology does memory work: the clockwork mechanism summons up a behind-the-times colonial world even as it smooths its narration.

Something similar happens in the life history of Marie Bong, formerly a teacher and principal at Katong Convent Girls' School in Singapore. (Although not exclusively, Singapore's oral history archive is significantly biased towards people with a distinguished public service record, together with famous businesspeople, musicians, and other celebrities.) Interviewed in her sixties in 1992, she places the gramophone within a rose-tinted scene from her 1930s childhood. Its appearance marks the passage of the decades, but also causes temporalities to overlap:

> We were able to sing all the A. A. Milne songs. I used to be able to play the piano, so I used to be able to play them on the piano also. We had records also. I remember a lovely collection of nursery rhymes we had. We had, you know, the kind of gramophone that you had to wind up.[15]

Recalling the turning of the handle adds sensorial depth to this memory while also bringing another time into the present of narration: the gramophone-specific temporalities of winding up, playing, and listening. She remembers Winnie the Pooh and his songs, made popular through piano sheet music and records: perhaps even the recorded voice of Milne's nine-year-old son, the real-life Christopher Robin, released by HMV in 1929.[16] In her recollection, discs nestle among a list of family possessions and materialize the sounds of a distant imperial past.

A final take on the gramophone comes from the conductor and choir master Paul Abisheganadan, who studied arts at Raffles College in the early 1930s. One of his British lecturers owned a collection of classical records and played them at a weekly high tea for students, which he held at his home: his wife served biscuits and cakes, and Beethoven was heard and discussed. The gramophone itself was "the wind-up kind, not an electrical gramophone even." And these wind-up gramophones were everywhere at Raffles College, as an audible presence marking the passage of the hours:

> At 4 o'clock there would be a gong after which you'd hear a tremendous amount of noise. Noise making again would cease immediately after dinner at 8 o'clock. You couldn't play a gramophone. I mention the gramophone because there was no such thing as radio in those days. I'm talking about the early thirties, you know, radio we didn't know anything about it until much later. So we had this wind-up kind of gramophone. Those of us who could afford to buy a portable HMV or Columbia portable gramophone kept it in our rooms with a few plates, 78-rpm gramophone records, which we treasured very, very much. But even these we could not play any music or anything like that after 8 o'clock at night. They were meant to be study hours.[17]

Gong and gramophone add texture to the student experience being recalled. Abisheganadan conjures up a daily release of energy, followed by its containment.[18] Students who could afford them kept portable gramophones, a relatively recent innovation of the Twenties and Thirties. By this point the true prize was not the gramophone, but the disc.

The Oral History Centre was established by Singapore's ministry of communication in 1979, just over a decade after the country's 1965 split with the Malaysian Federation to become an independent nation-state. As a government document of the period relates, one of the archive's founding aims was "to record the voices of people who have been eyewitnesses to events and developments that marked the growth of Singapore from a British Colony to an independent country."[19] In other words, oral history was conceived as a memory bank for a postcolonial nation-state. As throughout Southeast Asia more broadly, it became a tool for state building: a counter-archive to written records that would instead draw on the memories of its new citizens, as though to whisper a postcolonial state into being.

Over the decades, the Oral History Centre has interviewed roughly four thousand Singaporeans, as well as Britons and other Europeans who formerly lived and worked in Singapore. These interviews have been conducted in many languages—Mandarin, Malay, Tamil, Teochew, Hokkien, Baba Malay, Arabic, and more—but the majority in English, amounting to tens of thousands of hours of recordings.[20] At first recorded onto tape, all interviews have been digitized and can be consulted at the archive on CD; many of the interviews have been transcribed. In 2014 the National Archive put almost all of its collection (save for a few embargoes) on its website, making almost everything freely available online.[21] Not only that, but many of the recordings have been time-locked to their transcripts, enabling Internet users, regardless of their IP address, to search the archive by keywords and phrases.

The National Archive's enthusiasm for open access and hyperaccessibility comes with political implications.[22] Notably, such ease of access facilitates the writing of ultralocal histories.[23] At the same time, in making oral history readily available and audible online—albeit protected from further reproduction by lo-fi sound quality and rigorous digital rights management technology—the archive promotes an intimacy between citizen and state, a closeness that inspires a sense of national belonging even as it surveils. As Nien Yuan Cheng has pointed out, such intimacy has become a notable feature of Singapore's national identity as a "storytelling state"—one also exemplified by the Singapore Memory Project, an online database inaugurated in 2015, which invited citizens to upload a million memories in the form of stories, photos, sound recordings, and videos.[24]

What are you looking for—here, in this archive? Insofar as this question can be disengaged from personal and unfathomable psychological motives, it can invoke a broader historical dilemma: the seemingly inescapable condition in which the desire to find certain things, according to predefined categories, silently guides and structures inquiries into the past.[25] Of course, this has long been the case and perhaps always will be. But in the case of digital archives it has become an everyday and even mundane issue: one that prods and teases. Books, newspapers, and other printed materials have become rapidly searchable by keyword, with untold effects on historical method; and in the case of Singapore's National Archive of oral history, words have also become ways of rapidly sifting through sounds. The latter makes it more feasible than ever before to use oral history for a "secondary purpose"—that is, to read and listen across multiple oral histories to find out about something other than the speakers' primary purpose (often, but of course not always, to record the interviewee's life history).[26] And yet, our lately acquired ability to blaze through unimaginably large data sets—perhaps especially when it comes to oral history, which presents such powerful reality effects—inevitably short-circuits the hitherto seemingly neutral procedure of "finding" historical evidence.[27] When search results return so quickly, the act of searching may easily rebound on researchers themselves, bringing to the surface the aggravating issue of desire as constitutive of historical knowledge.

In this book I am exploring the relationship between format and listening, to show how materiality and infrastructure can inform aural experience even as listening routinely overspills its containers. And yet, listeners themselves prove oddly elusive. Perhaps this is what I wanted to find in turning to Singapore's oral history archive, as one of the few places where one can hope to find and compare historical experiences of the gramophone. Or perhaps I am indulging in a sound historian's daydream: of hearing listeners speak about their listening in their own words.

Abu Bakar Ali made a note to the future in the course of his interview: to remember that the gramophone was "a well-to-do man's object." His memory is unusual in speaking at a great distance from the perspective of gramophone ownership, placing the instrument in sharp relief. Yet, while obvious here, this theme of possession of gramophones or discs echoes throughout the other testimonies I have quoted, and adds an important dimension to the broader picture. Patricia Choo Neo Oh, for example, shows how gramophones and discs were not only for rich men; her Malay mother ruled the gramophone in her house, while schoolgirls used it to learn songs as they listened to discs and transcribed and shared song texts. And even though she had a gramophone at home, discs were for the most part too expensive; she borrowed them from a female relative who had married into money.

These memories might be understood in the context of the time in which they were recalled: from the perspective of a postcolonial present looking back, tensely and fondly, to a colonial past. For Douglas Hiorns, the winding up of the gramophone was an imaginative means of access to a boozy idyll long gone; for Marie Bong, turning the handle unlocked a golden childhood in which the gramophone was a musical toy. Amid a thick haze of reminiscence, though, we also encounter much more detailed memories: for example, that of a music student at Raffles College. Paul Abisheganaden recalled the Beethoven-fueled high teas held by his music professor, together with the much broader policing of the college through noise rules restricting gramophone use. The "treasuring" of discs took on additional meaning in this connection, as a way of signifying the social tensions between students and professors in the colonial university.

What larger conclusions can be drawn from these oral histories? On the one hand, they provide a complement to the work of Tan Sooi Beng, who argues that the shellac disc was a vehicle for "pan-Asian cosmopolitanism" in the colonial context of British Malaya (a place discussed in chapter 2).[28] In this context, "winding up" the gramophone in Singapore could also serve as a materialization of memory; it was a means of accessing and reframing a colonial past. On the other hand, these oral history interviews open doors onto wider, even global themes: the class distinction between gramophones and discs and the sheer expensiveness of the latter (a topic I will explore in another context in chapter 4), and also, more broadly still, the imaginative dimensions of listening to recorded sound. In this sense, "winding up" the gramophone can be a prelude to the second half of this book, which pivots from materiality and infrastructure now to explore three perspectives on listening—granted by a singer, a region, and a work of fiction.

CHAPTER 3

The Reproduction of Caruso

Even now widely considered one of the world's greatest tenors, Enrico Caruso was one of the most famous living Italians in the early twentieth century.[1] These claims to fame are not, though, the only reasons he continues to receive attention from historians. He was also the singer whose voice made listeners believe in, and pay for, music on record for the first time. Or so a well-known story goes. It is a story that took hold in the years after Caruso's death in 1921. In an early issue of *The Gramophone*, editor Compton Mackenzie wrote:

> If you are anxious to test the measure of Caruso's vitality, consider what he has meant to the gramophone. He made it what it is. For years in the minds of nearly everybody there were records, and there were Caruso records. He impressed his personality through the medium of his recorded voice on kings and peasants. Everybody might not possess a Caruso record, but everybody wanted to possess one, and a universal appeal such as his voice made cannot be sneered away by anybody. People did not really begin to buy gramophones until the appearance of the Caruso records gave them an earnest of the gramophone's potentialities.[2]

Note the distinction Mackenzie drew, in 1924, between hardware and software: Caruso's discs led to gramophone sales. By 1952, the idea that Caruso—the discs, the voice, the man—unleashed the power to create a musical medium was commonplace, so much so that *Life* magazine could refresh its readers' memory in the following terms: "So great was Caruso's prestige, even then, that the phonograph automatically became socially accepted."[3] Over the decades, this idea of Caruso's historical influence over listeners has been revived time and time again.[4]

The notion is alive and well in the twenty-first century, as scholars across the humanities reexamine sound reproduction technologies and the tricky issue of what made listeners pay attention to them.[5] In one of the most thorough accounts of Caruso's aural attraction, the historian David Suisman claims that his personality was in active synergy with an emerging star system.[6] Suisman argues that the singer became an early mass-media celebrity because his recordings were blessed with a highly distinctive and "manly" voice: listeners could recognize him by sound alone, and could associate that sound with a celebrity persona, awakening a desire to be similarly recognised (Suisman notes an early-twentieth-century cult of personality in North America that gave rise to countless manuals on how to become one's own personal brand through dress, comportment, and voice).[7] Caruso instigated a wave of consumption in gramophones and discs among the middle classes, establishing a pattern with far-reaching consequences for the development of the music industry. He provided, according to Suisman's narrative, an early demonstration of the fact that a sung performance could be mechanically reproduced while, crucially, retaining the performer's unique acoustic signature.

Suisman gives new depth to an old story. He explores Caruso's role in recruiting gramophone listeners, noting broader dynamics of celebrity at play within the North American mediascape. Yet his version of the story leaves Caruso's identity as an Italian in the United States largely untouched.[8] By contrast, in a more recent treatment of Caruso as the "first Neapolitan star," Simona Frasca explains how the Italian diaspora of which he was part shaped his celebrity, in large part through recordings.[9] Together with Italian and French operatic numbers, and popular songs in English, Caruso recorded several Neapolitan songs, sung in his Neapolitan mother tongue. His first Neapolitan discs date from the early 1910s, the peak years of mainly Southern Italian working-class emigrants arriving in the United States.[10] Frasca suggests that these recordings circulated widely among New York's *colonia*—the term used by elite Italians to refer to Little Italy—adding an important vector to Caruso's growing celebrity. A fresh tranche of consumers was drawn to Caruso by contemporary politics: in the context of settler-colonial racism, which framed Neapolitans as "darker" than white Americans, Caruso provided a positive image of the Southern emigrant by calling on Italy's prestigious operatic heritage.[11] To put this another way, his records enabled an assimilationist dream of acceptance within US society without any loss of Southern Italian identity.

Suisman and Frasca offer important reappraisals of Caruso's relationship with the gramophone: as the product of celebrity fascination among white middle-class society, while also catering to the desire for "whitening" among the Italian diaspora in the United States.[12] Both elements of historical explanation are called forth by the present-day scholarly agendas, and take on additional significance in an age of sound studies. Here, Caruso stories insistently raise questions of historical origin and narration: Can we identify the arrival of a moment when "music" placed on "record" engaged a listeners en masse for the first time? How should we tell the story of the emergence of mass listening? As we repeatedly turn to Caruso to answer these questions, his gramophone career comes to stand for the emergence of a consumer reflex, the desire to buy and listen to music on recordings, establishing the beginning of a story that leads—by way of tape, vinyl, and server farms—to the micromonetization of music in the present day.

In this chapter I want to amplify some of the awkwardness of this tale. In short, I will revisit a series of uneasy equivalences between Caruso and disc which, I would like to suggest, echo deeply in histories of listening and occlude the many and generative frictions between listeners and sound media that structure musical and sonic formats.[13] In particular, I will try to show how a shift in stories of Caruso's relationship with discs—and in the ways listeners paid attention to them—took place mainly after his death. Only then did discs, voice, and man come into narrative alignment, forging the shape of a story in which Caruso could be said to have brought a new musical consumer into being. These postmortem stories attributed grandiose powers to Caruso's voice to make musical media, yet paradoxically denied him agency in his own reproduction. He became the gramophone industry's unwitting rainmaker, whose voice just happened to resonate with technologies and listeners of the past.[14] By contrast, in revisiting Caruso's life through discs, I will reconstruct his agency in the making of the format. I will then go on to show how his death has lent force to those who, following Mackenzie's example, made claims about the singer's influence over gramophone listeners of yesteryear, even as his many entanglements with the Italian diaspora were largely forgotten.

Voice of Gold and Bronze

Caruso was born in Naples in 1873, to a working-class family. His father was a metal mechanic, a trade he encouraged his son to follow, apprenticing him at an early age to a factory that made metal (probably bronze) water fountains for the city. (Remember this last detail.) His mother, a cleaner, insisted that Caruso attend school in the evenings, where he sang in a cathedral choir and studied technical drawing.[15] (This last detail will also return.) Caruso's operatic breakthrough came in his early twenties at Naples's small Teatro Nuovo, with a minor role in Mario Morelli's *L'amico Francesco* (1894).[16] The opera was bankrolled by the little-known composer, and was performed only twice.[17] Nevertheless, the event provided a launchpad; a number of engagements followed, both in Italy and abroad. Before the nineteenth century was over, Caruso had appeared in Rome, Cairo, St. Petersburg, Moscow, and Buenos Aires.[18]

In 1900, Caruso sang for the first time at Milan's Teatro alla Scala, opening the new season in Italy's most prestigious opera house. It was an important milestone, drawing further international attention. In January 1902, after observing Caruso perform in Milan, a representative from London's Gramophone Company invited him to record ten numbers—an invitation that Caruso accepted.[19] The recording session took place a few hundred meters from La Scala: at the Hotel Milan, where Giuseppe Verdi had died the previous year. Caruso recorded well-known tunes—including "Questa o quella" and "Celeste Aida," staples by the recently deceased Verdi, perhaps intended as an homage. But his choice of repertoire came largely from operas composed in recent years, including the aria "Studenti, udite!" from Alberto Franchetti's *Germania*, which had premiered at La Scala only the previous month. In other words, his earliest discs envisioned the gramophone as, at once, a medium for archiving the canon and for broadcasting recent operas.[20]

What induced Caruso to record, where other opera singers had refused the Gramophone Company's offers? This question has been deeply pondered, giving rise to a potent mythology of its own.[21] Along with the cash, it is likely that the promise of fame provided an important incentive. Yet I would like to suggest that his familiarity with metals played a role. Caruso's early experiences in constructing water fountains meant that, unlike many other performers of the time, he was primed to understand the processes by which wax moulds were cast. In the Hotel Milan, for example, Caruso's voice was engraved in a wax master that would later, in a Gramophone Company factory, be cast in copper and then nickel: a process not unlike the casting of bells, coins, and indeed bronze water fountains. As I will go on to show, metal casting remained a constant theme throughout Caruso's musical career.

It was at least in part due to his Milanese discs that Caruso came to New York's Metropolitan Opera House for the first time in 1903. The Met's director, Heinrich Conried, was on a talent-scouting trip to Paris that summer when he heard of Caruso's growing reputation in New York; and on the strength of elite word of mouth, together with the testimony of recordings the tenor had made the previous year, he invited Caruso to join his company there.[22] For Conried, the endorsement provided by recordings would have been something of a novelty in the multistage rigmarole of selecting and hiring opera singers, offering him a further guarantee of Caruso's good voice. Yet, at this early moment in the gramophone industry, discs meant much more than just the sounds they contained. Like a *carte de visite*, discs called attention to a singer's increasing circulation on an international opera circuit. In this sense, the very sounds of discs marked an empty space in which a singer could be imagined and desired.

Ahead of Caruso's arrival in New York, his contract was negotiated by Pasquale Simonelli, a banker.[23] Simonelli was himself a relatively new arrival in North America, having migrated from Naples in 1897 to try his luck among New York's Italian elite—first as a language tutor and librarian, then as a clerk at the Italian Savings Bank.[24] He was well suited to Caruso's purpose: in addition to his Neapolitan credentials, he was a member of the Republican Party and had acquired other useful connections in the United States. Despite initial misgivings about the contract Simonelli created, Caruso was, later, deeply grateful to the banker—so much so that he gave Simonelli a gold medallion bearing his profile, engraved with the words "per ricordo" ("to remember me by").[25]

These personalized gold coins contain overlapping themes in Caruso's biography up to this point. He already knew about metalwork, of course; and the minting of medallions was customary for well-to-do personages across the long nineteenth century, functioning as both presents and souvenirs.[26] Caruso produced very small, inexpensive imprints of himself that could be produced at scale and more freely distributed. It was a practice he imported into the recording studio, as his first biographer, Pierre Van Rensselaer Key, recorded shortly after Caruso's death: "Often he came to the recording laboratory with little souvenirs for members of staff and the orchestra; and once he brought each of them a gold medallion with a bas-relief of his head on one side."[27] These mini-souvenirs complemented the making of discs—a mold of his profile, a mold of his voice—bringing two modes of portraiture into contact. Their conjunction represents Caruso's agency in his own reproduction. Doled out at the recording studio, coins symbolically repaid a debt to musicians and laboratory technicians in helping reproduce his voice. At the same time, these coins enlisted their recipients' services and good opinions as workers, recruiting them in the project of making a celebrity personality.

Circulation

The Simonelli medallion and its replicas present Caruso at the fulcrum of interlocking circulations: as a singer ascending through a cosmopolitan opera circuit, and as a famous Neapolitan in transit to and from an elite Italian community of bankers, doctors, and operagoers in New York. These areas of circulation were not entirely separate. Many people, including musicians and opera singers, belonged to both, and Caruso benefited from commanding audiences already familiar with or at least interested in opera, while also calling on ethnic pride from the Italian diaspora.[28] Yet his celebrity was the product not only of the combination between these two sets of listeners, but of productive frictions between them: frictions that supercharged Caruso's circulation through a clash of political interests.

Consider the most well-known anecdote about Caruso: the so-called Monkey House Incident of 1906, in which he was accused of sexually harassing a woman who then vanished before the trial.[29] On 16 November he was arrested in or near the Primate House of New York's Central Park Zoo on the charge of "annoying women," specifically a young woman called Hannah Graham.[30] The day after the arrest, the New York Police Department held a press conference in which the arresting officer revealed intimate particulars:

> [Caruso] wore a single-breasted overcoat, with a cane stuck upright in the pocket. His hands were in his pockets, and I never could make out . . . just how he used them to such annoyance, for he never took them out. After arresting him on Friday evening I examined the coat, and found that there was a slit in one of the pockets. Through this he could reach out a hand through the buttoned space.[31]

Two days later, another press conference was held at the Metropolitan Opera. Caruso was present but Conried spoke on his behalf, reading out a prepared statement that declared the tenor's innocence. As Caruso looked on, Conried reenacted a scene later described in the *Washington Post*:

> One of the reporters played "Mrs. Graham." Mr. Conried put both his hands in his pockets, looked at an imaginary monkey up near the wainscoting, and brushed gently against the reporter, instantly bowed and moved over toward the corner of the room.[32]

Except for a few remarks in French—Caruso could neither speak nor understand English, a fact that later became important to his defense—the singer remained silent; others spoke about him and on his behalf.

When Caruso arrived at Yorkville Magistrates Court a few days later, the room was packed with around six hundred people, including several prominent operagoers; there were many more on the staircase outside.[33] According to the *New York Times*, those present could be divided into "Italians," who shouted *Viva Caruso!*, and "Americans," who hissed.[34] The legal proceedings opened with a shock for the defense: the public prosecutor—and former police chief—James A. Mathot produced fresh allegations. Caruso had harassed not only Graham in the Primate House but others elsewhere: two "respectable" women, a "colored lady," and two girls.[35] Graham did not appear at any point during the trial, and Caruso's legal defense argued that no such person existed: the police, it claimed, were unwilling to produce the key witness for fear of exposing a long-standing scam in which they were actively implicated.[36] However, the police did produce another female victim, who alleged that Caruso had sexually harassed her. This new witness entered the court covered in a heavy white veil and never spoke; her name was never revealed. As she uncovered her face, Mathot asked Caruso, through an interpreter: "Do you recognize this woman?" Caruso replied no, he did not. Mathot went on to ask whether Caruso had once leaned against this woman's back in the Met's standing section during the second act of *Parsifal* (conjuring, for opera fans in the courtroom, Wagner's Flower Maidens, as perhaps an appropriately lurid accompaniment for a sexual misdemeanor). Caruso again answered no, he did not. His defense objected that Mathot was firing off questions "simply to get into the newspapers." The magistrate refused permission for Mathot to call a second, again anonymous, witness whom, it was suggested, Caruso had abused at a horse show.

Mathot's called a female witness to distract from Hannah Graham's nonappearance, as though to present a larger context for Caruso's alleged actions in the Monkey House: the very real problem of sexual harassment of women in New York, which Mathot smoothly combined with nativist fear of male immigrants.[37] Eliding the enormous differences between elite and working-class Italians in New York, the latter being primary targets of nativist fear, Mathot in his closing remarks directly addressed the wealthy Italians who had come to court to support Caruso:

> I am not here as a representative of the Police Department or as a defender of [the arresting officer], but I am here in the name of decency, and I ask, in the names of our wives and of our children and of every honest man in the community, that you give a decision that will impress on these misfit wretches, these perverts, the fact that they cannot insult honest women on our highways as they strive to do.[38]

Mathot's insult provoked an outcry from the gallery. The following day, the magistrate returned to declare Caruso guilty, sentencing him to a fine of a ten dollars, although sparing him severer punishments of imprisonment and hard labor.

In recalling in some detail this notorious episode from Caruso's early years in New York, I want to underscore the manner in which the singer was represented. He was largely mute, while extensive newspaper coverage reveled in contrasting Caruso's distinct personas as an opera singer, on the one hand, and as southern Italian in New York on the other. In all this, the fact that Caruso did not speak English well and mostly spoke through interpreters was somehow crucial. Journalists scanned his face for signs that he comprehended what was being said about him, remarking on his apparent boredom in constantly twirling his moustache.[39] The tenor's muteness called attention to his physical presence, creating an amusing distinction between his putatively transgressive body and his famous voice. His silence mirrored that of the veiled woman presented by the prosecution: she, too, became a muted body in the courtroom, the object of endless chatter and speculation.

Caruso had an opportunity to respond a few months later, when he began working as a caricaturist for the Italian-language satirical newspaper *La Follia di New York* (The Madness of New York). In January 1907, several weeks after the trial, the editor invited Caruso to supply sketches for the annual banquet of the New York Camera del Commercio, an important event in the *colonia*'s calendar. He drew prominent men in attendance—diplomats, ambassadors, aristocrats, and newspaper editors—and was published on the front page: pairs of tuxedoed figures occupied the corners, while the caricaturist himself appeared at the center, with his hands significantly planted inside his much-discussed pockets. According to the caption, Caruso stared menacingly at a certain "Cavaliere 'M'! A mystery!"[40] In veiled language easy to decipher for an Italian readership apprised of recent events, Caruso represented himself throwing a vengeful glance in Mathot's direction.

Following this debut as a caricaturist, Caruso supplied drawings for *La Follia* on a weekly basis for much of the rest of his life. Mainly featuring lawyers, businessmen, and musicians in New York, and occasionally famous women, these sketches were for the most part mild in their satire, serving to flatter prominent people in the *colonia* and its orbit. The tenor's secondary vocation became well known beyond the North American Italian press, and was soon monumentalized in a bilingual luxury edition spearheaded by *La Follia*. These books generated advance demand, as revealed by the following letter to the editor which appeared on the front page of *La Follia* in 1907:

> Dear Sir, I have received the three copies of "Follia" I requested, in which I admired the splendid caricatures by Caruso. Caruso is a wonderful man. A few days ago, I saw an advert for the "Book of Caruso" but the price ($50) put me off. If in said book there were SOME ORIGINAL SKETCHES DRAWN BY HIS OWN HAND, then I can see why it would have such great value.

> I do not know Enrico Caruso, nor had I ever heard him sing (an unpardonable error) before the last season; but, having to judge from the public that goes to the Metropolitan Opera House, I must deduce that he has many admirers and is very popular, more popular than one would think. AND THIS DESPITE ALL THE GOSSIP SPREAD ABOUT HIM LAST WINTER—WHICH, NEEDLESS TO SAY, I NEVER BELIEVED.
>
> With pleasure, I send you the two dollars for a year's subscription to "Follia." THERE IS NO PRICE NOT WORTH PAYING FOR A NEWSPAPER THAT HAS THE HONOUR TO PUBLISH ORIGINAL SKETCHES BY THE GREAT TENOR ENRICO CARUSO.[41]

This letter was signed by Helen Weston, introduced by the paper as a "signorina americana" who has "perfect knowledge of our language." The editor highlighted in capital letters what he took to be the take-home messages: the great expense of the volume was justified by the images' authenticity (perhaps she expected originals rather than copies); and that this operagoer—an American woman, no less—had never believed the rumors stemming from the Monkey House.[42]

Weston's letter also furnishes subtler information about the meanings and values that contemporaries ascribed to these caricatures. She presented herself as someone who hadn't heard Caruso sing until recently, thus positioning herself among a wide orbit of middle classes interested in opera but largely mystified by it. As her letter confesses—and this was perhaps the rule rather than the exception—she felt obliged to judge him, and his performance, from the reactions of others: to "deduce" (*arguire*) that he was widely admired. In other words, the singer remained unknowable even when present on stage, and even more so in recollection. Operatic fandom required more tangible, more easily legible supports, such as caricatures, which could create a record of operatic performance and provide a means of approach to a famous voice.

Masks and Doubles

The Monkey House Incident echoed throughout the cosmopolitan West. A sketch showing Caruso confronted by the veiled woman in court provided the front cover for Paris's *Monde illustré*. In-depth news coverage reached the notice of James Joyce, then living in Trieste, who later recycled the material for Leopold Bloom's trial in *Ulysses* (1922).[43] In New York, Caruso was no longer just a famous opera singer. He was, for example, the target of a scene in the 1907 *Ziegfeld Follies* in which he was "tried on stage (by a jury of twelve beauties) for his then famous antics"—a skit that featured the famous Broadway actor Anna Held (Florenz Ziegfeld's wife) as Mrs. Innocence.[44] The skit's main song, "My Cousin Caruso," was performed by Charles A. Bigelow, a well-known comic actor. Composed for the occasion by Gus Edwards and Edward Madden, "My Cousin Caruso" gives voice, in heavily accented English, to a Neapolitan immigrant to New York who claims family ties with the Metropolitan Opera's greatest star. Its melody quotes from the famous phrase from *Pagliacci*, "Ridi, pagliaccio, con il cuore infranto" (Laugh, clown, though your heart is broken), but is set to new words ("His voice so sad-a, Drive de ladies all mad-a") to envoice the immigrant's parody of his famous cousin.[45]

Such attention brought about a shift in the way Caruso was talked about, refreshing the opposition between his operatic voice and immigrant body established by the Monkey House fiasco and the subsequent trial—a split staged in the song through the double exposure of tenor and dubious cousin. Caruso not only was aware of such doubling but actively encouraged it. The musicologist Larry Hamberlin quotes extensively from an account of Caruso performing at a benefit concert, where Gus Edwards sang "My Cousin Caruso": "The audience howled at the catch lines, and Caruso screamed louder than anyone else at Gus's efforts to satirize him."[46] Such laughter might be read in many ways, signaling discomfort mixed in with apparent delight. For one thing, the evocation of Caruso's cousin as a Neapolitan type recalls blackface minstrelsy, a theatrical institution in the early-twentieth-century United States.[47] Laughter was more or less compulsory in this context as a way of communicating racist pleasure among audience members.[48] But, as the blackface tradition bears out, laughter can also fulfill functions well beyond the domain of humor.

As both the object and the subject of laughter, Caruso's racial identity was at once darkened and whitened.[49] In laughing, he became "whiter" in his identity as an opera star; in being laughed at, he became "blacker" through association with his biological relation. Once again, we find a split between body and voice: his body as the object of a racializing gaze; and his voice as the object of a racializing ear.[50] In another example of this phenomenon, Caruso later sculpted a miniature bust of himself in the act of laughing (figure 3.1), which again constitutes a multilayered performance of race. In the shape of a laughing Buddha, and intended to function as a decorative bookend, this statuette invokes orientalism and chinoiserie (and kitsch). Yet, with eyes closed and mouth open wide, and cast in blackened bronze, the object also cues blackface minstrelsy. Caruso-as-Buddha makes sidelong reference to the tenor's signature aria from *Pagliacci*, in which ambiguous laughter featured so prominently. No doubt this mini-bust was meant to be funny: it invites laughter from its beholder, even as it catches Caruso's own laughing mid-convulsion.[51]

Figure 3.1 "Caricature Self-Portrait Bust by Enrico Caruso" (1909), sculpture in blackened bronze. Museum number S. 104-2015. © Victoria and Albert Museum, London.

Eight impressions of the mold were struck in 1909 at the Roman Bronze Works, owned by the Genoese chemical engineer Riccardo Bertelli—the most important Italian foundry operating in early-twentieth-century New York. In the means and content of representation, these statuettes record a celebrity marked by recent events in the city. He is a laughing man encased in a metal body.

Caruso later participated in a silent film about his Neapolitan relative. Apparently inspired by Edwards and Madden's song, he starred in *My Cousin* (1918), in which the cousin is redeemed as a real, long-lost relative and a veritable dopplegänger. Produced by the prestigious Hollywood company Famous Lasky Players, the script was supplied by Margaret Turnbull, a Scottish writer on the staff. It was a Caruso extravaganza in which he appeared in both title roles: as the world-famous singer Cesare Caroli, and as Tommaso Longo, his cousin who (as an intertitle informs us) "carves out a meagre living sculpting models for the Italian plastering foundries" in New York. The film riffs on and literalizes a situation that will by now be familiar: of Caruso as a man with two bodies. In an important scene, the opera singer mimes "Vesti la giubba" (including the notorious hysterical laugh) on stage before a packed audience, even while his Neapolitan cousin looks down from the nosebleed seats.

In the 1910s many films revolved around human doubles, exploiting the medium to incorporate elaborate trick shots.[52] *My Cousin* turns on two such moments. The first comes shortly after Cesare's performance at the Met and takes place in an Italian restaurant: Tommaso orders a round of drinks for everyone in the house, and proposes a toast to the famous tenor. Cesare watches the scene with satisfaction from a private booth. He then makes to leave: in an extended shot, he walks from the deep background toward the exit, passing Tommaso on the way. As they approach each other, Tommaso enjoins the stranger (that is, Caroli, disguised by his hat) to raise a glass to Italy's beloved tenor. Once the singer has left, the restaurant's owner reveals to all that they have been in the presence of the great Cesare Caroli himself. A second example, again featuring two Carusos on screen at once (this time using a double rather than a trick shot) occurs near the very the end of the film, and visually enacts the long-delayed family reunion.

My Cousin was a disaster at the US box office. The film historian Giuliana Muscio argues that its failure was due to Caruso's unwillingness to participate in US stereotypes about violent Italians, along with the story's prevailing focus on Tommaso rather than Cesare, foregrounding the experience of Italian immigrants at the expense of screen time for the famous singer.[53] But there is another reason why the film failed to appeal, which has more centrally to do with the pleasures and dangers of doubling. It is significant, for example, that Tommaso makes casts for the Italian foundries, recalling both Caruso's father's trade and the singer's own mold-making proclivities. The opening scene of *My Cousin* reveals Tommaso at work in his studio surrounded by classical figurines in plaster waiting to be cast in metal, the largest of which is covered with a white sheet, later to be revealed as the cast of a life-size bust of Cesare Cairoli. During the course of the film, this bust becomes an important character

Figure 3.2 A still image from *My Cousin* (1918). This cross-fade shows Cesare Caroli (Caruso, seated) remembering meeting his cousin Tommaso (Caruso, standing) in a restaurant, but failing to recognize him. Tommaso's bust of Caroli also appears in this shot. The film is in the public domain; see https://commons.wikimedia.org/ (accessed 27 February 2020).

in its own right—a third Caruso, no less. Not merely a reproduction, it becomes an agent of recognition when it prompts Cesare to remember the chance meeting with his cousin at the restaurant, a memory visualized through elaborate crosscutting (figure 3.2).

When the two cousins finally meet in the closing scene, Cesare is accompanied by the cast of himself. As a street party unfolds in Little Italy, Cesare enters Tommaso's studio and, at long last, acknowledges his relative and offers him a lucrative commission to recreate the bust in marble. The pendulum swing between singer and cousin (original and copy) that extends throughout the film ends in the cousin's favor, inviting empathy with the plight of the penniless artist and, by extension, with Italian immigrants in general. This is an important reason why *My Cousin* was a flop, as Muscio suggests: it appeals to nonexistent empathy from mainstream white middle-class moviegoers of the time. But another reason was that in the late 1910s, at the height of Caruso's fame and prestige, North Americans found it hard to suspend disbelief and draw pleasure from the juxtaposition of two Carusos.

My Cousin reflects deeply on the politics of Caruso's reproduction.

A story of doubles and migrant circulations, it calls attention to the collective expenditure of attention involved in the replication of any famous personality, together with the more particular racial dynamics of repulsion and attraction engaged through Caruso's stardom around the Atlantic seaboard. An unapproachable distance separates relatives for most of the film: a distance that is ultimately overcome by way of a bust, the product of molding and metalwork, which prompts the famous singer to go in search of his audience member. *My Cousin* enacts a magical reversal of the celebrity dynamics by which an audience member comes to know an opera star, staging the fantasy of a celebrity in pursuit of his fan. In this way, the film pays homage to the larger patterns of economic migration that sustained Caruso's celebrity. And beyond this vast human circulation, it also stages a tribute to the materials through which "he" traveled. The film's true hero is neither singer nor cousin, but a bust, which stands in for the labor and materials expended in the reproduction of a famous personality through drawings, coins, statuettes, and discs.

Disc Life

To sum up the argument so far: placed alongside other visual media and plastic forms, Caruso's early circulation on gramophone discs appears different. In the recording studio, the singer offered small gold tokens bearing his profile: it was an exchange between craftsmen, a face for a voice. Next to his caricatures, discs could be understood as pictures: aural sketches of performance that overcame a passage across the footlights, at once acknowledging and inscribing the distance (noted in Weston's letter) between performer and audience member. Busts and statuettes, for their part, find analogies in the industrial processes by which discs were made and the human resemblances they enfolded. Wax masters were like plaster molds, waiting to be cast in metal, marble, or shellac mixtures; both discs and statuettes embodied desirable likenesses to body, mouth, and voice. As I now turn my focus to discs, I want to explore the possibility that the story of Caruso's discs need not be construed as a tale of drawing listeners to a new medium, and to suggest that at the turn of the century, discs were understood as yet another mode of celebrity, yet another means for transmitting the virtual person.

Caruso's most well-known disc can be productively reviewed and reheard in this vein. In 1904, shortly after his arrival in the United States, he recorded "Vesti la giubba" for a second time. More than any other record, this disc has been marked out for its power to attract listeners to the gramophone. It was, or so we frequently read, the first ever to sell a million copies, to "go platinum."[54] Early accounts from the trade press, by contrast, present a looser affinity between Caruso and early disc listeners—as when, in 1907, a Philadelphia-based gramophone salesman reported that his customers were requesting demonstrations from the tenor, though, he stressed, not any song or disc in particular.[55] Recorded in the pages of *The Talking Machine World*, this local snapshot cautions against reading "Vesti la giubba" as an acclaimed hit. More likely, it accrued its devotees over time as an eminently collectable operatic souvenir. That notwithstanding, "Vesti la giubba" became—as the *My Cousin* parody underscored—an aria and a role deeply linked with Caruso. A song about a clown applying theatrical makeup, it constructed the disc itself as a celebrity mask.

Such analogies between discs and other molds may seem fanciful at first blush. But they offer an alternative to the Caruso story outlined at the opening of this chapter: the potent myth, which has gathered reality through repetition, that Caruso's discs drew listeners to the gramophone for the first time. A useful point of contrast here is with historical advertisements, which might appear to echo a story of emergent mass listening. Ads bearing titles such as "Both are Caruso" and "Caruso's Glorious Voice Kept for Posterity by the Phonograph" stridently assert the equivalence between man, voice, and disc, and illustrate a dominant mode of gramophone listening under white male capitalism. With everyday accounts of listening widely scattered and hard to retrieve, historical adverts may thus be understood to provide access to the dominant logics of an historical, cultural marketplace. Yet the claim of equivalence between man and disc found in contemporary advertisements proves to be ambiguous. On the one hand, the ads' phatic assertions point to their opposites (as Jonathan Sterne has noted, the statement "Both are Caruso" immediately engages the reasonable suspicion that both are not, in fact, Caruso).[56] On the other hand, the very chattiness of ads distracts from quieter material contiguities.

The plastic analogies recovered in this chapter, by contrast, point to an historical epistemology for Caruso's recordings in which sounds were not merely the content of discs, but also an elaborate frame—alongside advertisements, record catalogues, and disc labels—for the personal properties contained within. By contrast, the indexing of the performer's body provided a more basic impulse for disc buying, persisting beyond the still evanescent if now repeatable temporality of listening, and the promised stimulation or delusion of the consumer's ears. Clearly, these desires cannot easily be separated: in discs, the urge toward capturing a celebrity's body and the possibilities of listening to a voice are closely entwined. Yet, Caruso's case indicates a larger pattern within the development of the gramophone industry, by which human capture provided the imaginative scaffolding for the ear-centric orientations, or what Sterne calls "audile technique." My argument draws inspiration from Stephen Best's explorations of early sound reproduction technology, which note the legal parallels in the United States between slaveholding and phonography, in terms of the seizure of human properties.[57]

A chance remark—again taken from the pages of *The Talking Machine World*—demonstrates the primacy of such bodily capture. Quoted in an interview in late 1906, an anonymous recording expert said: "No voice rings out better or with more realistic effect than Caruso's, and one could almost believe it was the man himself who was singing and not the record."[58] Coming from inside the gramophone industry, these words contain an early rumbling of the notion that the tenor's voice was especially suited to recording technology. In this sense, it could be read, alongside ads discussed above, as evidence for the special appeal of Caruso's discs to the ears. But the statement also and more straightforwardly expresses admiration at the outcome of industrial processes of sonic sculpture. It conveys pleasure at the second self that "rings" from record, the disc that "sings," with the emphasis falling not on the sensory means but on the industrial product, together with the act of recognition to which it gives rise.

The production of doubles had its correlate in New York's *colonia*, as we have seen. Not only did settler-colonial racism split the world-famous celebrity from the lowly immigrant, the voice from its body; it also created a biological tropology in which the split was given new shape and resignified through two bodies linked by putative family ties. Splitting and doubling prepared the way for the singer's reproduction in sound, loosening his voice from his body in advance of its circulation on disc, readying listeners to receive the singer's double in his absence. In other words, there was a busy dialectic between Caruso's presence, onstage and in "real life," and his absences materialized by plastic doubles. On the one hand, discs stood in for the opera singer as a performer; on the other, they substituted for a fast-growing body of migrant southern Italians moving across the Americas.[59]

Traces of this dialectic linger in Compton Mackenzie's words, quoted at the head of this chapter. Readers of *The Gramophone* were enjoined to "test the measure of Caruso's vitality": a life force that "made [the gramophone] what it is." Behind this claim lay the prejudices of Old Europe against Italian excess, as well as more recent racisms inspired by a perceived overabundance of European migrants crossing the Atlantic.[60] Mackenzie invoked this political geography:

> There has recently been a tendency to decry Caruso for his over-emphasis, his shouting, his almost ventriloquial ambitions, his coarseness, and his theatricality. No doubt, his singing possessed all these faults; but they were the faults of superfluous energy, of superfluous emotion, of superfluous vitality. They were inherent in his personality and therefore in his art. He should have pruned his style, the critics tell us. No doubt he should; but it is easier to prune a gooseberry bush in a backyard than a jungle in Guiana.

Caruso's theatrical presence morphs into the thriving life of the tropics, distantly foreshadowing Werner Herzog's *Fitzcarraldo*; the colonial passagework is sudden and unashamed.[61] Mackenzie summoned Caruso as a power as vital and inevitable as the jungle's growth—a transition between the opera singer and the densely thicketed rain forest that could only make sense alongside a surplus of southern Italian lives propelled around the Atlantic Ocean.

For Your Ears Only

At the time of his death, this vaunted vitality in Caruso's records was freshly recalled. There was an explosion of life-writing—newspaper articles, obituaries, biographies—which made passing mention of his recording activities, usually in the context of reports on his tremendous wealth.[62] A trope emerged of Caruso's "imperishable" and "indestructible" legacy in sound recordings, one summed up and immediately capitalized on in an Victrola advertisement that played on Caruso's deathlessness.[63] Less predictable and more variegated was the picture that emerged from his earliest biography—the result of a collaboration between Pierre Van Rensselaer Key and Bruno Zirato, Caruso's lifelong personal secretary, rushed into print shortly after his demise:

> Through "the machine" (as he termed the phonograph) he was available to the multitudes who could by no other means feel the spell of his voice and art. It seems a fitting medium to help keep our memory of him fresh: we have only to close our eyes—listening to his reproduced singing—to have him almost with us.[64]

Here, in death, we find the seed of a story about Caruso's life in discs: one to do with countless far-flung listeners, enchanted by his voice alone. But it is worth noticing the details. As Key invited his readers to close their eyes, he directed them not only in an act of listening, but in the reactivation of their memories. It was a graveside whisper to opera audiences

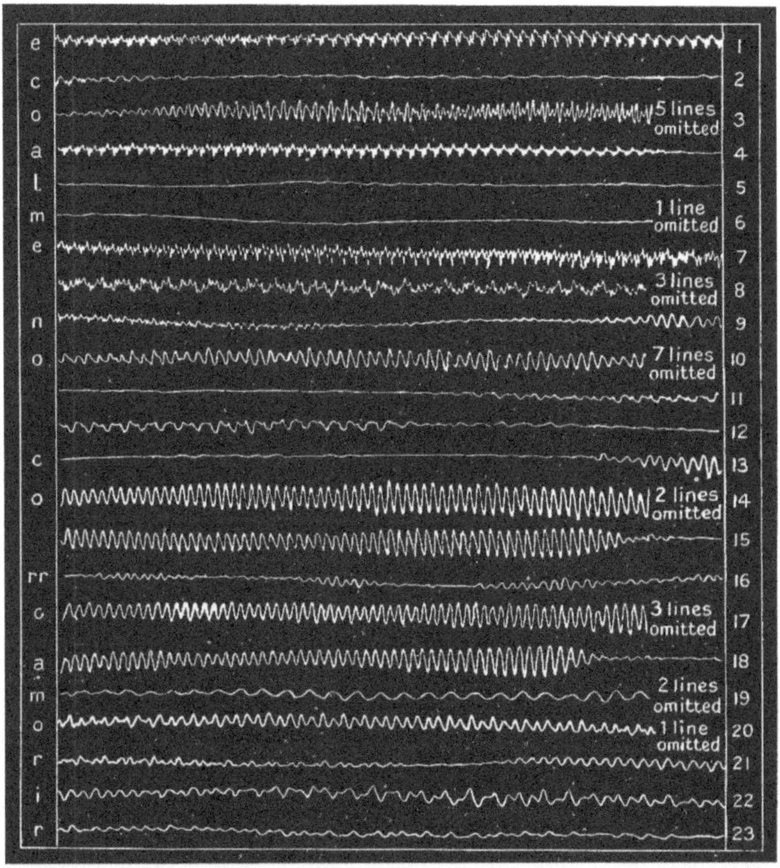

Figure 3.3 An early spectrogram showing Caruso's voice, reproduced from Edmund Wheeler Scripture, "The Curves of Caruso," *Musical Times* 65 no. 976 (1924): 518.

rather than to the untold multitudes, one that enjoined contemporaries to use recorded sounds to rekindle fond memories of a well-loved singer.[65]

Another window onto the fast-changing meanings of Caruso's discs comes from the unlikely realm of experimental phonetics. In 1924, Edmund Wheeler Scripture, a speech scientist, published a short vocal autopsy in *The Musical Times*.[66] Scripture employed an experimental setup he had honed over decades: a long transducing arm connecting a needle—dragged through the groove of a slowly turning gramophone disc, rotating once every four hours or so—to a stylus pulled over scrolling black smoked paper. In subjecting Caruso's discs to this apparatus, he produced an early spectrogram, mapping the frequency of sounds against their unfolding in time (figure 3.3). In particular, he based his analysis entirely on a five-second passage from near the end of Caruso's 1906 recording of "Di quella pira," a well-known aria from Verdi's *Il trovatore*, beginning with the onset of the aria's closing line, "Teco almeno corro a morir" ("I'll hurry at least to die with you").

These words were a topical choice in the wake of Caruso's death, even while Scripture pleaded for the scientific value of this short selection from the disc. There was, he claimed, an analytical utility in choosing to focus on the sustained (if notoriously inauthentic) high C (on "*teco*"), which demonstrated the perfect regularity of Caruso's waveform. What is more, the passage selected provided a compact demonstration of all the Italian vowels (all except "*i*" and "*u*" appear twice, allowing for ease of comparison on the page).[67] By this point in time, there had been a long tradition of wondering at powerful, manly Italian vowels in vocal pedagogy—a tradition to which Scripture contributes when he calls attention to the waveform's constant mobility of pitch:

> [Caruso] does not sing the exact notes indicated by the music as an organ or other mechanical instrument would. His voice rises and falls and twists around the tones instead of sticking to them. The result is that the song has nothing mechanical about it, but is full of *life and emotion*.[68]

And yet, Scripture's report reveals its author's penchant for the macabre—a preference dating back to his earliest experiments in transducing gramophone discs, when he focused on poetic declamations of "The Sad Story of the Death and Burial of Poor Cock Robin." Scripture's object was the voice of the poet beyond the text: an almost animal, bodily presence that could be approached through discs in their physical, physiological, and psychological dimensions. As described by Sterne, Scripture's writings are filled with pages "soaking in the metaphysics of presence"—utter conviction in the identity between voice and being.[69] The result, in Scripture's autopsy of Caruso, is an analysis of the once-living voice staged through a text about rushing into the arms of death.

Odd though it is, Scripture's vocal autopsy illustrates an evolving relationship between the tenor and his listeners. In the wake of his death, "life and emotion" became the conspicuous categories of Caruso analysis.[70] And in this sense, if in no other, Scripture's approach is emblematic of the retrospective impulses more broadly at work in the making of a musical medium: the imaginative and narrative structures that go hand in hand with audile technique. We have seen how, in Mackenzie's short obituary, Caruso "made the gramophone what it is" by interpellating the medium's listeners (hailing them into listening to the gramophone, as if for the first time). In a more scientific register, Scripture reimagined Caruso's discs in purely sonic terms, as if hearing the tenor's voice had always been the focus of attention for gramophone users and disc owners—both the medium and the message.

Reading on in Scripture's autopsy illustrates a basic difficulty of this approach: the sheer struggle of keeping Caruso's voice in focus for the ear, because sensory specialization proves hard to sustain. The speech scientist swerves, pausing to wonder over line 8 of his diagram, which, "according to the text [, . . .] must be a vowel curve, yet such a curve is an impossibility. It looked like a vowel curve produced by a violent wobbling of the tracing apparatus." Scripture goes on to dismiss the idea that such an error could have been produced by his faultless experimental setup. No, the "violent wobbling" must emanate from the singer himself:

> On listening carefully to the gramophone disc, I could hear that there was a difference in Caruso's voice at this point. He seemed to be crying. There was a tear in his voice, and this curve is the picture of a tear. How he did it, or how anyone can put a tear in the voice, is beyond imagination—but here is the registration of such a tear.[71]

Scientific listening morphs into a séance: the disc becomes a vehicle by which a once-living body, even its internal vocal behaviors, can be recovered and reexamined. One day in the future, aided by still greater powers of calculation, more mysteries might yet be revealed: "Still another secret of Caruso's voice—perhaps the most important one of all—lies in these curves. The melodious ring of his voice can be heard from the gramophone discs."[72]

Scripture was the first, though by no means the last, to summon Caruso from the grave.[73] He inaugurated a long tradition of autopsies and resurrections, both in voice science and in the recording industry.[74] In presupposing a three-dimensional body impressed in and forever after able to be reanimated from his discs, Scripture foreshadowed digital reconversion in the 1970s and beyond: the computational practices by which the voices of old singers are stripped of their noisy patina for the purposes of eternal exploitation in the marketplace.[75] Scripture marks an important development in Caruso's now posthumous career, in which he played the role not so much of a disembodied voice, but of something more like a "vocalic body": one now torn from the body of the migrant Southern Italians his sound once seemed to invoke.[76]

What Scripture most weirdly shows are the occult paths by which aural orientations may be reached—and, once reached, awkwardly maintained. This may be what the Caruso story of listeners drawn to the gramophone ultimately suggests: that ears are not easily annexed to a man or a technology, or even to a particular technique of the body, at least not for long. Such linkage requires constant assistance from advertisers, exegetes, historians, speech pathologists, and more. Caruso's discs—like all recordings, perhaps—have never been a straightforward object of audition, never only directed to listening ears. They were and are a site for listening's entanglements: the technical, narrative, and always imaginative means by which it is assembled ever anew.

CHAPTER 4

Gramophone vs. Gazooka

In October 1925, *The Gramophone* published a note on "A Working Man's Choice of Records." It explained a preference for shellac discs featuring military bands:

> Why? you ask, possibly with a superior smile. Well, in the first instance you can be fairly sure of a finished performance, whether it be an overture, a march, selections from opera or musical comedy, or a descriptive piece. Secondly, in the diversity of music recorded by military bands all tastes appear to be catered for. My third point is the question of cost, and I contend that you get good value for your outlay.[1]

The words—written by one Leonard F. Emms, then in his late thirties and resident in Stratford-upon-Avon—offered advice to fellow working-class gramophone enthusiasts on how to build a collection of discs and structure a listening program. First, he suggested, begin with a march, which "enlivens both you and your friends."[2] Next, proceed to a selection from an opera or musical: perhaps the Coldstream Guards playing "The Belle of New York," or the Grenadier Guards' "The Beggar's Opera," both discs priced at four shillings and sixpence.[3] "Then what do you want better than the 'Folk Song Suite' (Vaughan-Williams) as played by H. M. Life Guards . . . ?" This record, with the "sweetness of reed instruments" emerging in a medley on the traditional song "Green Bushes," dispels any condescending notion that "we admirers of military bands" want only the "blare of trombones or the clash of cymbals to colour our music."[4]

Emms's anticipation of a sneer was well-founded in addressing the readers of *The Gramophone*. Established two years earlier by novelist Compton Mackenzie, whom we met at the opening of chapter 3, the magazine had developed into a bastion of middle-class taste. It provided a steady stream of reviews to help its readers discriminate among an endless profusion of classical music on disc, now released monthly by major record companies like HMV, Columbia, and Parlophone.[5] Something like an early consumer watchdog, Mackenzie's journal surveyed the disc market through the eyes and ears of those predisposed to spend money on such luxury goods as shellac discs. In this context, then, Emms's article was an anomaly. He argued for the military band as a good option for working-class listeners, who, he anticipated, were likely to be unfamiliar with the shellac disc as a sonic format. The military band represented continuity in the face of technological novelty, and thus a degree of security when purchasing an expensive object (even if discs of military bands were often cheaper than other kinds, such as those featuring famous singers of the time). Equivalent to twelve US dollars in 2021, four shillings and sixpence was the average daily pay for a cargo worker on the railways, to give an example that was also a common form of employment in Stratford-upon-Avon.[6]

Another sidelong perspective on the British disc market comes from the *Gramophone*'s letters to the editor. In the same issue (October 1925), two readers wrote in response to a question—"Where are the ladies?"—posed two months before by a frequent contributor who wrote under the pseudonym "Scrutator." He remarked on the near-total absence of women's voices in the magazine: "Surely we have some fair readers in the fraternity, but if so, where are they? Have they no interest in the great affairs of state such as needle-track alignment, sound boxes, gaskets, etc.?"[7] Gladys M. Collin, writing from Manchester, responded by pointing out that the "fact that women enthusiasts do not write to *The Gramophone* does not mean that they do not exist."[8] Unlike certain male contemporaries, she suggested, women did not feel the need to exhibit their passion across the pages of a magazine. What is more, women's relative silence should not be interpreted as a lack of interest in gramophones, or (as Scrutator's longer argument had implied) in "serious" music. On the contrary, Collin noted that in her routine visits to "a neighbouring industrial town" to attend gramophone concerts, she had been "struck by the preponderance of women, many of them poor, *all of them silent and attentive*, who have been drawn there to *listen*, and certainly not to *see* or be *seen*."[9]

Printed beneath Collin's letter was another response to Scrutator's question, from Francis E. Terry of Streatham, a district of London. Taking a different tack, Terry began by accepting that "women do generally seem to be less interested in gramophones than men."[10] But since middle-class women were frequently obliged to listen to their husbands, fathers, or sons discourse at length about such "absurd interests" (his comparisons were with golf and stamp collecting), women were inoculated against them. He went on to draw connections between the masculine grip over the gramophone and the political economy of the age. The instrument belonged to a professional and managerial class: men whose lives were ruled by the distinction between work and leisure, creating an allotment of time in which to enjoy recorded music. By contrast, the lives of middle-class women were not often structured around such oscillations between office and home; their musical interests were instead more serious investments in the acquisition of socially useful skills: in singing or playing musical instruments, rather than in recorded music. Terry also considered the situation of working-class women, briefly noting the many duties, both at home and at work, that prevented them from acquiring musical skills (the ability to "read a score silently" was mentioned elsewhere in his letter), let alone building libraries of shellac discs.[11]

In this chapter I want to consider more deeply the relationship between recorded music and social class, along with crosscurrents of gender and race, to probe the gramophone's status as a mass medium. Taking a prompt from Emms, Collin, and Terry, and the various pathways and obstacles between working-class listeners and mediated musical experiences they outlined, I want to suggest ways in which shellac could at times aspire to "mass" import—a term I will take to be a euphemism for the working classes during the period in question. But I want also to insist on the many gaps, significantly but not exclusively having to do with the format's expensiveness, between the working classes and mediated listening in the British 1920s and '30s. Ultimately my goal will be to consider the format's place in a political history of listening, and my site of particular attention will be South Wales, one of Britain's prime sites of mining fossil fuels. In a coalfield society, the unlikeliness of the relationship between listeners and gramophones was acute. If the cost of a disc were the equivalent of a day's labor for a railway worker, then a coal miner would have worked half a week for the same amount (to say nothing of the expense of the gramophone itself)—assuming that such work were available during the 1920s, a time of widespread unemployment and depressed wages.[12]

South Wales is a useful place to think through the history of the format in other ways. On the one hand, local newspapers have become more readily available in recent years, placing the UK gramophone press in a new light. Reviews of the latest releases on disc were published not only in *The Gramophone* (established in April 1923), but also in several regional newspapers, including the *Shields Daily News* (from 1922), the *Burnley News* (1923), the *Dundee Courier* (1924), the *Leeds Mercury* (1924), and the *Northern Whig* (1925)—the last based in County Antrim in Northern Ireland—to name only some early examples. In what follows, I focus on the *Glamorgan Advertiser*, a local paper published in Maesteg, and its unusually long column dedicated to disc reviews.[13] But I will also make extensive use of fictional treatments of sound and listening, conveyed through the writings of Gwyn Thomas (1913–81), a novelist and playwright as well as radio and TV broadcaster, who grew up in Cymmer, near Porth, in the Rhondda Valley. Music was central to Thomas's writings about Wales, and it makes his novels and plays a useful resource for thinking about the sound and the politics of the format. His fiction also provides a revealing counterpoint to more obviously factual archives of listening.

In 1926: The Gazooka Year

Before homing in on the gramophone, I want to consider another instrument of listening—one that better sets the scene for interwar South Wales. I refer to the gazooka: a kind of mirliton, which, like a paper-and-comb, transforms the humming of its player into a searing, raspy buzz. Also known as the "gazook," the instrument's name stabilized in later reminiscences, and appears to have been a corruption (a playful mishearing?) of "kazoo." Indeed, gazookas were kazoos, sometimes with the addition of a tin horn.[14] This instrument became the sonic signature of the general strike of 1926, when hundreds of gazooka-wielding "jazz bands" took to the streets of South Wales (figure 4.1). On 3 May, in response to demands from the South Wales Miners Federation (SWMF) and other mining unions for higher wages, coal owners shut their doors to workers across the United Kingdom. A declaration of war by mine owners (the heads of private companies), this lockout threatened to go on until the unions would accept both cuts in pay and a lengthening of the working day. On 4 May, the Trades Union Congress—an umbrella organization representing interests of mining, railways, and other heavy industries—called a general strike, which halted UK railway transport for nine days. A historical achievement, the strike was nevertheless unsuccessful—Stanley Baldwin's Labour government failed to improve pay and working conditions, prompting miners across the UK to continue striking into the summer and autumn. In South Wales, many coal miners, almost all of them allied with the SWMF, refused to accept the proposed work conditions until November, thus leaving their families without an income.[15]

The appeal of gazookas in 1926 is, on one level, easy to understand. The instruments required no special musical training. In a region deprived of a major employer, gazookas were a means of collective music making to while away the hours made suddenly, endlessly, available. Yet, the proliferation and intensity of gazooka-based entertainments is worth pondering. An important if not sufficient historical context to explain the rise of the gazooka can be found in a recent history of South Wales car-

Figure 4.1 *Western Mail* (21 July 1926), 10. Original caption: "A jazz band from Williamstown marching through the streets of Cowbridge collecting in aid of the miners' distress fund." By permission of the Llyfrgell Genedlaethol Cymru / National Library of Wales.

nivals and fetes. In the early twentieth century, the SWMF, sometimes together with local branches of the Labour Party, took charge of organizing Labour Day processions in towns throughout the region.[16] This date took on special significance in 1926, when larger-than-usual crowds gathered to watch the parades. Indeed, so successful were the Labour Day parades that they inspired countless further carnivals during the six-month strike, often with the purpose of raising funds for local canteens and soup kitchens. For example, on 19 June, the *Merthyr Express* reported on a recent procession through the streets of Troedyrhiw, headed by the chief constable of the police and the town band, followed by "three jazz bands" who produced "queer and grotesque noises" by means of "a variety of obsolete and improvised instruments."[17] Not yet branded with a name, the gazooka can be glimpsed through an emergent association with "jazz"—itself a fuzzy category in interwar Britain, as Catherine Tackley has shown, often carrying subversive undertones.[18]

"Jazz" bands featuring gazookas appeared in another carnival that took place on the same June day in 1926, this one in Bargoed, at an event organized to support the local canteen fund. As in Troedyrhiw, thousands lined the streets to watch a procession headed by a brass band, followed by several characters in costume, including "comic bands" playing "jazz."[19] The procession led from the church to the football ground, where participants were awarded prizes. The best comic band was judged to be the "Saveloy Banana Band," which had already won no fewer than twenty-one such competitions. A deliberately mangled reference to the Savoy Orpheans—the most famous British dance band of the later 1920s, largely responsible for relaying ideas of American jazz to UK audiences via the wireless—the band's name hints at the repertory being hummed into gazookas. Other prize winners included "Indian Temple" and "Welsh Tableau" (in the category of best tableau), "Glaxo Baby" and "Golliwog" (for comic dress), and "Coalowner and Miner" (for best original idea)—the last featuring a coal owner dragging "a long chain attached to the miner's neck." Of course there were many other acts that won no prizes but nevertheless caught the public's eye, such as a "tiny little tot" dressed up as child actor Jackie Coogan in Charlie Chaplin's *The Kid* (1921).

As the strike went on, the carnivals gained in importance, both as a way of raising funds for soup kitchens and as a means of protest and entertainment. Toward the end of July, Maesteg held a long procession, attended by thousands of onlookers, that included

> fairies, gypsies, collier boys, a nurse and a wounded soldier, Irish colleens, a wasp, a sunflower, a savage lady, a pillar box, an absent-minded beggar, Red Indians, quaint little couples, a navvie's jazz band, with barrow, spades and pickaxes, the "music" they produced being weird and wonderful.[20]

The procession began at 11 a.m. and was led by a woman and two men on horseback, followed by the Maesteg Catholic Mission Prize Band. Immediately following them was a "a striking tableau, representing an injured miner in a hospital ward, with a doctor, a nurse and an ambulance man in attendance. On a placard was displayed the words: 'One way in which the miner pays for coal.'"[21] Further along in the parade, another scene depicted a colliery owner "driving a team of colliers in chains"—under the banner "THE PRICE WE PAY FOR COAL"—immediately followed by impersonations of the president and the secretary of the Miners' Federation of Great Britain, Herbert Smith and A. J. Cook.

Over the course of the summer of 1926, jazz bands playing gazookas took on a life of their own, independent of overtly political demonstrations. In August, a gigantic flower show was held by the Horticultural

Society of Aberdare. Thirty-three jazz bands, each containing fifty to eighty members, gathered to compete from towns around South Wales, watched by an audience of roughly fifteen thousand. A write-up for the *Merthyr Express*, titled "Jazz Fever," reported: "One would have imagined that Aberdare was oblivious to the grim realities of the coal stoppage for the spirit of light-hearted revelry mingled with the strains of popular ragtime music until long after dark."[22] A relatively external observer—the judge of a male voice choir competition held earlier in the day, who had been brought in from the Carmarthenshire town of Ammanford for reasons of impartiality—opened his adjudication wryly: "I have heard so much jazz since I have been in Aberdare that this beautiful singing came as a welcome antidote."[23] A journalist for the *Merthyr Express* echoed his opposition between "the blatant medley of a jazz band" and "the majesty of the male voice choir," but reluctantly admitted that the bands eclipsed the choirs: "In the evening the programme reached somewhat of an anti-climax when jazz bands held sway and the spirit of carnival seemed to hold the town enthralled."[24] During the evening, at the fair ground, prizes were awarded to the top three bands—the "Toreadors" of Foundry Town, Aberdare; the "Sheiks of Harem Band" of Ferndale (a town in the Rhondda Valley); and the "Kentucky C—ns" of Miskin, Pontyclun (also in the Rhondda)—with special prizes given to the Aberaman Welfare Ladies Band and the Cwmbach Ladies.[25]

Parading for the purpose, or sometimes under the pretext, of raising money for strikers' canteens, the gazooka bands became the object of a moral quandary. Near the end of July, a Welsh-language editorial in the *Pontypridd Observer* grumbled:

> Nid oes un gair gennym yn erbyn y Carnivals yma fel y cyfryw, os nad oes tuedd i'w cario ymlaen i ormodedd. Nid pobpeth ynddynt, hefyd, sydd yn dangos y chwaeth oreu, fel y mae gwaetha'r modd. Pwy ddydd, yn y Porth, yr oedd un peth yno yn hollol amddifad o chwaeth, ac yn ymylu ar fod yn watwarus. Cariant luman ac arni'n argraffedig "Y Ffug Briodas," gyda dyn mewn gwisg offeiriad a'r Beibl yn ei law. Mewn lle arall, yr oedd Jazz Band yn cario lluman a'r geiriau "Myfi yw bara y bywyd." Y mae pethae fel hyn yn anfoesol a gwatwarus dros ben. Yn awr, chwi fechgyn y Rhondda, disgwyliwn bethau gwell oddi wrthych chwi; os ydych am ychwaneg o garnivals, carier hwynt yn ymlaen yn "weddus ac mewn trefn."
>
> (We have nothing to say against the Carnivals as such, as long as they don't tend to be excessive. Sadly, not everything about them shows good taste. One day, in Porth, there was something utterly destitute of taste, bordering on contempt: they carried a flag bearing the words "The False

> Bride," with a man dressed in minister's clothes and a Bible in his hand. Elsewhere, there was a Jazz Band carrying a flag with the words "I am the Bread and the Life" written on it. Things like this are immoral and contemptuous indeed. Now, you Rhondda boys, we expect better things from you; if there are to be more carnivals, carry them out "decently and in good order.")[26]

Taking a conservative line, this commentator was clearly rattled by the skewering of the church—whose solidarity with the strikers had been less than firm—along with the apparently blasphemous association between jazz and the mysteries of the transubstantiation. Quoting at the end from Corinthians 14:1, a chapter that forbids preaching at the temple in foreign tongues, this editorial brandished a caution against idolatry. It was also a warning to "chwi fechgyn y Rhonnda" (you Rhondda boys) to keep their political demonstrations within the bounds of intelligibility.

In other words, the jazz bands of South Wales threatened to become an end in themselves, even as gazookas became a feature of everyday life, well beyond the official carnivals. Less amply documented, since carnivals always invited an extensive report in local newspapers, roving gazooka bands were glimpsed on the streets of South Wales as early as May—for example, in the chance observation that "funny bands attract[ing] much attention" wandered from Fair View toward Blackwood.[27] In July, at a football awards ceremony at Mountain Ash, two men came forward to collect their medallions in "stone age costume," which they had been wearing prior to the event, as they paraded the football pitch as part of a jazz band.[28] Reflecting on the permeation of the bands throughout the valleys, an editorial in the *Merthyr Express* speculated on what had become a generalized mania for carnival:

> It is the direct outcome of the coal stoppage. The men are bored with this long period of idleness, and are glad of anything that will help "kill time" and make the dreary hours move a little quicker. . . . Surprising ingenuity is displayed in the get-up of the various characters, some of them being fearfully and wonderfully made, and one often wonders how people who have been idle for seventeen weeks can produce such elaborate, and in many instances, gorgeous costumes, which must have cost a considerable amount. These carnivals have evolved many jazz bands with mysterious "musical" instruments, which might be more fitly described as instruments of torture, and which fill the air with their ear-splitting din.[29]

Arising from the exceptional circumstances of the strike, the gazooka's tone was ill-keeping to the ears of this newspaper commentator. But, as he was forced to concede, it was well-diffused and incredibly popular—not least because, by invoking "jazz," it was a means of offending establishment sensibility. Unfortunately, beyond the occasional references to "ragtime," itself a floating signifier in 1920s Britain, few observers recorded which tunes any given band played. Yet corroborating evidence, such as the bands' names and their companions in the parades, points toward a vital interface with US popular culture. I'll shortly go on to examine a fictional treatment of the carnivals that was more specific, though in some ways misleading, about choices of tune. Even without such specificity, however, larger patterns of cultural transfer can be inferred. With the widespread adoption of carbon microphones after 1925, both in recording studios and radio booths, gramophone discs from the United States were relayed across the world airwaves with a new electronic accuracy. The rise of the gazooka in South Wales was a local response to this large-scale shift; it was a way of handling (both grasping and failing to grasp) "jazz." In other words, the gazooka not only produced raucous noises but was an instrument of listening attuned to its moment.

As the counterpoint to town brass bands and male voice choirs, the sounds of the gazooka also signaled the distant power of US media to frame and reshape local representations of the "the world." (This cultural influence of US media in South Wales should be contrasted with political sympathies, which were closer to Russia following a huge Soviet donation of more than a million pounds to the striking miners.)[30] Thickly populated by national and ethnic stereotypes, the South Wales carnivals drew freely on contemporary fantasies about racialized others. The primary motors of such acts of exoticization were, of course, US slavery and British imperialism; popular US gramophone discs relayed by radio, in concert with US silent films, were the vehicles. This cultural influence explains the prevalence and popularity of "Red Indians" and blackface minstrels in 1926 South Wales, the latter standing out among other exotic figures on parade as a constant feature from one carnival to the next.

A Story of Coal

The gramophone whirs in the background of a celebrated radio play, Gwyn Thomas's *Gazooka: A Story of Coal*, which tells the story of a Rhondda community during the 1926 strike. Commissioned by BBC Radio Wales, *Gazooka* was first broadcast in 1953 and often repeated during the 1950s and '60s, following a warm reception in the radio press.[31] In the period after the Second World War, the play tapped a rich vein of nostalgia for interwar South Wales—much like Dylan Thomas's contemporary and now better-known *Under Milk Wood* (1954). Both works used radio as a means of access to a past recently lost. *Under Milk Wood* opened with a montage of dreams narrated by the dreamers themselves, the sleeping inhabitants of an imaginary town ("Llareggub" = "Bugger All" in reverse) on the outskirts of Swansea. Dylan Thomas channeled radio to summon the atmosphere of an historical community; his play amplified dreams to make audible the jostling of unconscious minds. More straightforwardly, Gwyn Thomas's *Gazooka* conjured the past through an instrument and its sound: one preserved over the years by radio through gazooka broadcasts. Radio schedules advertised "gazooka" shows in midcentury Britain, as a way of filling empty airtime. Yet behind this screen of radio reminiscence, the gramophone also played a role in *Gazooka*'s narrative.

Set in a rundown estate of terraced houses, ironically named Meadow Prospect, the play opens amid a moral crisis. A notorious local figure—Cynlais Coleman the Comet, so named for his abilities as a runner—has established a gazooka band of young men who, lacking costumes, wear almost nothing. They march around the estate and into the mountainside, wearing loose-fitting white sheets in an (again loose) interpretation of Sufi whirling. Headed by Coleman himself, playing the Mad Mahdi—in tribute to the Nubian leader Muhammad Ahmad, who led a ten-month siege against the British army at Khartoum in 1884—the band marches to the tune of the "Colonel Bogey March"—played at an excessively slow tempo, as if "to squeeze every last drop of significance out of it."[32] The ranks of out-of-work young people daily frolicking through the hillsides create consternation among the older residents, as members of the Meadow Prospect Discussion Group—"a harassed and anxious fringe" who gather weekly at the library at the miners' institute to debate political and philosophical issues—strive to rehabilitate Coleman's band so that it can compete alongside two others from the area in a coming regional competition. These other local gazooka bands are the all-female Britannias, who play "Rule Britannia" while draped in Union Jacks, and the Boys from Dixie, dressed entirely in black, including blackface makeup (the narrator briefly wonders where they found the cork to burn).[33] Both bands are led by Georgie Young the Father Flung, another infamous local figure, who served in one of Britain's African campaigns long ago. His military past explains his enthusiasm for imperial pageantry: "It gave Georgie some part of his youth back to have this phalanx of darkened elements wheeling and turning every whipstitch at his shout of command."[34] As a result of Georgie's excessive zeal, both the Britannias and the Boys from Dixie fall apart on the day of the competition, leaving the only hope of victory to Coleman's band, now reformed

Figure 4.2 The Bull Fighters at the Fforchneol Arms, Cwmaman. Two men in the center of the front row support a "bull's head"; "the matador," wooden sword in hand, stands behind. Amgeuddfa Cwm Cynon / Cynon Valley Museum, image ACVMS 2009.208. Reproduced with the permission of Rhondda Cynon Taf County Borough Council Heritage Service.

as the Meadow Prospect Matadors. Figure 4.2 shows an outfit similar to the one Thomas had in mind.

The gramophone enters the story at this point, amid a community discussion over an appropriate melody for a band to hum through gazookas. A local choir director suggests an Iberian folk tune, but Coleman insists on the Toreador Song from Bizet's *Carmen*. This choice initially garners support from the discussion group—"Let's lift the tone of the carnivals; I'm for the operatic tune," one key member opines—but the chairman, Gomer Gough the Gavel, has another idea: "I'm One of the Nuts of Barcelona," a song made popular on radio and disc.[35] This choice comes as a surprise from the aged and serious-minded Gomer, but the proposal is ultimately accepted. "I'm One of the Nuts of Barcelona" refers to the chorus of a contemporary popular song, "Barcelona," written by the British lyricist Huntley Trevor: an elaborately xenophobic number, including crudely transcribed foreign accents, concerning an Italian womanizer in Spain.[36] The music was written by Tolchard Evans, a well-known composer of popular songs (most notably "Lady of Spain" in 1931), born in London in 1901. Minus the lyrics, the song was recorded by the Savoy Orpheans, which, as mentioned previously, was a jazz band popular in interwar Britain, largely heard through recordings and radio performances.[37] Advertised on the label as a "quick one-step," the musical arrangement included a large brass section, piano, and guitar, and featured solos by muted trumpet, trombone and—to exhibit the increased bandwidths of frequency made recordable by the electrical microphones—a cello playing in the low registers.[38]

Thomas's deployment of "Barcelona" in *Gazooka* was apt. On a local level, its use reflected a wave of Spanish immigration into Rhondda towns such as Maerdy, which gave rise to a heady mix of xenophobic fear and communist solidarity in coal mining communities in the late nineteenth century. Yet the choice of disc also had much more contemporary resonance, and reflected an international scene for popular music. Released in April 1926, "Barcelona" could anchor the play's 1950s radio listener in the months of the strike. Perhaps more importantly, the sound of the record bore an affinity with the explosion of so-called jazz bands across South Wales: the nasal quality of the gazookas reflected the prominent use of muted trumpets in "Barcelona," which struck a similarly playful tone in recalling Dixieland improvisation. In addition to its capacity to evoke an historical atmosphere, the song and record served a narrative function in allowing Thomas to stage a community debate over an appropriate melody for the Matadors. In the story, the choice of "Barcelona" represents the local ascendancy of "jazz" over "opera," even if this triumph comes about in an unexpected way. The jazz record is championed by Gomer, an intellectual, who binds himself (according to the strictures of dialectal logic) to a coming "age of clownish callowness," while its rival ("Votre toast" from *Carmen*) is promoted by Coleman, the area's troublemaker-in-chief.[39]

While "Barcelona" became a popular hit during the months of the 1926 strike, its use in the play must be understood as an attempt on the part of a writer in the 1950s to convey the spirit of an event that was within living memory for some of his listeners. After all, the opening lines begin with an invocation of memory, brought about by a sound:

> Somewhere outside my window a child is whistling. He is walking fast down the hill and whistling. . . . He is moving through a fan of light from a street lamp. His head is thrown back, his lips protrude strongly and his body moves briskly. "D-I-X-I-Even Mamee, How I love you, how I love, my dear old Swanee . . ." The Mississippi and the Taff kiss with dark humming lubricity under an ashen hood of years.[40]

Composed by George Gershwin in 1919 and committed to disc by Al Jolson the following year, "Swanee" sends the first-person narrator back in time: "The sound of it promotes a roaring life inside my ears. Whenever I hear it, brave ghosts, in endless procession, march again."[41] The whistling marching boy foreshadows the carnivals to follow in the play, while the mention of "Swanee"—more recently revived by Al Jolson's turn in the film *Rhapsody in Blue* (1944)—hints at blackface performance as an important component of a historical reality. Inflected by more recent events, the whistling conjures up a fantastical geography, a "dark humming lubricity" that evokes the riverine networks along which the melody flowed.[42]

Primarily addressed to radio listeners of the 1950s, *Gazooka* also presented a sustained reflection on listening in 1926. Indeed, the play homed in on the sounds and silences of the 1926 strike as an explanation for the sudden proliferation of character bands. As Thomas's narrator put it:

> No smoke rose from the great chimneys to write messages on the sky that puzzled and saddened the minds of the young. The endless journeys of coal trams on the incline, loaded on the upward run, empty and terrifyingly fast on the down, ceased to rattle through the night and mark our dreams. The parade of nailed boots on the pavements at dawn fell silent. Day after glorious day came up over the hills that had been restored by a quirk of social conflict to the calm they lost a hundred years before. [. . .] out of the quietness and golden light, partly to ease their fret, a new excitement was born. The carnivals and the jazz bands.[43]

Here Thomas invokes a famous myth: the glorious summer of '26. This fantasy is often repeated in oral histories. As Sue Bruley has shown, the weather was not especially fine that year.[44] As Bruley also points out, though, miners and their families were more able to appreciate whatever fine weather there was, precisely because of the stopping of work. The same point applies to Thomas's recollection of the silences of the strike. An interruption of the working day created an experiential void—one marked by widespread fear among mining communities that they could lose their livelihoods altogether—and from this silence came the bands, an outburst of "rapture."[45]

Beyond the silence of the strike, close listening illuminated the bands' rise in another way. In deploying songs made popular by the gramophone and wireless, *Gazooka* insists on its grounding in 1926 as an historical moment, not only in South Wales but also on a global stage. To put this another way, the play aspired to represent an episode in which the Welsh working class restaged the world for themselves. It not only recalled a series of bizarre and racist parades, but reassembled the modes and media of spectatorship that brought fragments of the world to Wales in the first place. It is telling in this respect that *Gazooka* took pains to notice, if only in passing, that the hard-won matador costumes were inspired by a showing of *Blood and Sand*—a 1922 American silent film starring Rudolph Valentino—at a local cinema in 1925.[46] The choice of "Barcelona" underlined another mechanism of globalization: one that had precious little to do with Spain and everything to do with the US entertainment industry's interface with European markets in the age of the carbon microphone.

Gazookas belong to this evolving context, as an instrument of listening through which global sounds, mediated by American cinema and British radio and sound recording, were in turn resignified by the Welsh working class. By imparting a veneer of noisy interference over massed voices, the instrument mimed the very conditions of audibility of media. The gazooka was in this sense a technique for getting hold of sounds heard via the radio, a gramophone manqué. Such use had an ambivalent politics both in the play and in historical practice. As a means of invoking "jazz," the gazooka was, at one and the same time, a general signifier of disobedience, an opportunity for racial masquerade, and even a way for coal miners to identify with enslaved peoples of West Africa. Particularly early on in the summer of 1926, the carnivals saw colliers in "blackface" hauled through the streets by mine owners. In the 1953 play, meanwhile, the Boys from Dixie distill the broader tensions between the patriotic and anti-imperial. On the one hand, the band's prominence in *Gazooka* references currents of racism released among the South Wales working class.[47] On the other hand, the blackening of their faces inevitably recalled a local reality, in the shape of the white miner caked in coal dust—the central figure in the world-historical drama of the strike.

In Praise of Listening

Having explored the gramophone's mediating role in South Wales carnivals, I now want to focus on a source more centrally about listening to shellac discs: a column published in the *Glamorgan Advertiser,* a weekly newspaper. Headquartered and printed in Maesteg, a town fifteen miles from Porth, where Gwyn Thomas grew up, the *Advertiser* took its primary materials from day-to-day life in the Llynfi, Ogmore, Garw, and Avon valleys, presenting a local view from amid a cluster of working-class communities. Founded shortly after the First World War, it gave voice to a "new world of ideals, powers and destinies which is opening for the human race."[48] A regular column dedicated to disc reviews began in 1926, aiming to fill "a particularly big gap in places like Maesteg, Bridgend, Porthcawl, and the districts around, where opportunities to hear the world's great artists are few and far between, and the best in chamber music and orchestral music is little but a name."[49] Entitled "Gramophone Notes," this column was at first monthly, but from 1927 was published roughly every other week, sometimes even weekly, averaging a thousand words each time. It typically began with an important classical release—for example, the first electrical recording of Grieg's Piano Concerto (as a four-disc set) in 1927, or the first more or less complete recording of Wagner's *Die Walküre* (fourteen discs) in 1928—offering an introduction to the composer and the work, along with a generally positive evaluation of the performance and the quality of the recording.[50] After that, there were short comments on other notable classical discs, making sure to point out occasions on which local artists, such as the soprano Gwladys Naish or the pianist Marie Novello, released records. More frequently, the reviewer—writing under the pseudonyms "Stylus" (1927–30) and "Under the Needle" (1931–35)—focused on famous or up-and-coming performers across Europe and the United States. "Gramophone Notes" almost always concluded with a rundown of popular and dance music. Sometimes cordoned off from the rest of the column by the subheading "THE LIGHTER SIDE," US popular music (foxtrots, jazz, Broadway hits) dominated, together with British bands and comedians made popular by the wireless.

Routinely appearing on pages 2 or 7 of the *Glamorgan Advertiser*, "Gramophone Notes" occupied conspicuous space in the eight-page newspaper (the front and back pages were plastered with local advertisements, as was typical in papers of the period) and often stood apart from its surroundings. When it appeared on page 7, the column nestled with reports of regional cricket matches, car accidents, proceedings of the Maesteg magistrates' court, and other local stories. When it was on page 2, by contrast, it featured with more important local stories, which in practice meant reports on conditions in the coal industry. This parallelism was more or less inevitable during the strike. On one page, for example (figure 4.3), the column could be found between "Band Sunday"—a report on a brass-band parade and a public meeting at Maesteg's Town Hall sponsored by the Royal Antediluvian Order of Buffaloes, a philanthropic organization inspired by Methodism—and "Coal News," a detailed account of an emergency meeting called by the local parliamentary representative, also held at the Town Hall later the same Sunday. These columns made for unlikely bedfellows: commentary on recent recordings of Grieg's "Norwegian Dances" and Wagner's "Siegfried Idyll" jostled alongside an account of a nonconformist sermon and an MP's speech to miners, focusing on Labour's campaign to amalgamate three thousand privately owned mines across the country into a national syndicate.[51]

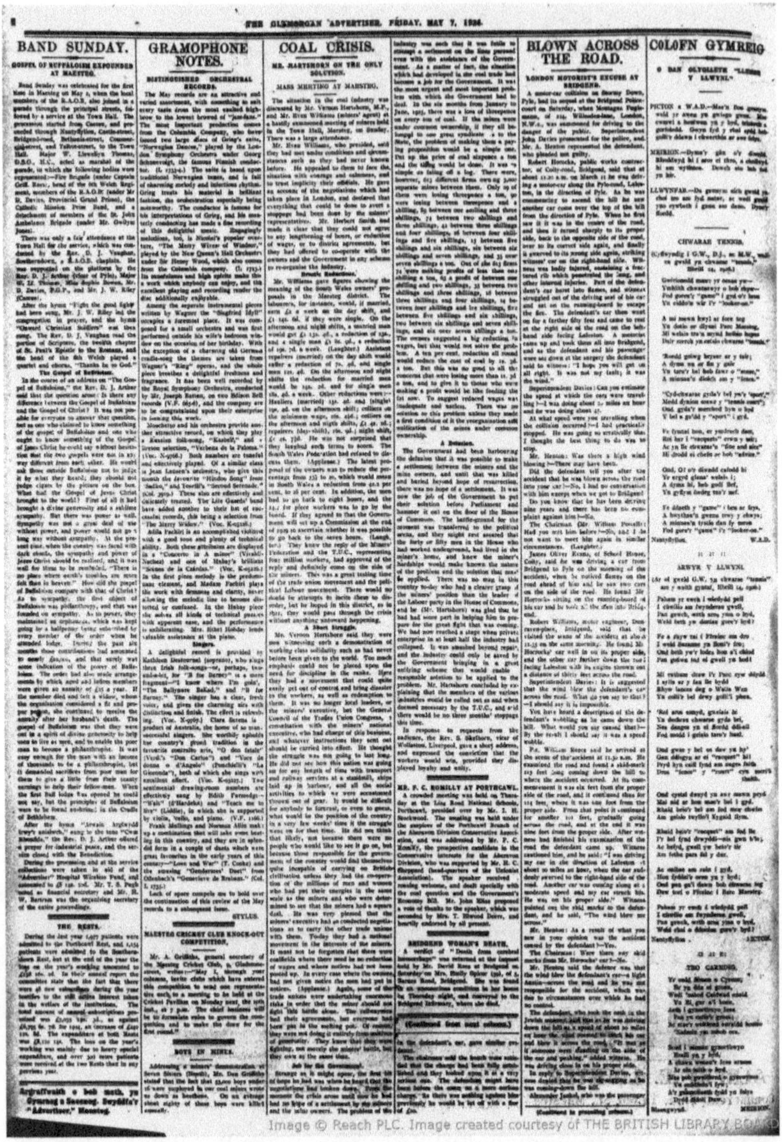

THE GLAMORGAN ADVERTISER, FRIDAY, MAY 7, 1926.

BAND SUNDAY.

GRAMOPHONE NOTES.

COAL CRISIS.

BLOWN ACROSS THE ROAD.

COLOFN GYMREIG

Figure 4.3 *Glamorgan Advertiser*, 1 May 1926, p. 2. Courtesy *Glamorgan Advertiser* / Reach PLC. Image supplied by the British Newspaper Archive.

On one level, it is of course unsurprising to find diverse happenings clustered on a newspaper page. On this same page, for example, were many other reports—one featuring a reckless motorist from London hauled before the local magistrate—as well as a regular fixture, the “Colofn Cymreig” (Welsh-Language Column). The latter was present in every issue of the *Advertiser*; it always appeared flush to the right or left of the page, and featured poems written by locals.

Viewed up close, then, the newspaper page evoked the multiplicity of everyday life. On the macroscopic level, though, the arrangement of articles represented patterns that repeated over many issues. In particular, "Gramophone Notes" routinely shared a page with the "Colofn Cymreig." While the two columns were of course different in purpose—not to mention language, tone, topicality, and regional focus—they shared a common function in establishing space for culture and aesthetics alongside, yet distinct from, local and national news. This separation of functions is instantiated in figure 4.3, and it was a dependable feature.[52] For example, "Gramophone Notes" never referenced the strike throughout a six-month upheaval in 1926; and, if Stylus frequently alluded to the "slender pockets" of his readers, then the political life of South Wales entered the column only a handful of times in its decade-long run.

Occupying a space adjacent to both politics and daily life, "Gramophone Notes" projected a particular image of the reader as a listener. I would like to consider the column published in April 1928 in these terms. It began with a reflection on the centenary of Schubert's death, an occasion that, the writer hoped, might convert "low-brows" to the classical cause by way of the composer's famous tunefulness. Such listeners were, Stylus proposed, "mostly over-modest people who shrink from a symphony or a string quartet because they fear they will be unable to understand it or to discern its beauty or charm."[53] They might even find themselves "paralyzed by fright" when confronted by such music. Yet, with its profusion of melodies, Schubert's Ninth—the leading topic of this column—could ease the transition from terror to delight: "The veriest tyro in musical appreciation can find in it an abundance of pleasure. The whole symphony is full of the most charming tunes—tunes that one can 'get hold of' and whistle in the bath or hum in the street."[54] Stylus provided a brief history of the piece—a guide for the uninitiated in an era before sleeve notes. Next came two subsections dedicated to recent gramophone curiosities: the appearance on disc of "TWO FEMALE VIRTUOSOS" (cellist Guilhermina Suggia and violinist Erika Morini) and a section devoted to "BELLS." HMV had released a series of records of the Loughborough War Memorial carillon, featuring a fantasia of popular songs, along with a disc devoted to the ten-and-a-half-ton "Great Peter" of the York Society of Change Ringers. A closing paragraph listed "vocal gems" by "the Salon Group of Singers" and "the Cocoanuts"—the latter having recently debuted at the Garrick Theatre in London—and a foxtrot ("When day is done") played by Paul Whiteman's orchestra.

Week after week, month after month, the column outlined parallel shifts downward—both through the prevailing hierarchies of musical genre and in terms of cultural function, as education for the man on the street segued into tips as to the latest curiosities, dances, and popular songs. In 1931, when Stylus's pseudonym was changed to Under the Needle (perhaps indicating a change of author), the column began to lead with popular music, probably reflecting editorial pressures as well as broader cultural shifts.[55] Yet even while the shape of the column changed, the weight of the discussion—the sheer expenditure of words—was still devoted to classical music. This much was consonant with the column's founding mission: to negotiate the formidable distances between inhabitants of South Wales and the classical music scene, thereby bringing the supposedly uninformed listener closer to a metropolitan ideal. But this mission was conducted semi-independently of listening practice, since readers could enjoy "Gramophone Notes" without necessarily becoming owners of gramophones or consumers of discs. After all, the column was in the first instance a mode of reading rather than of listening. A continual stream of fresh releases on disc provided an ever-renewing prompt for Stylus to introduce, and for readers to learn about, classical works in a place where such knowledge was difficult to obtain.

Given this educational purpose, together with a focus on Central Europe and North America, it is small surprise that South Wales itself featured only rarely in "Gramophone Notes." One such special occasion was inspired by an unusual intersection of these interests: a concert given by the Cardiff Instrumental Trio in Maesteg in 1929. Supported by the Welsh National Council and the Carnegie Trust, this concert was freely given for the public as part of a series of performances of chamber music in "distressed" industrial areas.[56] It took place at Norths Memorial Hall—the working men's institute named after Norths Navigation Company, the local coal owner—and it was reportedly packed. Perhaps because of this, it necessitated a warning:

> At the outset Mr. [Joseph] Morgan [the trio's pianist] warned the audience that the music they were to play could not be termed popular. They had taken as light pieces as they could find from the works of the great classical masters written for the trio. Beethoven, whom Mr. Morgan described as the great democrat of music, was the first composer represented in the programme. He tried, said the speaker, to express things in music in a simple, fundamental way, which enabled them to be understood by the man in the street without great musical culture.[57]

Thus verbally prepared, the first item was the last movement of the composer's Trio in G major (op. 9, no. 1). The Cardiff Trio went on to ransack other four-movement works for their scherzos and finales—including Haydn's "Gypsy" Rondo (the finale of Hob. XV/25)—in an effort to keep things "light." At the close of the concert, one Mrs. W. W. Paddison proposed a vote of thanks on behalf of the institute to the Cardiff Trio. She paid special tribute to the way in which the Maesteg audience had listened: "You have proved yourselves musicians every one."[58]

In the following issue of "Gramophone Notes," Stylus capitalized on the event to celebrate "CHAMBER MUSIC FOR ALL":

> Many music lovers shrink from chamber music in the belief that it demands special faculties. . . . The fallacy of this belief has been exposed many times in this column, and an additional proof of its falsity was given at the chamber-music concert held at Maesteg last week, when a crowded audience—not more than half a dozen members of which had had any musical training, probably—listened with keen attention and deep appreciation to a programme of trios by the greatest classical composers.[59]

No special aptitude was required, then. All that was needed was an "ear for a tune," even if learning and experience would result in a fuller appreciation. Stylus suggested that the gramophone could make an important contribution to this end in offering the uncultivated listener an opportunity to acquire a musical education. This was, of course, a gramophone trope; but in repeating it here, Stylus echoed a proposal made during the Maesteg concert, whose organizers announced that "the free loan of wireless sets, gramophones, and gramophone records" could lead to the creation of listening clubs throughout the district.[60]

The people of Glamorgan were in this sense a few steps ahead of the Cardiff missionaries. For one thing, gramophones were often mentioned in the newspapers of the time, usually to thank particular individuals for supplying recorded musical entertainments as part of small amateur concert programs (a wider phenomenon, previously explored in Singapore in chapter 2). Furthermore, the fantasy of local listening clubs had already been partly achieved, in Glamorgan and across the United Kingdom, as gramophone entertainments came to fulfill an important function in working men's institutes, particularly for the retirees among their members. In 1928, the Nantyffyllon Lounge Society—a local wing of the Maesteg working men's institute, which met in a library—began a series of gramophone concerts catering to elderly residents:

> The society is doing a noble work in supplying entertainments to occupy the leisure hours of the old veterans of the mine. Recently Mr. Richard

> Rees gave them an excellent gramophone recital, comprising items by the greatest artists in the world.[61]

Other similarly brief bulletins on the Lounge Society's activities centered around the gramophone, and routinely mentioned how appreciatively the audience listened.[62] For example, in November 1928, following the death of one of its members, the Lounge Society gathered in the library to commemorate the deceased with speeches and disc selections from Handel's *Messiah*. A bulletin in the *Advertiser* noted that on this occasion, "There were some ladies present, together with several visitors from Maesteg, and all expressed themselves as being delighted" by what they had heard.[63]

The death of a miner at an old age was something worth celebrating at a time when fewer than half of pit workers lived to collect a pension.[64] Still, as a means of celebration the gramophone remained conspicuous in this commemoration, as in many other meetings of the Lounge Society. Its recurrent mention in otherwise nondescript reports singled out an object of local pride—something to be held up as a feature of the library rather than as the possession of an individual, even while recital givers (such as the above-mentioned Mr. Richard Rees) contributed discs and were routinely thanked. At the same time, this playing of discs, in Nantyffyllon as in countless other places, provided the occasion for a formulaic compliment to listeners of the community. This seemingly obligatory praise might be understood in various ways: as condescending to the "old veterans of the mine," for example; or, more elaborately, as an almost necessary gesture, given the trials of patience these supposedly uncultivated listeners had willingly endured. Such praise recalls the image of the listener projected elsewhere throughout "Gramophone Notes": the kind of person who might be seized with terror on being confronted by classical music, but who might, given the chance, learn to enjoy humming the tunes of a symphony in the bath.

Opera in the Terraces

"Gramophone Notes" on the one hand, *Gazooka* on the other—two sources yield contrasting snapshots of an historical listener in the Welsh valleys. If the newspaper column carried aspirations of working-class uplift, the play staged a more unruly set of listening subjects, able to mobilize mediated sounds in unpredictable ways. Both projected fantasies of different kinds: one of the working-class (largely white, largely male) listener brought into communication with high culture via the gramophone; the other, of a community in possession of the power to rewrite (for amusement and perhaps advantage) semiotic codes transmitted by the media. The two documents also present contrasting types of evidence: as part of a newspaper, the column bears a stamp of historical specificity, while the belated radio play has an indirect, artistically mediated purchase on past events. And yet, fiction comes closer to addressing the question posed at the outset of this chapter, since *Gazooka* illustrates not only possible connections between gramophone discs and "mass" listening, but also the gaps across which those connections were made. Pushing beyond a paradigm of individual ownership over media artifacts, the play suggests more complex routes of listening along which sounds were (over)heard and remade.

This theme of access to recorded sound was treated more fully in Thomas's first published novel, *The Dark Philosophers* (1946).[65] Again, his story unfolds in an estate of terraced houses—referred to throughout as the Terraces, and bearing a strong resemblance to *Gazooka*'s Meadow Prospect—in the Rhondda Valley. But this time it takes place in the 1930s, in the context of British rearmament after 1934, which saw the transition from endemic unemployment to tentative employment, often in arms factories, in South Wales as in other places. Yet the novel insists on its grounding in the Terraces; the narrative never exits this space. In this respect, it resembles certain Depression-era novels from the United States—as described by Michael Denning in *The Cultural Front*—which were also deeply anchored in working-class environments, and similarly eschewed didactic juxtapositions of the middle and working classes familiar from a previous generation of writers.[66] Thomas drew no lessons from the contrast between the haves and have-nots; the novel was rhetorically addressed to a working-class readership, whom he sought to enlist through humor and "dark philosophy."

The gramophone's entry into this story comes as the eponymous dark philosophers—a group of four men, Walter, Ben, Arthur, and John, all in their mid-thirties—meet at an Italian café in the Terraces that specializes in tea and hot cordials. The café is owned by one Idomeneo Faracci, an Italian worker indentured to a Fascist overlord by means of an elaborate stove, the loan of which creates a constant debt, and which significantly bears a logo of Italian Fascism. Idomeneo has an "old cabinet gramophone" in the back room, and a collection of records including "very sweet arias from operas, also duets, trios and choirs."[67] Together with the loud hiss of Idomeneo's stove, which routinely interrupts their discussion, these discs comprise the soundtrack to an unlikely symposium, as well as an opportunity for singing along. Idomeneo often takes the baritone part in ensembles numbers, while a sixteen-year-old carpenter apprentice called Willie sings tenor, much to the enjoyment of audiences in the café.[68]

This gramophone-supported singing, together with the hissing stove, continually prompts topics for debate. After belting out an unspecified aria, and following a crest of high spirits, Willie slumps, looks "sadly at the stove," and reflects:

> We feel warm and happy now and that is good. The music reaches us and we are willing to hear all the things it has to tell. But, hell, man, what about all the people around us, most of the people in these Terraces for a start, whose lives are sad and ugly because they never understand what all this music means?[69]

As the discussion falters, all that can be heard in the café is the "roaring of angry, complicated draughts through the twisted air shafts of the stove."[70] Meanwhile, John—the narrator, speaking on behalf of the other men, using the first-person plural—inwardly connects the music they have heard with the position Willie outlines:

> We cursed within our own minds the sterile cold and loneliness we had lived in for many years when misery and anger had killed the memory of all such loveliness as that music within us, and we thought sorrowfully of all those many voters lying around about us in the Terraces who had been made numb and stupid by poverty, dead even to divine beauty created by man.
>
> Many of Idomeneo's records were worn and very often all the music you heard from some of the older ones was a scratch that went up and down to a certain beat, like a hoarse ghost following the music about, quarrelling with it.[71]

In this pensive but noisy atmosphere, John mulls common feelings of humiliation given rise by a long spell of unemployment: the loneliness, the numbness—feelings represented elsewhere in the novel through the stiffness and inefficiency of the laboring body.[72] As a remedy, opera is bittersweet, raising larger questions about the structural absence of beauty in the Terraces ("put up so that people could eat and breed in between shifts"), along with the mediated nature of its rare appearance.[73]

As if in response to thoughts left hanging in the air—air made dense and smoky by Idomeneo's stove—Willie makes a constructive proposal: that the café-goers each contribute sixpence (half a shilling) every week to save up for new discs. Before long, the men find themselves at a gramophone shop in a nearby town, where the manager is happy, if surprised, to welcome this "band of voters from the Terraces":

> We would listen to dozens of records before choosing the one we wanted, so on those Friday evenings when we had money to go the gramophone shop, we always had a very good concert in addition to the pride of actually being able to buy something that did not have to be eaten or worn.[74]

When these operatic records, selected for the opportunity of singing along in harmony in the café, are played back, Idomeneo explains the plot and significance of the words; he shadows the bass while Willie learns the tenor.

Crucially lacking a soprano, Willie brings along his friend Margaret, who impresses the men not only with her voice but with her political acumen. Margaret's mother is bedridden, and Margaret is her only caregiver. She asks the men to pay her mother a visit to cheer her up—an invitation they reluctantly accept, fearing that their bedside manner will be too clumsy. To supplement the conversation, records are played on Idomeneo's gramophone, even as incidental sounds once again cut across the music: this time, noises made by an irritated and willfully ill-mannered subletter who rents two of the four rooms in Margaret's mother's house. At first they hear his bedpost tapping slowly yet rhythmically against a partitioning wall. He is apparently having sex. Margaret looks embarrassed but her mother merely shrugs, her thoughts on the subletter having "gone far beyond the stage of speech."[75]

As this plot summary of *The Dark Philosophers* might suggest, broader philosophical themes are rehearsed through the gramophone and through other noises that interfere with playback. The sound of opera in an Italian café among the Terraces cues a debate on the nature of beauty in an ugly world and, more particularly, on the ways in which the eruptive nature of beauty reveals such familiar ugliness for what it is. This thought occurs first to Willie, the idealistic youngster; but while his idea seems naive, it proves hard to dismiss. The discussion group conducts a philosophical experiment to test Willie's notion: they carry Idomeneo's gramophone to Margaret's mother, who is a prime example of one of the more wretched residents of the Terraces. The sight of them carrying the gramophone through the streets on a Sunday morning draws "many a dark and intolerant glance" from worshippers on their way to chapel.[76] The result, in the acoustic bleeding through the walls—the music in one direction, the subletter's noises in the other—makes an obvious point: that these houses were not built with loud entertainments in mind. It is telling that a small act of coercion is required to keep the music playing.

Ben, the most violence-positive among the philosophical friends, subdues the subletter through force—suggesting the more broadly contrived nature of the situation, and the sheer willfulness required to bring a little beauty into the lives of the poor.

Thomas's equation of beauty with Italian opera, a famously exclusive art form, is of course a relic: a remnant of historical attitudes, if not specific to opera, then more generally toward beauty, routinely associated with high culture in the period before and immediately after the Second World War. It was in this very British context—and with the industrial proletariat of South Wales in mind—that Raymond Williams's interventions in cultural theory, in treating "culture" as "ordinary," could resonate so powerfully.[77] And yet, while Thomas's reflections on beauty are of their time—and of course are outdated, more than seventy years on—his exploration of the uses of the gramophone, in the wake of the cultural theory of Williams and Stuart Hall, strikes a more contemporary note.[78] Key is the singing that goes along with the playing of shellac discs, which implies the transformation of a medium of listening into a means of performance. Not everyone in the novel can sing or wants to, of course, but conversation with Idomeneo provides other learning opportunities. An uncommon Italian name, *Idomeneo* is of course also the title of an opera by Mozart. In the novel, Idomeneo represents a fragile means of access to high culture by way of diaspora. On the one hand, the dark philosophers learn about Italian-language opera; on the other, singing along to shellac discs deepens the friends' understanding of the Italian diaspora, as they discover the dangerous conditions under which Idomeneo has come to be in Wales.

Beyond the singalong, another abiding reflection on the gramophone lies in the medium's relation to what is perhaps the core theme of *The Dark Philosophers*—the means of persuasion by which the working classes conspire against their own interests, together with the tactics by which such auto-oppression can be corrected. It is significant in this respect that Willie is thrown into the philosophers' midst by the gramophone: first as a tenor, then as an antagonist to their socialist convictions. Willie, in turn, brings Margaret to the café and subsequently leads the philosophers' gramophone-wielding expedition to visit her mother. Back at the café, and much later in the novel, it is after the playing of a disc ("Qual'occhio" from the love duet in act 1 of *Tosca*) that Willie finally abandons his belief in progress and the good intentions of local powers that be. The crux of the novel, his moment of political conversion is prepared by the creation of an environment of collective listening—to a disc he and the other men have jointly purchased several weeks before. The group that forms in the café around the acts of buying, playing, and singing along with shellac discs provides a study in community building: one established around material objects, of course, but also around collective experiences of beauty and feelings of pride.

Mass Aurality

In placing gramophone discs in the hands of workers, *The Dark Philosophers* brings this chapter full circle, returning to a theme that has been a constant throughout: the politics of access to sound media, together with the techniques of listening by which audible contents can be grasped. This issue of access is not reducible to shillings and pence. A lack of spending power was, of course, a powerful disincentive to gramophone consumption for the working classes during the interwar years. But grasping sounds was also a matter of aesthetic practices: of singing, humming, whistling, and parading—as bodily means of handling listening. This is perhaps one reason why melody has emerged as an important musical parameter across different sites of gramophone activity, both fictional and nonfictional: in the unisonous buzz of the gazooka bands, in Stylus's promotion of Schubert's tunefulness, and in the dark philosophers' café-based singalongs. On one level, this much is unsurprising: melody has played this role of rendering music malleable since long before the gramophone. Yet within a historical media context, a primeval capacity to absorb and redeploy musical sounds through melody acquired new political charges and potentials. In an environment of gramophones and radios linked by electrical transduction of sounds via the carbon microphone, the ability to grasp melodies, to take them into the body, was the first step in rendering them in plastic form for future manipulation.

Another theme of this chapter, closely related to the questions of access and ownership, has been the politics of musical genre: the notorious standoff between classical and pop. In the carnivalesque world of *Gazooka*, the ascendancy of "Barcelona" over "Votre toast" represented the upending of cultural and political hierarchies. In the *Glamorgan Advertiser*, meanwhile, classical music ceded ground much more slowly and reluctantly. As noted above, it was only after 1931 that "Gramophone Notes" began to lead with reviews of popular music; and even then, the bulk of commentary was reserved for exegesis of classical masterpieces. If nowadays this age-old contest between classical and pop may appear artificial or invidious, then under the star of mid-century modernism the battle raged in earnest. I would like to suggest that it took on a lease of life in the interwar period through disc-based discourse, which in referencing a standardized media format unlocked possibilities of side-by-side comparison.[79] This much may be true not only of the *Glamorgan Advertiser* but also of many other local papers, where the reviewing of discs rehearsed and intensified the divisions between classical and pop. Shellac discs could be called upon to sustain such a discourse because within an intermedial network dominated by radio, they were more tangible (if always phantasmatic) receipts: commodities that, in reifying aural experience, more readily supported an aestheticizing register of discussion.

If shellac discs polarized these basal musical genres in the interwar years, then the classical/pop binary was not the only axis around which the politics of the medium turned. Not only "jazz" carried hopes of political revolution, but also classical music imported into working-class contexts. While Stylus's column strikes the historian attentive to the cost of living as oddly unrealistic—expounding as it did, for more than a decade, on the notion of workers becoming gramophone aficionados—this very unreasonableness contained, beyond an atmosphere of condescension, a revolutionary hope of disrupting the political and aesthetic order by which classical music was shuttled toward middle-class ears. This fantasy did sometimes become reality—as witnessed, for example, in the Lounge Society meetings held at Nantyffyllon's library. But even here it retained a frisson of unlikeliness, if not impossibility. Such gramophone concerts inspired commentary on how well—attentively, delightedly—the working classes listened. Though deeply patronizing if glanced from the trenches of contemporary culture wars, such comment carried a subversive intent in pressing the injustice of reserving cultural treasures for the well-to-do.

This was also the line of interrogation pursued in the philosophical nerve center of Idomeneo's café. Here, outrage at beauty's absence was more fully and melodramatically expressed, and proactively remedied through experiments in group listening. A work of fiction, of course, *The Dark Philosophers* nevertheless supplies the most direct comment on the political nature of a mass medium. It does so because as a novel, it renders an entire social world in the subjunctive mode: its value as an historical document of listening lies in the way it identifies potential uses of the gramophone in coalfield society that might otherwise fly beneath the radar of written archives.[80] Read alongside contemporary newspapers, the novel suggests ways in which the medium was, or might become through use, political—not only as a groundswell of popular music, but as a way of placing classical music in working hands; not only through individual possession of media artefacts, but through collective ownership and enjoyment. An historical and philosophical novel, it proposes gramophone-inspired emotions of beauty and pride as a boon for the dominant structure of feeling in coal country—what Thomas elsewhere describes as a "daily war on the battlefield of dignity."[81]

Beyond South Wales, and even beyond the sinuous geography of coal, there are wider implications here for the history of the shellac disc as a format. In this sense the gazooka stands for something larger: the more-than-technological techniques by which the working classes handled listening in the early days of interlinked sound media. As an instrument in South Wales, the gazooka was more "mass" than the shellac disc. Yet, through its networked relation to the shellac disc, the gazooka demonstrated how one mode of listening could be mimed and absorbed by another and take on wider political significance. Through the gazooka, the gramophone became at once "mass" and distant; it distilled the central paradox of the format's widespread inaccessibility. This curious fact was elsewhere and otherwise noted by the readers who wrote to *The Gramophone* in 1925, observing the remoteness of the gramophone from the lives of working-class women, and those women's efforts to overcome that distance. It cues a dimension to the politics of listening that always exists in the frictions between mass audiences and mediatic objects.

CHAPTER 5

Being and Listening

This last chapter considers a single song and a particular disc, together with a self-consciously individual listener. It concerns the political and aesthetic consequences of friction, of record wear. As gramophone advertisements warned, a single rotation with the wrong needle could ruin a disc forever, whereas careful handling could lead to thousands of playbacks (figure 5.1).[1] One, or thousands. Either way, friction placed an upper limit on the disc's life span, creating an arc over listening experiences as sounds wore down over the course of their use. The listener under scrutiny in this chapter was in some ways deeply unusual, as we shall see. But I will be suggesting that his idiosyncratic listening style speaks to a wider condition: one structured by the frictional boundary between songs and shellac mixtures. I will be using "/" as shorthand for multiplicity throughout this chapter, as a needle-like sign that can also stand for the boundary between sounds and vibrations, to evoke the capacity of friction to generate connection and contamination across difference, even as that boundary constantly disintegrated in sound.

The disc I want to explore is partly real and partly imaginary. It surfaces in the pages of Jean-Paul Sartre's debut novel, *Nausea* (*La Nausée*, 1938), a loosely autobiographical work in the form of a diary, which unfolds against the backdrop of the fictional French city of Bouville—literally, Mudtown, a parody of 1930s Le Havre, where Sartre worked as a high school teacher.[2] Written from the first-person perspective of one Antoine Roquetin, a former globetrotter turned local historian, the diary follows the trajectory of his mysterious illness, "*la nausée*": attacks of overwhelming dizziness that cause familiar objects to dissolve as sights, smells, and sounds blur into each other. A few days into his diary, Roquetin discovers a temporary cure for his illness in a shellac disc: an "old ragtime with a vocal refrain," called "Some of These Days."[3] On hearing it, he is comforted by memories, recalling having heard it for the first time many years ago, in 1917, whistled on the streets of La Rochelle by American soldiers. Roquetin notes that this disc, one of the oldest in

Figure 5.1 Part of a double-page spread wartime advertisement for Pathé's equipment, titled "The Biggest Thing Any Phonograph Can Claim" (that "after a thousand performances, Pathé discs show no perceptible wear"). *Talking Machine World* 13, no. 4 (April 1917): 22.

the café's collection, is a "Pathé record for sapphire needle." Pathé was a popular brand in the United States and France in the period after the First World War, known for its supposedly frictionless interface with ball-tipped needles (a claim illustrated in figure 5.1).[4] As the melody returns to Roquetin through the medium of the shellac disc, in the present of the café—on a particular evening in 1932, according to his diary—it casts a spell, counteracting his sickness and reanimating his body: "God! That is what has changed, my gestures. This movement of my arm has developed like a majestic theme, it has glided along the song of the Negress; I seemed to be dancing."[5]

Nausea has inspired reams of interpretation over the years, not least because as Sartre was the most public of intellectuals in postwar France, his novels and plays can offer an attractive point of access to his more technical philosophical writings. In 1953, Iris Murdoch published an early appraisal of Sartre's output through the lens of his fiction: she argued that *Nausea* represented a new kind of "philosophical myth, which shows to us in a memorable way the master-image of Sartre's thinking."[6] Murdoch underscored the use of music in the novel, which, she claimed, played a role similar to that of the geometrical figure in classical philosophy: music, like the circle, stood for essence, even the Platonic idea. According to her interpretation, this kind of "music" could not be touched by existing things; reduced to its essence in melody, understood as a *series* of notes, it created a vanishing point within a world crowded by objects. Taking a Murdochian approach, but further highlighting the meanings attached to the song Sartre chose, Mark Carroll has shown how the invocation of North American jazz mattered deeply.[7] Broadly agreeing with Murdoch that "Some of These Days" allows for a "flight into an imaginary realm," Carroll additionally underscores the significance of jazz in Sartre's world as both a signifier of an exotic Other and, more unusually, a banner of freedom.

Here, as throughout the vast exegetical corpus that encircles *Nausea*, Sartre's many references to sound reproduction technology tend to disappear in the act of interpretation. At best, gramophones and discs become incidental to the Platonic idea of song—or even, in Carroll's analysis, the Platonic idea of jazz, or even of "Some of These Days." Yet I want to suggest that gramophone paraphernalia was an important means through which Sartre rehearsed philosophical concepts about the relation between things and nothings, the immanence of transcendence. In other words, I want to show how "Some of These Days"—as a "songish formation" of ideas, materials, and practices—belongs to and reflects upon the gramophone age.[8] Wielded as a philosophical tool by Sartre, the disc speaks to the historical conditions of a format in which shellac discs created streams of sounds that flowed in certain directions and with definite speeds. Not only as ideas but as plastic materials, particular songs—understood as hybrid temporal entities that emerge between acts of composition, performance and listening, together with the materialities and infrastructures that sustain such acts—crumbled, as sound, into shellac mixtures.

Song/

It is hard to disentangle life from fiction, especially where music is at stake.[9] But there was undeniably a real song, and a real disc, at the base of Sartre's novel. I can start with the famous song, whose music and lyrics were penned by the Black composer Shelton Brooks. Born in 1886 in Amherstburg, Ontario, within a community established by African Americans who fled US slavery, Brooks and his family moved in 1901 to Detroit, where he later emerged as a vaudeville entertainer.[10] Brooks published "Some of These Days" in 1910, by which point it had already become a popular work. The song featured swung rhythms, chromatic harmonies, and a classical tonal structure: a refrain that modulates to and from the relative minor. As Michael Graber has shown, Brooks's song drew on the model of Frank Williams's "Some o' Dese Days" (1905).[11]

Another source, channeled by Brooks and Williams alike, was the eponymous hymn "Some of These Days," which entered North American church services in the late nineteenth century.[12] The connection between the hymn and the song is faint but hard to dismiss. Brooks retained the repeating initial phrase, its rhythm—three short upbeats followed by a long downbeat—together with the key signature and pitch, now inflected with a defining chromatic lower neighbor note. Yet everything else—time signature, harmonization, key structure, and so on—was different (compare figures 5.2 and 5.3). A forensic musicologist might conclude that his borrowing from the hymn was small, even unconscious, rather than a concerted act of musical reference.

This distant, yet undeniable sonic connection between hymn and song opens up political meanings. In a widely circulated sermon, "The Signs of a Brighter Future for the American Negro," the minister and equal rights leader Francis J. Grimké selected "Some of These Days" as the accompanying hymn. Through the hymn, the phrase became a musicalized cliché: an everyday phrase locked to a melodic fragment.[13] It became anchored to a series of political sentiments and affects, as well as to theological and political axioms. For example, Grimké's sermon outlined reasons for optimism: increases in property ownership, advances in education, belief in the "ultimate triumph of right," "faith in the power of the religion of the Lord Jesus Christ to conquer all race prejudices." His sermon steadily built toward an indictment of white American cultures of worship at the turn of the century:

> It is an apostate church, utterly unworthy of the name it bears. Its spirit is a mean and cowardly and despicable spirit. [. . .] And yet with 135,667 preachers, and more than 2,000,000 church members in this land, this

Figure 5.2 "Some of These Days" by Frank Lebby Stanton and Joseph Lincoln Hall, a hymn and distant precursor of Shelton Brooks's famous song

Figure 5.3 Shelton Brooks, "Some of These Days" (Chicago: Will Rossiter Co., 1910), p. 2; mm. 23–31

> awful, black record of murder and lawlessness against a weak and defenseless race, still goes on.[14]

Echoing the words of the abolitionist Theodor Parker in "The True Idea of a Christian Church" (1846), Grimké declared that if he thought such racial violence could not be ended, "I would never enter the church but once again, and then to bow my shoulders to their manliest work, to heave down its strong pillars."[15] His sermon nevertheless closed with cautious optimism, in anticipating the rebirth of Christianity in the United States: an image of hope that communicated profound mourning. He drew powerfully on the hymn, which also opened with optimism ("Some of these days all the skies will be brighter") and similarly ended with grief ("Some of these days! Let us bear with our sorrow").

In Brooks's composition, the continuation of "Some of these days . . ." changed again—". . . you'll miss me honey."[16] What was in a church service the collective invocation of hope, and what became in Grimké's sermon the call for an end to a murderous white hegemony, was now replaced by the harangue of an abandoned lover. Distanced from its religious and political meanings, grief nevertheless bled over from hymn to song in the anticipation of heartbreak it both scripted and enacted.[17] Popular on the vaudeville stage were early performances of the song in signature acts by Diana Bonnar, whose portrait adorned the cover of the sheet music, and Hedges Brothers and Jacobson, a male vocal trio.[18] This early appropriation by white performers was mirrored in the song's rapid reception by the phonograph and gramophone industries. The American Quartet—an all-male vocal group renowned for its distinctive, close-textured harmonies, later to be reclaimed as an early example of barbershop singing—released "Some of These Days" on shellac disc in 1910, the same year in which Brooks's score was published.[19] In 1911 at least two more recordings appeared: a shellac disc by the British-born soprano and prolific recording artist Elise Stevenson, accompanied by vocal quartet; and a wax cylinder by the Jewish and Ukrainian-American singer Sophie Tucker.[20]

Tucker seized on Brooks's song, not only in recording it but in her stage act. "Some of These Days" became her signature song on vaudeville and burlesque stages both in the United States and across Europe. Born in 1886, Tucker was the child of Ukrainian immigrants who opened a working-class Jewish restaurant in Hartford, Connecticut, around 1890. She married in 1903 and had a child in 1905; two years later she left her family to pursue a singing career in New York, with the hope of escaping poverty and making money to send home. She made her first vaudeville appearance at Keith and Proctor's 125th Street Theater (previously the Miner's Theater), in blackface. According to her autobiography, this was not a personal decision, but was forced on her by the theater's manager, due to her "ugliness."[21] Tucker continued to perform in black- and brownface, and with a broad southern US accent, during an extended tour with the Gay Masqueraders, a burlesque troupe, in 1908. Yet at some point around 1909, she refused to wear blackface makeup any more. She claimed it had been, for her, a humiliating acceptance of her "ugliness": a general judgment conferred on her physical appearance by various men of the theater world. In other words, Tucker was troubled by the personal implications of blackface, yet unconcerned by its racial politics; and in this respect she was not unusual among white performers. Minstrelsy offered her a path into show business, albeit an unconventional one for a woman—blackface performers were overwhelmingly male—and perhaps a sly means of capitalizing on her weight.[22]

By the time Tucker met Brooks in 1910, when the composer sought her out to promote his latest song, she had already appeared at the Ziegfeld Follies and was, by her own admission, already behaving like a "star." Indeed, it was only through the intervention of the Black singer and minstrelsy performer Molly Elkins—Tucker's travel companion and perhaps lover—that she agreed to meet Brooks at all.[23] Later she recalled being glad she did:

> The minute I heard "Some of These Days" I could have kicked myself for almost losing it. A song like that. It had everything. Hasn't it proved it? I've been singing it for thirty years, made it my theme song. I've turned it inside out, singing it every way imaginable, as a dramatic song, as a novelty number, as a sentimental ballad, and always audiences have loved it and asked for it.[24]

This passage compactly illustrates the thoroughgoing absorption of the song into Tucker's personal mystique. Through a heavy scrim of reminiscence, two features of her account are nonetheless clear. First, she recognized the song's value only through the ears of Elkins, elsewhere referred to as her "maid." Second, despite her immense success, she felt no debt of acknowledgment, let alone money, to Brooks beyond this brief mention. Tucker's autobiography, from which this extract comes, significantly bore the title *Some of These Days*. Yet she chose Jack Yellen—the Jewish composer of another hit song, "My Yiddshe Momma"—rather than Brooks as the autobiography's dedicatee.[25]

Many years later, in 1931, around the time Sartre graduated from the École normale supérieure, Tucker made her debut performance in Paris at the Théâtre de l'Empire:

> I sang song after song, still with my eyes and heart on the galleries. When I swung into "Some of These Days," the house went wild. Then I sang the chorus in French, and it brought a terrific laugh and applause from all over the theater.[26]

Before Tucker crossed the channel from England, the song's chorus had been translated for her by none other than the British heiress Edwina Mountbatten, in collaboration with her friend and fellow socialite Hugh William Osbert Molyneux, 7th Earl of Sefton. Tucker's aristocratic translators, together with her lack of familiarity with the language, hint at reasons why her rendition of the chorus in French inspired an eruption of laughter. Another explanation for such strength of reaction is suggested by her experience at another concert a few weeks later in the Netherlands. Her rapturous reception was later explained to her by a local:

> "Dear Miss Tucker, if you could understand Dutch, you would have heard the words the entire audience let out in one gasp at your entrance: 'My God! She's a white woman!'" It seems the Dutch thought from my phonograph records and my syncopation and deep voice that I was a colored star. The Dutch shopkeepers advertised my records: "By the American Negro Singer—Sophie Tucker."[27]

With few images of the singer in circulation, disc vendors found it convenient to believe, or expedient to pretend, that Tucker was African American. This produced a widespread assumption among record listeners, in the Netherlands and perhaps across Europe, that they were hearing a Black singer. Onstage, of course, the pretense was instantly disturbed—in this case, with eruptive effect—and in this respect, theater audiences in Holland were not so different from US audiences of blackface performances decades before. One of the most popular moments in Tucker's act for US vaudeville crowds came usually near the end of a blackface set, when she partly removed a black glove to flash white skin.[28] While these early audiences likely "knew" all along that Tucker was a large white woman in blackface, the disruption of a fantasy of blackness could reliably provoke a response.[29]

Tucker's race remained a topic of conversation throughout the 1920s and '30s in the United States, where she was now a major celebrity. Such discussion interlocked with "Some of These Days" in complex ways. In 1929 a reader from St. Paul, Minnesota, wrote into the *Chicago Defender*'s "Defender Forum"—an important area of discussion on African American topics—with a simple request for information: "Please tell me if Sophie Tucker is a Negro."[30] A few years later, in the same "Defender Forum," another reader asked if "Some of These Days" had been written by a white man.[31] Such straightforward queries suggest that the gramophone created uncertainty around the song's composer and most famous performer—together with the need to resolve the ambiguity. Another remark, from later in the decade, highlights the role of sound reproduction in all this while suggesting how such talk more broadly functioned as celebrity gossip. When Tucker met the actor Luise Rainer for the first time in 1937, in Hollywood, the latter declared: "I've heard you on the phonograph and radio, but I thought you were a Negro."[32] In relaying this encounter, the *Defender* glossed Tucker's reaction: "The well-known blues artist, who is a friend to the actual profession and has appeared on many benefits side by side with race artists, took this remark as more or less a joke."[33]

/Disc

Having outlined the song's early reception, I want to explore the possibility that Sartre, like Rainer and so many others, knew next to nothing about it. In other words, I would like to suggest that the genesis and reception of "Some of These Days"—precisely because it was a song he encountered mainly if not exclusively through a shellac disc—remained a closed book to Sartre, as to many European audiences. With no accompanying images or text beyond a standardized disc label containing the names of musicians, the shellac disc was a format prone to a high degree of contextual loss. I noted above in passing that Sophie Tucker, the singer who staked out exclusive ownership of the song, was in Paris around the time Sartre graduated from Paris's leading university. But there is no reason to believe that he might have seen her at the Théâtre de l'Empire in 1931, or even heard about her European tour. Indeed, had Sartre known of Tucker's European tour, it is likely that *Nausea* would have been a very different novel. Among other things, it would have obliged the proto-existentialist author, deeply committed to truthful observation, to confront the many and lively connections between French and US jazz.[34] In other words, it is precisely Sartre's lack of knowledge about this widely circulating song that speaks through in the novel.

For example, circulation on recordings—wax cylinders in the first instance—can help explain how it was that "Some of These Days" became the antidote to Roquetin's illness. In the novel, Sartre's protagonist remembers hearing the song for the first time in in 1917 in La Rochelle. This was also the year in which Sartre himself was newly present in the town, after his mother—Anne Marie née Schweitzer, cousin of the famous Albert—remarried and moved her family there. Toward the end of the First World War, US servicemen were present in La Rochelle, where they established a large car manufacturing plant to supply the Allied troops, and conceivably brought the song (its sheet music, cylinders, and even discs) with them.[35] It is at least possible, then, that twelve-year-old Sartre encountered the melody here at this time, whistled by US soldiers, as in the novel. He became significantly reacquainted with the song a decade later, during his time as a university student in Paris, having embarked on his famous relationship with Simone de Beauvoir. In an autobiography, she recalled "Some of These Days" being among a series of shellac discs that comprised the soundtrack of their student days, in which the song figured alongside a miscellany of emerging jazz standards and Broadway hits.[36]

It may be impossible to know which recording of "Some of These Days" Sartre and de Beauvoir heard. Following a number of danceable instrumental covers, including one by the Original Dixieland Jazz Band in 1922, a fresh tranche of recordings featuring vocalists was made in the later 1920s. The first and best known of these was the 1926 "foxtrot" created by Ted Lewis's orchestra, featuring Sophie Tucker—who had recorded it on wax cylinder sixteen years before, as previously noted. After a lengthy instrumental introduction, as was standard in dance songs of the period, her rumbling voice entered at the song's refrain. Lewis's arrangement—his uncredited violin and trumpet players, in particular—no doubt deserve some of the credit for the song's immense success.[37] But fame accrued mainly to the singer. Tucker went on to record "Some of These Days" with other bands several times in the years and decades that followed.[38] Nevertheless, the recording by Tucker and Lewis was not the only version on the market in the 1920s. It inspired a rash of recordings by, among others, Ethel Waters (1927), Vaughn de Leath (1927), Betty Morgan (1927) and Diana Dell (1928).[39]

This lineup includes the likeliest candidates for the recording found among Sartre and de Beauvoir's collection, and thus the real-life counterpart to Roquetin's beloved disc. Impossible though it may be to pin down one disc or another as *the* version echoed in the story, the exact performance inscribed on disc—even the copy's minute physical characteristics—came to matter a great deal in the book. As previously mentioned, Sartre introduces it as a "Pathé record for sapphire needle" released after the First World War.[40] Near the end of the book he again stresses the disc's age, as Roquetin prepares to leave Bouville forever, while fretting that he will be unable to find the record elsewhere: "It is very old, even too old for the provinces; I will look for it in vain in Paris."[41] As the story reaches its dénouement, with his nausea worse than ever, Roquetin visits his local café to hear the record one last time. He sits at his preferred spot and writes in his diary as he listens: "The truth is I can't put down my pen."[42] As the disc plays the story out, it becomes timelocked to Roquetin's diary, in which the pace of reading mimics the unfolding of the song, played twice over and heard, as it were, in real time.

Roquetin's diary offers a rare account of the disc listener in process. His first impression on hearing "Some of These Days" is a feeling of shame.[43] Up until the moment the music begins, he has been living in an ugly world. But the song he now hears, like a "little jeweled pain which spins around above the record and dazzles me," opens a portal to another reality:

> [. . .] It spins gaily, completely self-absorbed; like a scythe it has cut through the drab intimacy of the world and now it spins and all of us, Madeleine, the thick-set man, the patronne, myself, the tables, benches, the stained mirror, the glasses, all of us abandon ourselves to existence; because we were among ourselves, only among ourselves, it has taken us unawares, in the disorder, the day to day drift: I am ashamed for myself and for what exists *in front* of it.
>
> It does not exist. It is even an annoyance; if I were to get up and rip this record from the table which holds it, if I were to break it in two, I wouldn't reach *it*. It is beyond—always beyond something, a voice, a violin note. Through layers and layers of existence, it veils itself, thin and

> firm, and when you want to seize it, you find only existents, you butt against existents devoid of sense. It is behind them: I don't even hear it, I hear sounds, vibrations in the air which unveil it. It does not exist because it has nothing superfluous: it is all the rest which in relation to it is superfluous. It *is*.[44]

The novelist delves deeply into contemporary imagery of shellac discs (see again figure 5.1). The "sapphire needle" noted earlier in the story becomes a "little jeweled pain" (*petit doleur de diamant*) and then a "scythe" (*faux*) that slices through the present.

This passage is historically rare, then, in two different ways at once: both as a diary of listening and as an account of listening in real time to a particular shellac disc. Roquetin's diary is also deeply idiosyncratic in the way Sartre articulates this listening experience. In Roquetin's confession of shame in the presence of recorded music, "Some of These Days" not only becomes an object of audition but acquires the ability to see and hear the listener himself, suddenly revealed in his drab surroundings. The sudden exposure and shame induced by the playing of the disc gives rise to a revenge fantasy: Roquetin imagines breaking the disc, as though to reduce it to the level of other merely existing things. Yet even as he envisages this possibility, he realizes that the exercise would be futile, because the musical event that the disc relays is immortal.

To state the obvious, Sartre is working out larger philosophical claims through Roquetin's nauseated ears.[45] The song, incarnated in the disc, becomes a tool: one that enables Sartre to articulate a division (an act of dividing that itself takes place in time) between present and past, self and other—a division that nevertheless evokes a stable, objective relation between the subject and the past, the subject and the other. The shellac disc seems to illustrate a connection between these otherwise uncommunicating regions. In storing and releasing sounds from the past, the disc functions as testimony to the enduring reality of an expressive event. And yet, and this is critical, such testimony must inevitably deteriorate over time:

> And there is something that clutches the heart: the melody is absolutely untouched by this tiny coughing of the needle on the record. It is so far—so far behind. I understand that too: the disc is scratched and is wearing out, perhaps the singer is dead [. . .] But behind the existence which falls from one present to another, without a past, without a future, behind these *sounds which decay from day to day, peel off and slip toward death*, the melody stays the same, young and firm, like a pitiless witness.[46]

Through the decomposition of the shellac disc, Sartre lays out, for the first time, an existentialist vision of truth in a godless world, the disc standing as the "pitiless witness" (*témoin sans pitié*), an objective memory to guarantee order in a world in constant flux. Yet of course the disc also contains the seeds of that vision's undoing, since an act of faith is required to believe that the melody stays "the same," fixed through the disc for all eternity, even while the disc itself wears down.

Being and Listening

There may be nothing else quite like Roqutein's listening diary in the attention he lavishes on a shellac disc, and in the far-reaching implications he draws from the experience. But its sheer, dogged eccentricity can nevertheless point to its relevance as a document of listening—its self-flagellating honesty casting light on broader political and material conditions of an historical format. There is, of course, the unusual attention Roquetin directs toward gramophone brands, needles, and turntables. Sartre also discloses an interest in the actions and consequences of friction—in "sounds which decay from day to day, peel off and slip toward death," emphasized in the previous long quotation. In this way Sartre evokes a broader historical experience of listening to music on disc: one attuned to the consequences of repeated playback. He shows how shellac mixtures gave rise to overlapping temporalities, the time of playback superimposed over the aging of the disc itself. Through the avatar of Roquetin, Sartre offers a portrait of a *kind* of disc listener intimately familiar with the format's contradictory experiences of both permanence and the steady disintegration of sounds over time.

These experiences echo deeply into Sartre's future. In celebrated passages from *Being and Nothingness* (1943), he returned both to music and to the café environment to describe through-time acts of negation in more abstract terms. There is no longer any mention of gramophones, of course. As befits a more serious philosophical work, both music and café are reduced to mere examples of more widely observable realities. I will consider two brief examples. The first involves the café and a friend called Pierre:

> I am meeting Pierre at 4 o' clock. I arrive quarter of an hour late: Pierre is always punctual; will he have waited for me? I look at the room, the customers, and I say, "He is not here."[47]

As the philosopher scans the café, its "customers, its tables, its seats, its mirrors, its light, its smoke-filled atmosphere, and the sounds the fill it" dissolve into to an undifferentiated background.[48] This background in turn recalls *Nausea*'s café, whose atmosphere was similarly evoked by a blurred background of "tables, benches, the stained mirror, the glasses." And it is against this background that Sartre, the philosopher, constantly expects Pierre to manifest, even though Pierre never appears:

> [. . . The café] makes itself the ground for a specific figure, it bears it everywhere in front of it, it presents me with it everywhere, and this figure, sliding constantly between my gaze and the real, solid objects of the café, is precisely a perpetual dissolution: it is Pierre, detaching himself as a nothingness against the ground of the nihilation of the café.[49]

Appearing in a chapter titled "The Origin of Negation," this passage presents Sartre's concept of nothingness for the first time. Making use of the well-known phenomenological distinction between figure and background, he explains how Pierre continues to haunt the café for as long as his absence nihilates the café (as background). Even more abstractly, Sartre goes on to say that such absence, as an example of nothingness, should be understood as a dynamic negativity, "a perpetual dissolution"—a vacuum rather than a void.

The second example concerns music, and again involves Pierre—Sartre's philosophical John Doe who haunts *Being and Nothingness*. This time, Pierre is dead. His figure nevertheless emerges in a part of the book devoted to temporality, in a section dedicated to the being of the past:

> I can say of Pierre, who is dead, that "he liked music." In this case both subject and attribute are in the past. And there is no current Pierre to be the starting point from which this past-being could arise. [. . .] a taste for music has never been *past* for Pierre. Pierre has always been the contemporary of this taste, which was *his* taste; his living personality has not survived him, and neither has he survived it. It follows that, in this instance, what is past is Pierre-liking-music.[50]

In this set of reflections, Sartre's examines a quirk arising from his broader metaphysical outlook, according to which the existence of the past comes to depend on witnesses who can verify its being. In this instance, the philosopher herself must stand as witness to Pierre-liking-music, and to Pierre's past-being more generally:

> Today I am the only one responsible, in my freedom, for the being of Pierre who is dead. And those dead people who have not been rescued and carried aboard by some survivor's concrete past are not *in the past*; rather, they—and their pasts—have been annihilated.[51]

With these examples of negation before us, we might return to *Nausea*'s anguished close, which circles around the same theme. As mentioned above, as the story comes to an end, Roquetin "livestreams" his diary, frantically writing while listening in real time in the café. He listens to "Some of These Days" and fantasizes wildly about the circumstances that gave rise to the performance he hears on disc. He imagines and invents the song's composer: "a clean-shaven American with thick black eyebrows on the twenty-first floor of a New York skyscraper. [. . .] He is sitting, in shirt-sleeves, in front of his piano; he has a taste of smoke in his mouth and, vaguely, a ghost of a tune in his head."[52] His thoughts home in on the "worn-out body of this Jew with black eyebrows which [the song] chose to create it."[53] He yearns to be present at this moment of inception: he wants to hear this composer "*through* the melody, through the white acidulated sounds of the saxophone"—and similarly to behold "the Negress" *through* her voice. In the end, he admits that all this is pure invention. Roquetin wishes he possessed some biographical facts, to imagine the song's creators more accurately. And yet, whatever he may choose to imagine, these individuals have been immortalized: "So two of them are saved: the Jew and the Negress. Saved. Maybe they thought they were lost irrevocably, drowned in existence. Yet no one could think of me as I think of them, with such gentleness."[54]

Here the emphasis is squarely on the "I": Roquetin inhabits the role of the witness who testifies to the reality of individuals lost in the flux of the past. But were these musicians really so irretrievably lost? Could Sartre have at least tried to track them down? In the willfulness of its mistakes of musical reference, *Nausea*'s ending has long perplexed.[55] But perhaps, among the errors and agonies, we can find the outline of an historically emergent mode of listening, a phenomenology of recorded sound for the gramophone age. To recall its key features: the onset of "Some of These Days" slices through the present "like a scythe." All at once, the café and everything in it become the background for the song as figure. For as long as it plays, the disc creates a "perpetual dissolution" of the café; and for a short while after it stops, the song—its singer, its musicians, its composer—are ghosts: absences that energetically fail to appear against the undifferentiated sounds, sights, and smells of the café. This movement between playing and stopping, listening and nothingness, is the narrow window within which Roquetin writes his diary. It is also the prompt for his feverish imaginings as he yearns to attach bodies, both sexed and raced, to musicians he hears but does not see. Ultimately the sounds slip away and Roquetin is left as a witness—a human counterpart to the more "pitiless witness" that is the disc itself—who is able to save the singer—and, through her voice, the composer —from oblivion. After all, Roquetin wants to be rescued from oblivion himself; he is a witness who desperately craves witnesses. On the final page of the novel, he reveals that this is what motivated him to write his diary in the first place: the hope that one day readers "will think of my life as I think of that of that Negress: as something precious and at the same time legendary."[56]

/

Throughout this chapter, I have been claiming that Sartre's elaborate, fictional, and philosophical description of listening to "Some of These Days" recast something much more common, even ordinary. More strongly, I have been suggesting that it was this mundane experience of recorded sound that gave rise to his philosophical jargon: that there is direct path between *Nausea*'s gramophone needle—a "scythe that slices through the present"—and the no-thing that separates past from present in *Being and Nothingness*. This was a concept designed to resolve a technical problem of temporal multiplicity, which phenomenologists had been pondering at least since Husserl's and Bergson's work on time consciousness. In outline, Husserl's adoption of a mathematical concept—Bernhard Riemann's notion of continuous manifolds—was meant to explain how the experience of duration, in the now, constantly rolls over into the future through an ongoing synthesis of present and past.[57] As though to dispense with such heavy-duty theory, however, Sartre replaced Husserl's time synthesis with nothingness—a notorious if more lightweight concept that, in its negativity, explained connection across difference as a charged lack.[58] Yet while the idea can be tracked through intellectual history, its emergence was achieved through fiction and by means of an everyday engagement with sound technology.

I have already suggested one way in which nothingness more broadly applied to historical experiences of listening to discs: in the electrical absences that occurred, at least for a short while, in the moments after a record stopped. Sartre evoked a listener newly and more sharply divided between temporalities of playback and retention—a break no longer smoothed over by the presence of musicians falling silent, or by an audience's applause. This was a historical experience that gave rise to conceptual invention, and it shows one way in which the gramophone industry and philosophical daydreams could become entwined.[59] Another source can illustrate the two-way traffic between culture and conceptual invention, and, more particularly, the kind of residual thinking inspired by Brooks and Tucker's song/disc. In a 1926 review of "Some of These Days," published in a newspaper roughly six months after its US release, a journalist remarked:

> ... Je ne sais pas d'accents plus émouvants que ceux de Mlle Sophie Tucker, qui chante, avec le jazz de Ted Lewis, *Some of these days.* Mystérieux appels d'autant plus déchirants que nous pouvons, à notre fantaisie, *envelopper cette voix dans un être imaginaire.*[60]
>
> [. . . I do not know of a voice more moving than that of Miss Tucker, who sings, with Ted Lewis's jazz, "Some of These Days." Its appeals are mysterious—and all the more heartbreaking because we can, according to our fantasy, *envelop that voice in an imaginary being.*]

This reflection occurred in an overview of the latest disc offerings from the Columbia label: Lewis and Tucker's record featured alongside releases by the cabaret singer Maurice Chevalier and the tenor Georges Thill. Next to these more local celebrities, Tucker presented an enigma: a voice in search of a body.

Sartre played out the implications of this kind of listening exercise. *Nausea* likewise enveloped a recorded singer in an imaginary being, and did so according to a particular fantasy of Blackness. On the one hand, this was a general response to the nothingness produced by the disc itself: the absence of contextual information about the song and its singer. On the other, Sartre's was a culturally distinctive response to this absence, informed by transatlantic conventions of blackface performance.[61] As Jennifer Lynn Stoever argues, a "sonic color line" was constructed through techniques of listening, blackface minstrelsy among them, that trained listeners to discriminate between Black and white in the United States. Stoever explores how such listening was "both informed and was informed by emergent sound technologies."[62] Additionally, as Matthew Morrison shows, the embodied and sonic legacies of blackface performance (which he terms Blacksound) date from the early nineteenth century and echoed long afterwards, and well beyond the US.[63] Sound technologies provided for the global circulation of North American techniques of racialization, even while such entrainment produced unpredictable effects in different places.[64]

Heard through the shellac mixture and between political worlds, jazz could become a listening game for some Europeans, as though to mimic distinctions between black and white rehearsed in the United States. For Sartre, at least, such listening could also become something more. His novel pushed to the limit an exoticizing paradigm that lingered over "imaginary beings" (as per the record review quoted above) by insisting on the disc as an interface with an individual whose absence was viscerally present. This was a metaphysical requirement. Ultimately, there could be no such thing as *êtres imaginaires* in his philosophy—either something existed or it was nothing. Such vivid imagination of real others was to become the foundation of his later political commitments. There is a direct continuity, in other words, between the Sartre who described listening to "Some of These Days" over the gramophone and the Sartre who went on to read the poetry of Négritude as legible blackness, with profound implications for anticolonial thought.[65]

For this reason if no other, nothingness has much to recommend it as a perspective on historical experiences of listening within an international disc network whose center of gravity lay in the United States. Nothingness, in this sense, provides a way to focus the racial charges that thrummed across an endemic lack of context. To recap the case of "Some of These Days": even before the song's annexation by the recording industries, the composer decisively altered the key phrase in the hymn from which it derived, which itself had gathered antiracist significance by the turn of the twentieth century. These antiracist meanings receded into the background through stage acts by white singers in vaudeville, and then into a deeper obscurity through recordings that began circulating on shellac disc and wax cylinder after 1910. A decade or so later, and through the medium of shellac alone, "Some of These Days" became an international hit, even as its sound traveled extensively and independently of the musicians who made it. In other words, by the time Sartre picked up the disc, the song—its sounds, its words, its affects—had already leaped between contexts more than once. The shellac disc was only the last stage in a process of contextual loss and recapture: only the latest dive into nothingness, to reemerge, inevitably, with somethingness.

A concept that emerged in the interstices between a song and a disc, nothingness can point beyond the context of the particular song/disc relation explored in this chapter.[66] It gestures to much broader ways in which a multiplicity was held in tension as countless songs were materialized in many more discs, even while the distinction between song and material container was reliably kept distinct by listeners. Nothingness can evoke the generative lack in that imaginative separation: a historically emergent idea of song as sound and nothing more, achieved over a backdrop of the disc as a vanishing mediator. Or to put this differently, nothingness offers an interpretative key to a historical style of listening across difference, according to which the forgetting of materiality became the frangible condition for a full-blown hallucination of absent others.

It is with a shellac-enabled vision that I would like to close. Some years after Sartre's *Nausea*, and as the gramophone era came to an end in the United States, Ralph Ellison's *The Invisible Man* (1952) appeared.

Famously, it opens with the titular character listening to a recording of Louis Armstrong's "Black and Blue" (1929). In a "hole" in the ground below New York City, in the basement beneath a block of apartments, the invisible man has taken up residence; this space, abandoned and forgotten "since the nineteenth century," is illuminated by 1,369 filament light bulbs, using power tapped from the Monopolated Light and Power Company—an infrastructural hack that also allows him to play Louis Armstrong on an electrical disc-playing machine. And it is from this dazzlingly bright, warm, and comfortable "hole" in time that he begins to tell his story:

> I am invisible, understand, simply because people refuse to see me. Like the bodiless heads you see sometimes in circus sideshows, it is as though I have been surrounded by mirrors of hard, distorting glass. When they approach me they see only my surroundings, themselves, or figments of their imagination—indeed, everything and anything except me.[67]

As his story unfolds, he listens closely to "Black and Blue," and begins to hear sounds and voices well beyond and beneath it. Indeed, he becomes absorbed in the disc's vibrations and feels himself pulled downward into levels of unsound below the audible range:

> So under the spell of the reefer I discovered a new analytical way of listening to music. The unheard sounds came through, and each melodic line existed of itself, stood out clearly from all the rest, said its piece, and waited patiently for the other voices to speak. That night I found myself hearing not only in time, but in space as well. I not only entered the music but descended, like Dante, into its depths.[68]

Beneath "Black and Blue" he hears "an old woman singing a spiritual," and below that, on a still deeper stratum, a girl "the color of ivory" pleading "in a voice like my mother's" for herself before slaveholders. And finally, on the deepest level of all, he hears the words that begin a sermon: "Brothers and sisters, my text this morning is the 'Blackness of Blackness.'"[69]

Ellison's *The Invisible Man* is one of the most celebrated novels of the postwar United States, and its central idea of invisibility has long been hailed for its power to evoke the condition of Blackness. And while this is neither the time nor the place to launch a discussion of another, much longer novel, I would like to point out some features it holds in common with Sartre. My hope, then, is not to end this book with a last word, but to show how some ideas I have been exploring here might be tested against gramophone cultures more broadly.[70] First, and most straightforwardly, both Sartre and Ellison choose shellac discs from the recent past featuring jazz. Second, both use particular discs to stage fantastical acts of listening: visionary auralities that peer through sounds to the human bodies from which they must have emanated. I have said enough about Sartre's hallucination of a Black singer and a white Jewish composer. Of course, Ellison makes no such error. But the structure of an imaginative leap in the presence of recorded sounds remains in place: while listening, in an almost tactile relation to sound, the invisible man evokes a larger African American social body and political history, to which the sounds he hears are connected as if materially. As Nicole Brittingham Furlonge shows, Ellison beholds Armstrong's "Black and Blue" not so much as an item for silent contemplation and abstract enjoyment, but as a way of materializing a racial identity—that of being Black in postwar America—as a vibrational practice.[71]

In closing, I want to pause over this moment of imaginative leap—because what Sartre and Ellison shared, if in different ways and with starkly different results, was an insistence on the reality of a virtual musical experience. Their common interest in listening beyond and beneath sounds represented an alternative to the kind of heaven-bound transcendence championed by an earlier generation of musical aesthetics, encouraging instead a kind of listening that could slide along endless chains of indexical connection within this world. And this can offer one last—and, I think, hopeful—perspective on the format: that listening across difference in the shellac network was always, potentially, connection. For what ultimately underpinned these slippery visions of bodies in the gramophone age was friction—the force of the format that endowed imaginative claims with purchase. After all, even ideas about nothing must come from somewhere.

Acknowledgments

Some sections of this book have been previously published elsewhere. A version of chapter 1 appeared as "Shellac as Musical Plastic" in *Journal of the American Musicological Society* 74, no. 3 (2021): 463–500; and a version of chapter 3 was published as "The Reproduction of Caruso" in *Cambridge Opera Journal* 33, no. 1–2 (2021): 161–79. Those articles are reproduced here with permission.

This book has explored an old, heavy format, but it belongs to an older and heavier one: the academic monograph. My decision to write a monograph about gramophone discs might have portended a rare and solitary act. But looking back, I'm glad to report that there has been not too much solo about the "mono" in this case, and I am gladly reminded of the many friendships and debts that have made it possible.

First, I must acknowledge the support of a Leverhulme Early Career Research Fellowship held at King's College London between 2016 and 2019. The Department of Music at KCL is an incredible place to work, with so many kind and intrepid souls. I'm especially grateful to Martin Stokes, an inspiring mentor and guide, as well as to Katherine Butler-Schofield, Amy Blier-Carruthers, Oskar Cox-Jensen, Joseph Forte, Andy Fry, Kathy Fry, James Grande, Katherine Hambridge, Matthew Head, Jo Hicks, Tom Hodgson, Fred Moehn, Daniel Leech-Wilkinson, Ditlev Rindom, and especially Flora Willson. It is a pleasure to acknowledge Roger Parker's wonderful advice and interventions at many junctures along the way.

This project followed me beyond King's to the University of California, Berkeley. This book would not be as it is, for better or worse, without a graduate seminar I co-taught with James Q. Davies on sound reproduction ecologies. I'm also grateful to Susan Bay, Annie Greenwood, Virginia Georgallas, Melanie Gudesblatt, Marta Meazza, Rosie Ward, and Parkorn Wangpaiboonkit. I have been motivated and enlightened by Daniel Brownstein, Zhuqing (Lester) Hu, Alessandra Jones, Franz Nicolay, Kirsten Paige, Danni Simon, Maria Sonevystky, and Emily Zazulia. In addition to editorial guidance, Nicholas Mathew and Mary Ann Smart have provided me with much encouragement and insightful feedback.

I gratefully acknowledge the office space and library access provided to me as a visitor of the Institute of Advanced Study in Princeton during a four-month stretch. My especial thanks to Nicola di Cosmo and Myles Jackson, and to members of Myles's History of Science workshop—particularly Andrea Bohlman, who responded to chapter 4 via audio link while driving from Princeton to Chapel Hill. My thanks, too, to librarians at the Oral History Centre, National Archives of Singapore; to Jesus College, Cambridge, for funds to travel there; and to Dr. K. K. Sharma, Dr. Niranjan Prasad, and Dr. A. Mohanasundaram at the Indian Institute of Natural Resins and Gums, for entertaining strange questions about shellac. I'm grateful to Joanna Hughes at the EMI archives, as well as to librarians and archivists at Odessa's Museum of Sound and the Llyfrgell Genedlaethol Cymru (National Library of Wales). Marta Tonegutti has been a patient and generous editor, while Renaldo Migaldi, Meredith Nini, and Kristin Rawlings have provided careful editorial guidance; and I must thank anonymous readers who devoted much time and energy to this manuscript on behalf of the University of Chicago Press.

Beyond these institutions, many other individuals have also had a tangible impact on this book. Carlo Cenciarelli, Ellen Lockhart, and Ben Walton have been constant supportive friends and readers over the years. Fellow travelers in shellac history Kyle Devine, Vibodh Parthasarathi, and Elodie Roy have provided me with an incredibly convivial network. I must also thank Olenka Kleban for showing me around a bell foundry in Berkeley, decisively changing the direction of my thoughts on Caruso's reproduction—as did important feedback from Siel Agugliaro and Davide Ceriani. Many thanks for support on language matters from Caroline Murphy, Min-Erh Wang, and Xiaoyan Tan. I will be forever grateful to Sunny Mathew and his family for allowing me to stay for awhile at his Museum of Discs and Machines.

Returning to the topic of format, I have often wondered whether an acknowledgments section should include or be supplemented by its opposite: an unacknowledgments section, nominating those who have in various ways frustrated the book's progress. To be sure, such entities exist, and it is tempting. . . . And yet, as this book comes to an end, I am left with only gentle feelings. Almost everything I have written falls from a happy cloud of conversation with Delia Casadei. May the mists ever rise. I dedicate this book to my mother Janice, whose support means everything; to my sister Rhianne and her children, Ella and Elijah; and to Gwen, my nan, whom we miss every day.

Notes

INTRODUCTION

1. One measure of this expansion is the mushrooming of record shops in US and European urban centers, See, for example, the interactive map produced by Thomas Henry, "Disquaires de Paris: 120 ans d'enregistrement sonore," published online at http://disquairesdeparis.fr/ (accessed 10 July 2020).

2. The use of gramophones in place of priests in churches was noteworthy around 1900 (and a trope), as in the following comment: "A gramophone will in future occupy the pulpit daily, whose brazen tongue will pour forth sermons by all the best preachers." See [untitled], *The Singapore Free Press and Daily Advertiser*, 15 May 1900, p. 3.

3. See, for example, Michael S. Kinnear, *The Gramophone Company's First Indian Recordings, 1899–1908* (Bombay: Popular Prakashan, 1994), 9–20. Early attempts by Western record companies to record outside their colonies have been less studied.

4. My use of "global perspective" in this context bears resemblance to Georgina Born's recent theorization—which itself draws on Tariq Jazeel's reformulation of Gayatari Spivak's idea—of "planetarity" in music studies, as an alternative concept of the universal in its mediation of cultural singularity. See Georgina Born, *Music and Digital Media: A Planetary Anthropology* (London: UCL Press, 2022), 13–15. See also Tariq Jazeel, "Singularity: A Manifesto for Incomparable Geographies," *Singapore Journal of Tropical Geography* 40, no. 1 (2019): 5–21.

5. On formats, see Jonathan Sterne, *MP3: The Meaning of a Format* (Durham, NC: Duke University Press, 2012). For global perspectives on media, see Richard Maxwell, *The Routledge Companion to Labor and Media* (London: Routledge, 2015); see also Lucie Vágnerová, "'Nimble Fingers' in Electronic Music: Rethinking Sound Through Neo-Colonial Labour," *Organized Sound* 22 (2017): 250–58.

6. Following the Second World War there was a plunge in sales of 78s, a period which also saw the rise of long-play vinyl records. Shellac discs continued to be mass-produced for Indian markets into the 1970s. Yet, in India as elsewhere, the format would be mostly forgotten by the end of the twentieth century. See G. N. Joshi, "A Concise History of the Phonography Industry in India," *Popular Music* 7, no. 2 (1988): 147–56.

7. While the material sources of LP records (polyvinyl chloride and polyvinyl acetate), magnetic tape (polyethylene), and compact discs (polycarbonate and acrylic) in synthetic plastic are in many ways obvious, streaming is routinely framed as "immaterial" due to the absence of a physical record. Yet, as Kyle Devine has pointed out, streaming may in fact be significantly more materially intensive than these other music media. See Kyle Devine, *Decomposed: The Political Ecology of Music* (Cambridge, MA: MIT Press, 2019), 129–64.

8. For an overview of current responses to this challenge, see Elodie A. Roy, "Introduction: Entangled Phonographies" in Elodie A. Roy and Eva Moreda Rodríguez, eds., *Phonographic Encounters: Mapping Transnational Cultures of Sound, 1890–1945* (Oxford, UK: Routledge, 2022), 1–13.

9. Tan Tong Seng 陈仲生, interviewed by Bonny Tan at the Oral History Centre, Singapore, 2004. National Archives of Singapore, accession no. 002826, reel 7 of 25. Web 15 January 2020; translated by Xioayan Tan.

> 那时候有录音带了，有一种叫做 . . . . 不是我们cassette（匣式录音带）你知道吗？以前一种转筒的、滚筒的，圆形的滚筒，很古老，用线圈做成的滚筒录音带。不过这个不是民间用的啦，多数人家这个好像商业用的，还是国防国家用的。不过他们是以那个录了去改成是唱片还是怎么样啦弄进来。有些就立刻有些懂得音乐就把它写成谱，就一直传了咯，很快的，一下子你手上就有这些歌曲（笑）。这个《黄河大合唱》，我小学还没有毕业，好像四年级的时候，我就会唱了咯，那时候才几岁？[. . .] 在战前我妈妈是家庭主妇，那么我父亲就在外工作，早出晚归，那么她又跟我们这几个孩子，她很无聊你知道吗？我爸爸知道，就买一个留声机，用这个手搅的发条那种留声机，买来给她听。而没有钱买唱片，每一天或是两天，就有这个用三轮车推了很多唱片来租，出租的，好像一张唱片不懂一分还是两分？你去唱，唱了就拿回来，就再换几张去。所以我那时候听周璇的歌曲也是听到烂熟，听这个抗战歌曲也是听到烂熟，都是78转，都是用这个留声机来听的。哇，那时候多数听抗战歌曲已经录在这个78转（唱片）里面了。战前就有78转，百代（唱片公司）出版的。

10. See Elodie Roy, "The Sheen of Shellac: From Reflective Material to Self-Reflective Medium," in Antje Krause-Wahl, Petra Löffler, and Änne Söll, eds., *Materials, Practices, and Politics of Shine in Modern Art and Popular Culture* (London: Bloomsbury, 2021), 105–22.

11. See David Suisman, *Selling Sounds: The Commercial Revolution in American Popular Music* (Cambridge, MA: Harvard University Press, 2009), 277.

12. By contrast, matrix numbers—indicating the metal stamper used to press the disc—were pressed onto the disc itself, usually in the empty space between the paper label and the grooves.

13. Emile Berliner, "The Development of the Talking Machine: Read before the Franklin Institute of Philadelphia, May 21, 1913," in *Three Addresses* (Washington: [publisher not identified], 1913), 32.

14. Berliner, "Development of the Talking Machine," 32.

15. On technologies as the products of "male birth," see Jonathan Sterne, *The Audible Past: Cultural Origins of Sound Reproduction* (Durham, NC: Duke University Press, 2003), 180–81.

16. On the "habitual reliance of the production/consumption dichotomy," which stresses the contributions of inventors and entrepreneurs over other actors and agents, in telling the history of the phonograph and gramophone, see Lisa Gitelman, *Always Already New* (Cambridge, MA: MIT Press, 2008), 61–62.

17. Emphasis added. Berliner, "Development of the Talking Machine," 33.

18. See Roland Gelatt, *The Fabulous Phonograph: From Edison to Stereo* (New York: Appleton Century Crofts, 1966). For a more recent example, see "From Phonoautographs to MP3s: A History of Recording Formats," https://www.bl.uk/history-of-recorded-sound/articles/timeline-of-formats (accessed 19 Feb 2022).

19. This is an example of what Paul Théberge called "transectorial innovation." See Paul Théberge, *Any Sound You Can Imagine: Making Music/Consuming Technology* (Hanover, NH: Wesleyan University Press, 1997), 12 and 58–69.

20. Berliner, "Development of the Talking Machine," 35.

21. Berliner, "Development of the Talking Machine," 35–36.

22. Around 1900, Berliner abandoned vertical (hill-and-dale) grooves in favor of horizontal ones. The agitation of the groove from side to side meant that both discs and needles wore down more evenly.

23. Berliner, "Development of the Talking Machine," 36.

24. Berliner, "Development of the Talking Machine," 36.

25. As the editors put it, "If infrastructures represent the sine qua non of media content in the final instance, then formats represent the necessary forms of structuring and delivering media that coordinate between infrastructures and users." Alexandra Schneider, Axel Volmar, and Marek Jancovic, eds., *Format Matters: Standards, Practices, and Politics in Media Cultures* (Lüneburg, Germany: Meson Press, 2020), 7.

26. Schneider, Volmar, and Jancovic, *Format Matters*, 7.

27. Jacob Burckhardt, "Format und Bild," in Maurizio Ghelardi and Susanne Müller, eds., *Jacob Burckhardt Werke: Kritische Geamtausgabe*, vol. 13 (Munich: C. H. Beck, 2003), 506–16.

28. Jonathan Sterne, *MP3: The Meaning of a Format* (Durham, NC: Duke University Press, 2012), 11.

29. Schneider, Volmar, and Jancovic, *Format Matters,* 11.

30. Erika Balsom, "Instant Failure: Polaroid's Polavision, 1977–1980," *Grey Room* 66 (2017): 9.

31. Balsom, "Instant Failure," 9.

32. Sterne, *MP3*, 8.

33. The same holds true of shellac discs, and "format wars" raged around the turn of the twentieth century. See Allen Koenigsberg, ed., *The Patent History of the Phonograph, 1877–1912: A Source Book* (New York, APM Press, 1990).

34. Schneider, Volmar, and Jancovic, *Format Matters*, 17. For another lineage, which highlights the historical continuity between player pianos, phonographs and gramophones, see Timothy Taylor, "The Commodification of Music at the Dawn of 'Mechanical Music,'" *Ethnomusicology* 51, no. 2 (2007); 281–305.

35. See Adnan Akay, "Acoustics of Friction," *Journal of the Acoustical Society of America* 4, no. 111 (2002): 1525–48.

36. Sterne, *Audible Past*, 26, 84, 216–23.

37. On the disposability of shellac discs, and musical media more broadly, see Devine, *Decomposed*, 38.

38. Steven Feld, "Pygmy POP: A Genealogy of Schizophonic Mimesis," *Yearbook for Traditional Music* 28 (1996): 1–35.

39. By contrast, on "schizochronia," the annexing of the world's times, see Jairo Moreno, "Imperial Aurality: Jazz, the Archive, and U.S. Empire," in Ronald Radano and Tejumola Olaniyan, eds., *Audible Empire: Music, Global Politics, Critique* (Durham, NC: Duke University Press, 2016), 143–48.

40. Benjamin Piekut and Jason Stanyek, "Deadness: Technologies of the Intermundane," *TDR/The Drama Review* 54, no. 1 (2010): 4–38. The authors' quarrel is not with Feld, but with R. Murray Schafer, who coined the term "schizophonia." See R. Murray Schafer, *The New Soundscape: A Handbook for the Modern Music Teacher* (Scarborough, ON: Berandol Music Limited, 1969), 42.

41. Piekut and Stanyek, "Deadness," 19.

42. Michael Denning, *Noise Uprising: The Audiopolitics of a World Musical Revolution* (London and Brooklyn, NY: Verso, 2015).

43. Denning, *Noise Uprising*, 40–45.

44. Denning cites Attali as a spiritual forebear. See Denning, *Noise Uprising*, 10. However, as Shayna Silverstein points out, he "not only echoes Jacques Attali's universalist history, but also repeats the latter's problematic conceptual mapping of noise as oppositional to music." Shayna Silverstein, "Michael Denning, Noise Uprising: The Audiopolitics of a World Musical Revolution," *Twentieth-Century Music* 14, no. 1 (2017): 164. See also Jacques Attali, *Noise: The Political Economy of Music* (Minneapolis: University of Minnesota Press, 1985).

45. Kyle Devine and Alexandrine Boudreault-Fournier, eds., *Audible Infrastructures: Music, Sound, Media* (Oxford, UK: Oxford University Press, 2021), 4.

46. In an important work of postcolonial anthropology, and with sound reproduction in mind, Michael Taussig defined "mimesis" as the nature that culture uses to create second nature. Here I treat the "shellac disc" in a similar way. See Michael Taussig, *Mimesis and Alterity: A Particular History of the Senses* (London and New York: Routledge, 1993), 70.

47. On the concept of assemblage in music studies, see Georgina Born, "On Musical Mediation: Ontology, Technology and Creativity," *Twentieth-Century Music* 2, no. 1 (2005): 7–36; and her more recent "Introduction: Music, Digitization and Mediation—for a Planetary Anthropology," in Georgina Born, ed., *Music and Digital Media: A Planetary Anthropology* (London: UCL Press, 2022), 24–28.

48. For Deleuze, a multiplicity consists of different elements (sensible, conceptual, virtual) coming together in a distinctive way. The combination has no prior identity, but contains an indeterminacy that "renders possible the manifestation of a difference that is liberated from all subordination." The ele-

ments of the multiplicity are mutually determined "by reciprocal relations that do not admit of independence," and the network of relations implied by the multiplicity actualize themselves in spatiotemporal relationships, even as they generate terms and forms by which they are understood. See Gilles Deleuze, *Différence et Répétition* (Paris: Presses Universitaires de France, 1968), 236–40. On multiplicity as it was subsequently developed by Deleuze in relation to through-time musical experience, see Michael Gallope, *Deep Refrains: Music, Philosophy, and the Ineffable* (Chicago: University of Chicago Press, 2017), 208–9.

49. Ana María Ochoa Gautier, "Acoustic Multinaturalism, the Value of Nature, and the Nature of Music in Ecomusicology," *Boundary 2* 43, no. 1 (2016): 107–41.

50. Eduardo Viveiros de Castro, *Cannibal Metaphysics: For a Post-Structural Anthropology*, trans. Peter Skafish (Minneapolis: Univocal, 2014).

51. Bruno Latour memorably described Viveiros de Castro's perspectivism as a "bomb with the potential to explode the whole implicit philosophy so dominant in most ethnographers' interpretations of their material." Bruno Latour, "Perspectivism: 'Type' or 'Bomb'?" *Anthropology Today* 25, no. 2 (2009): 2. See also Jonathan Sterne, "'What Do We Want?' 'Materiality!' 'When Do We Want It?' 'Now!,'" in Tarleton Gillespie, Pablo J. Boczkowski, and Kirsten A. Foot, eds., *Media Technologies: Essays on Communication, Materiality and Society* (Cambridge, MA: MIT Press, 2014), 119–28.

52. See Carolyn Abbate, "Sound Object Lessons," *Journal of the American Musicological Society* 69, no. 3 (2016): 793–829. See also Delia Casadei, *Risible: Laughter without Reason and the Reproduction of Sound* (Berkeley: University of California Press, 2024).

53. Andrea Bohlman and Peter McMurray, "Tape; or, Rewinding the Phonographic Regime," *Twentieth-Century Music* 14, no. 1 (2017): 3–24.

54. A deconstructive approach to sound by way of inscriptive technologies remains a central topic. See Deborah Kapchan, ed., *Theorizing Sound Writing* (Middletown, CT: Wesleyan University Press, 2017), 1–22.

55. On the persistent, aggravating issue of material form within philosophical deconstruction, see Catherine Malabou, "The End of Writing? Grammatology and Plasticity," *The European Legacy* 12, no. 4 (2007): 431–41. I'm grateful to Delia Casadei for bringing this article to my attention and for inspiring the present argument about the need to move beyond inscription in sound theory.

56. Anna Lowenhaupt Tsing, *Friction: An Ethnography of Global Connection* (Princeton, NJ: Princeton University Press, 2005), 1–18.

57. Tsing, *Friction*, 4.

58. David Novak and Matt Sakakeeney, *Keywords in Sound* (Durham, NC: Duke University Press), 1.

59. Charles Babbage, *The Ninth Bridgewater Treatise: A Fragment* (London: John Murray, 1837), 109–10.

60. Babbage, *Ninth Bridgewater Treatise*, 109–10.

61. Babbage, *Ninth Bridgewater Treatise*, 109–10. On the longer history of

such theorizing, see James Q. Davies, *Creatures of the Air: Music, Atlantic Spirits, Breath, 1817–1913* (Chicago: University of Chicago Press, 2023).

62. John Picker, *Victorian Soundscapes* (Oxford, UK: Oxford University Press, 2003), 15–19.

63. On musical remedies to industrial pollution, and the anthopocenic logic that underlies such operations, see James Q. Davies, "Elijah's Nature," *Nineteenth Century Music* 45, no. 1 (2021): 49–64.

64. Babbage, *Ninth Bridgewater Treatise*, 218.

65. On this broader issue, see Amy Cimini and Jairo Moreno, "Inexhaustible Sound and Fiduciary Aurality," *Boundary 2* 43, no. 1 (2016): 5–41.

CHAPTER 1

1. *Making a Record* lasts three and a half minutes, and was probably intended as part of a series of shorts before a feature film; it is not known who directed, produced, or commissioned it, or even when it was released. Two copies are preserved in the archives of British Pathé (*Making a Record*, film ID 1008.13, canister EP 306). Film documentary took on the trappings of a genre in the late 1920s; see Betsy A. McLane, *A New History of Documentary Film, Second Edition* (London: Continuum, 2012), 73–78. On the importance of short films within a well-balanced program, see Richard Koszarski, *An Evening's Entertainment: The Age of the Silent Feature Picture, 1915–1928* (Berkeley: University of California Press, 1990), 163–80.

2. The film can be viewed online for free at www.britishpathe.com/video/making-a-record/ (accessed March 30, 2020).

3. See Susan Schmidt Horning, *Chasing Sound: Technology, Culture, and the Art of Studio Recording from Edison to the LP* (Baltimore: Johns Hopkins University Press, 2013), 18–22.

4. See Loiperdinger, "Industriebilder," in Uli Jung and Martin Loiperdinger, eds, *Geschichte des dokumentarischen Films in Deutschland: Kaiserreich 1895–1918*, vol. 1 (Stuttgart, Germany: Reclam, 2005): 324–32.

5. Subsequent longer documentaries about disc making would fill in some of the missing stages. Examples include *Command Performance* (sponsored by RCA Victor, William J. Ganz Production Co., 1942), Library of Congress, Prelinger Archive, https://archive.org/details/CommandP1942 (accessed 31 March 2020). The basic template of *Making a Record* remained intact, however; the gramophone disc was made visible as the product of Western labor, inviting surprise and awe at a modern convenience. Sound studies' programmatic focus on Western technology—in the already classic work of Jonathan Sterne, Emily Thompson, Karin Bijsterveld, and Trevor Pinch, among others—is interrogated in Steingo and Sykes, "Introduction: Remapping Sound Studies," in Gavin Steingo and Jim Sykes, eds., *Remapping Sound Studies* (Durham, NC: Duke University Press, 2019), 5–17. See also Jonathan Sterne, *The Audible Past: Cultural Origins of Sound Reproduction* (Durham, NC: Duke University Press,

2003); Emily Thompson, *The Soundscape of Modernity: Architectural Acoustics and the Culture of Listening in America, 1900–1933* (Cambridge, MA: MIT Press, 2002); and Karin Bijsterveld, and Trevor Pinch, eds., *The Oxford Handbook of Sound Studies* (Oxford, UK: Oxford University Press, 2012).

6. For an indicative list of materials, see Emile Hemming, *Plastics and Molded Electrical Insulation* (Chicago: Chemical Catalog Company, 1923), 153–54. I am grateful to Duncan Miller, founding owner of Vulcan Records, Sheffield, for telling me about his twenty-first-century experiments in making shellac discs.

7. See Thomas Walker Page et al., *Barytes, Barium Chemical, and Lithopone Industries* (Washington: Government Printing Office, 1920), 9–11; and Oscar Berninghaus, *The Story of Barytes: Where and How It Was Found and Its Importance to the World's Industries* (St. Louis, MO: DeLore, 1920), 7.

8. See Alvah Horton Sabin, *The Industrial and Artistic Technology of Paint and Varnish, Second Edition* (New York: Wiley and Sons, 1917), 201–2; and Nicholas Eastaugh et al., *Pigment Compendium: A Dictionary of Optical Microscopy of Historical Pigments* (Oxford, UK: Elsevier, 2008), 216.

9. See William Gervase Clarence-Smith, *The Economics of the Indian Ocean Slave Trade in the Nineteenth Century* (London: Routledge, 2013), 4; and Hideaki Suzuki, *Slave Trade Profiteers in the Indian Ocean: Suppression and Resistance in the Nineteenth Century* (New York: Palgrave, 2017), 148.

10. For a map of lac-producing regions, see A. J. Gibson, "The Story of Lac," *Journal of the Royal Society of Arts* 90, no. 4611 (April 1942): 324.

11. See Christopher Alan Bayly, *The Birth of the Modern World: Global Connections and Comparison, 1780–1914* (Malden, MA: Blackwell, 2004), 172–77.

12. An earlier argument for the historical investigation of shellac (ahead of the rise of "green" media studies) was put forth by Vibodh Parthasarathi, "Not Just Mad Englishmen and a Dog: The Colonial Tuning of Music on Record, 1900–1908," working paper no. 2/2008, Centre for Culture, Media and Governance, Jamia Millia Islamia, New Delhi (2007), 29–30.

13. Jacob Smith, *Eco-Sonic Media* (Berkeley: University of California Press, 2015), ch. 1.

14. Kyle Devine, "Decomposed: The Political Ecology of Music," *Popular Music* 34, no. 3 (2015). See also Devine, *Decomposed*, ch. 1.

15. Elodie A. Roy, "Another Side of Shellac: Cultural and Natural Cycles of the Gramophone Discs," in Kyle Devine and Alexandrine Boudreault-Fournier, eds., *Audible Infrastructures: Music, Sound, Media* (Oxford, UK: Oxford University Press, 2021), 209–28. On vibrant matter, see Jane Bennett, *Vibrant Matter: A Political Ecology of Things* (Durham, NC: Duke University Press, 2010), ch. 1. See also Roy, *Unsettled Matter: Shellac in Visual and Sonic Culture* (Amsterdam: Amsterdam University Press, 2023).

16. Roy, "Another Side of Shellac," 221. Emphasis in original.

17. Anna Lowenhaupt Tsing, *Friction: An Ethnography of Global Connection* (Princeton, NJ: Princeton University Press, 2005), 1–18. Devine also cites Tsing

on friction in this context, but to underscore the audibility of colonial violence in the hiss of gramophone records. Devine, *Decomposed*, 76.

18. The figure of 30–40 percent comes from Dorothy Norris, *Lac and the Indian Lac Research Institute* (Calcutta: Criterion, 1934), 10.

19. Arjun Appadurai, "Introduction: Commodities and the Politics of Value," in Arjun Appadurai, ed., *The Social Life of Things: Commodities in Cultural Perspective* (Cambridge, UK: Cambridge University Press, 1986), 3–63.

20. See, for example, Eliot Bates, "The Social Life of Musical Instruments," *Ethnomusicology* 56, no. 3 (2012): 372.

21. Appadurai, "Introduction: Commodities and the Politics of Value," 41.

22. See Marcel Mauss, "Les techniques du corps," *Journal de psychologie normale et pathologique* (1935).

23. On listening as a technique of body, see Sterne, *Audible Past*, 1–30, chs. 2–3.

24. Christopher Small, *Musicking: The Meanings of Performing and Listening* (Middletown, CT: Wesleyan University Press, 1998), 1–18.

25. Tsing, *Friction*, 51–54.

26. Tsing, *Friction*, 51–54.

27. See, for example, Sujit Sivasundaram, "Sciences and the Global: On Methods, Questions and Theory," *Isis* 101, no. 1 (2010): 146–58.

28. Kapil Raj, "Beyond Postcolonialism . . . and Postpositivism: Circulation and the Global History of Science," *Isis* 104, no. 2 (2013): 345.

29. Gramophone markets developed rapidly in India at the beginning of the twentieth century. In India as in many other places, however, gramophone discs were luxury articles marketed toward wealthy audiences. Even when the technology became more affordable during the 1920s, and later with the rise of radio, gramophones and discs were still considered too great an expense by the vast majority. See Kinnear, *Gramophone Company's First Indian Recordings*, 35–59; and Parthasarathi, "Not Just Mad Englishmen."

30. For an early identification of this etymology, see A. D. Imms and N. C. Chatterjee, *Indian Forest Memoirs: On the Structure and Biology of Tachardia lacca, Kerr., with Observations on Certain Insects Predaceous or Parasitic upon It* (Calcutta: Superintendent Government Printing, India, 1915), 1.

31. See Y. D. Mishra and P. Kumar, "Lac Culture," in Omkar, ed., *Industrial Entomology* (Singapore: Springer, 2017), 109–11.

32. See John L. Brockington, *The Sanskrit Epics* (Leiden, Netherlands: Brill, 1998), 28–29.

33. Abū al-Faẕl ibn Mubārak, *Ā'īn-i Akbarī*, second edition (Lahore, Pakistan: Sang-e-Meel Publications, 2004), 196. I am grateful to Katherine Butler-Schofield for advice on the quoted translation from Persian. Lac varnishers were among the lowest-paid workers on the building site, together with water carriers, well diggers, and bamboo cutters.

34. Daniel Defoe, *A New Voyage around the World by a Course Never Sailed Before; Being a Voyage Undertaken by Some Merchants, Who Afterwards Proposed the*

Setting Up an East-India Company in Flanders (London: Bettesworth and Mears, 1725), 177.

35. On this larger history, see Sudipta Sen, *Empire of Free Trade: The East India Company and the Making of the Colonial Marketplace* (Philadelphia: University of Pennsylvania Press, 1998), 1–19.

36. Nancy Lee Peluso, “What’s Nature Got To Do With It? A Situated Historical Perspective on Socio-Natural Commodities,” *Development and Change* 43, no. 1 (2012): 84.

37. See Marianne Webb, Lacquer: *Technology and Conservation; A Comprehensive Guide to Technology and Conservation of Asian and European Lacquer* (Oxford, UK: Butterworth Heinemann, 2000), 103.

38. Chemical analyses occasionally detect traces of shellac on historical instruments, such as a seventeenth-century harpischord by Girolamo Zenti. See Franca Falletti, Renato Meucci, and Gabriele Rossi Rognoni, *Marvels of Sound and Beauty: Italian Baroque Musical Instruments* (Milan: Giunti, 2007), 125.

39. On “vernice indiana,” see Merrifield, *Originial Treatises*, 2:695–97. In the seventeenth century, European travelers to India observed the material in use as varnish applied to a range of wooden objects and as a significant export to China and Japan. See *The Voyages and Travells of the Ambassadors sent by Frederick Duke of Holstein [. . .] containing a Compleat History of Muscovy, Tartary, Persia. [. . .] Whereto are added the Travels of John Albert de Mandelslo, (a Gentleman Belonging to the Embassy) from Persia into the East Indies*, second edition (London: John Starkey and Thomas Bassett, 1669), 122; and Jean-Baptiste Tavernier, *Travels in India*, vol. 2 (Cambridge: Cambridge University Press, 2012), 20–23.

40. Jean-Baptiste Tavernier noted connections between lac-turnery and toymaking in the seventeenth century. Tavernier, *Travels in India*, 2:22. See also Jeffrey Y. Campbell, *Women’s Role in Dynamic Forest-Based Small-Scale Enterprise: Case Studies on Uppage and Lacquerware from India* (Rome: Food and Agricultural Organization of the United Nations, 1991).

41. See, for example, “New York Letter,” *Paint, Oil and Drug Review*, 2 September 1891, pp. 14–15.

42. See Hemming, *Molded Electrical Insulation*, 16; and Hemming, *Plastics*, 179. There were close links between telephone and gramophone research. Emile Berliner, the gramophone’s inventor, drew on his experience as a laboratory chief at the Bell Telephone Company when he decided to switch from vulcanized rubber to shellac as a binding agent for disc molds in 1895; Berliner, “Development of the Talking Machine,” 192. Berliner’s well-rehearsed version of events, according to which telephones gave birth to discs, aligns with other North American narratives of technology in which the inventor plays the role of midwife. See Sterne, *Audible Past*, 180–81.

43. See Percy H. Walker and Lawrence L. Steele, *Shellac* (Washington: US Deptartment of Commerce, Bureau of Standards, 1922), 280.

44. See Robert Douglas Friedel, *Pioneer Plastic: The Making and Selling of Celluloid* (Madison: University of Wisconsin Press, 1983), ch. 1.

45. See Jeffrey Meikle, *American Plastic: A Cultural History* (New York: Rutgers University Press, 1995), ch. 1.

46. Wiebe E. Bijker, "Social Construction of Bakelite," in Wiebe E. Bijker, Thomas P. Hughes, and Trevor Pinch, eds., *The Social Construction of Technological Systems: New Directions in the Sociology and History of Science* (Cambridge, MA: MIT Press, 2012 [1987]), 155–82.

47. Elizabeth Brownell Crandall, *Shellac: A Story of Yesterday, Today, and Tomorrow* (Chicago: Day, 1924), 42. See also William E. Titsworth, The *Story of Shellac* (New York: William Zinsser & Co., 1928).

48. Crandall, *Shellac*, 41.

49. Edward Hicks, *Shellac: Its Uses and Applications* (New York: Chemical Publishing, 1961), 113.

50. Hicks, *Shellac*, 114.

51. The comparison between shellac and Bakelite consists in the novel chemical means of control over the "condensation reaction" between aldehydes and phenolics. See Bijker, "Social Construction of Bakelite," 162.

52. Western scientists have long been on the "knowledge periphery" when it comes to insects. See Edward Melillo, "Global Entomologies: Insects, Empires, and the 'Synthetic Age' in World History," *Past & Present* 223 (2014): 233–70.

53. George Watt, ed., *Economic Products of India Exhibited at the Calcutta International Exhibition, 1883–84* (Calcutta: Superintendent of Government Printing, 1883), vol. 1, pt. 1.

54. The entry "*Coccus lacca*" is in volume 2 (1889) and the entry for lac in volume 4 (1890); see also R. S. Chakravarthy, "Watt's Dictionary: A Landmark in the Study of the Economic Plants of India," *Economic Botany* 29, no. 1 (1975): 31–38.

55. See Londa Schiebinger and Claudia Swan, introduction to *Colonial Botany: Science, Commerce, and Politics in the Early Modern World* (Philadelphia: University of Pennsylvania Press, 2005); and Lucile H. Brockway, *Science and Colonial Expansion: The Role of the British Royal Botanic Gardens* (New Haven, CT: Yale University Press, 2002), 83–86.

56. In addition to the largely foreign use of shellac as a varnish, Watt noted its extensive local use in making "bracelets (*chúris*), rings, beads, and other trinkets worn by women of the poorer classes," as well as an interregional lacturnery business: Watt, *Dictionary*, 4:575.

57. Watt, *Dictionary*, 4:572.

58. Watt, *Commercial Products of India*, 1053–65.

59. Watt, *Commercial Products of India*, 1059.

60. See Anantanarayanan Raman, "Discovery of *Kerria lacca* (Insecta: Hemiptera: Coccoidea), the Lac Insect, in India in the Late 18th Century," *Current Science* 106, no. 6 (2014): 886–90.

61. My comments are based on conversations that took place in 2018 with Dr. K. K. Sharma, Dr. Niranjan Prasad, and Dr. A. Mohanasundaram, scientists at the Indian Institute of Natural Resins and Gums, in Ranchi, Jharkhand, for-

merly the Lac Research Institute. For a historical view on cultivation methods, see the articles by biochemist Motnahalli Sreenivasaya discussed below.

62. Watt, *Dictionary*, 2:411.

63. Watt, *Commercial Products of India*, 1060.

64. Under the subheading "Uses of Lac," in a subsection devoted to Europe and America, Watt noted, "Large quantities are employed as a stiffening material in hat-making, as a cement, as an ingredient in lithographic ink; and as modern demands it may be mentioned that lac is largely employed in the manufacture of gramophone records, as an insulating material in electric appliances, etc. Through the last-mentioned utilisation a fresh impetus has been given to the traffic, which perhaps largely accounts for the recent expansion of the exports from India." Watt, *Commercial Products of India*, 1064.

65. C. M. Harlow and H. A. F. Lindsay, *The Indian Forest Records: Report on Lac and Shellac* (Allahabad, India: Pioneer Press, 1921), 58–63; see also Crandall, *Shellac*, 30–34.

66. Harlow and Lindsay, *Indian Forest Records*, 61.

67. Harlow and Lindsay, *Indian Forest Records*, 62.

68. Harlow and Lindsay, *Indian Forest Records*, 17. Company stores were also used on occasion.

69. Harlow and Lindsay, *Indian Forest Records*, 2–3.

70. Harlow and Lindsay, *Indian Forest Records*, 5.

71. Kamal Nayan Kabra, *Dependence and Dominance: Political Economy of a Tribal Commodity* (New Delhi: Indian Institute of Public Administration, 1983), 26–27.

72. Kabra, *Dependence and Dominance*, v–vi; Bhalchandra Pundlik Adarkar, *Report on Labour Conditions in the Shellac Industry* (Simla: Government of India, 1945), 36.

73. See Christopher A. Bayly, "The Origins of Swadeshi (Home Industry): Cloth and Indian Society, 1700–1930," in Appadurai, ed., *Social Life of Things*, 285–322; and Priyamvada Gopal, *Insurgent Empire: Anticolonial Resistance and British Dissent* (London: Verso, 2019), ch. 5.

74. Harlow and Lindsay, *Indian Forest Records*, 96–97. This report also stressed the need to circumvent the countless middlemen who traded in lac and shellac, presenting a larger picture in which cultivators were cheated by a high number of mercenary intermediaries.

75. Harlow and Lindsay, *Indian Forest Records*, 81.

76. Kabra makes the same general point about lac's recent history: Kabra, *Dependence and Dominance*, 5.

77. Norris, *Lac*, 13–14.

78. Norris, *Lac*, i.

79. Harlow and Lindsay recommended Jabalpur rather than Ranchi as their preferred site. Harlow and Lindsay, *Indian Forest Records*, 97. For a map of lac-producing regions, see Gibson, "Story of Lac," 324.

80. Norris, *Lac*, 6.

81. See Norris, *Lac*, 6.

82. Norris, *Lac*, 10.

83. "Even in the gramophone trade efforts have been made to produce lac free records and for this purpose cellulose derivatives, resorcinol resins and phenol formaldehyde resin have been used." Norris, *Lac*, 12. Yet Norris could still write in 1934, "In this industry however the shellac record still stands supreme" (ibid.).

84. See Malathi Ramanathan and B. V. Subbarayappa. "Indian Institute of Science: Its Origins and Growth, 1909–1947," in Uma Das Gupta, ed., *Science and Modern India: An Institutional History, ca. 1784–1947*, vol. 11, pt. 4 (Delhi: Pearson Longman, 2011), 871–926.

85. Motnahalli Sreenivasaya, "Industrial Outlook: Crisis in the Lac Industry," *Current Science* 1, no. 4 (1932). Sreenivasaya noted an additional cause of the industry's likely demise: that Indian manufacturers failed to cater "sympathetically, intelligently and honestly" to foreigners—especially North Americans—through the absence of legal standardization of the product and the widespread use of adulterants, making it inevitable that the gramophone industry would seek to replace shellac with either cellulose-based plastics or "quick curing resins" (111, 112). Norris made similar predictions; Norris, *Lac*, 12.

86. "Before the advent of the gramophone, the demand for lac was very limited, being utilized in a few of the finishing industries." Sreenivasaya, "Industrial Outlook," 112.

87. Sreenivasaya, "Industrial Outlook," 111.

88. Sreenivasaya, "Industrial Outlook," 111.

89. See Lal C. Verman, "The London Shellac Research Bureau," *Current Science* 5, no. 1 (1936): 41.

90. Sreenivasaya suggested that "electrical appliances, switches, plugs, etc., with dials, stands and other artware could be manufactured": Sreenivasaya, "Industrial Outlook," 113. On the broader issue of national self-reliance through industry, see Bayly, "Origins of Swadeshi."

91. Motnahalli Sreenivasaya, "Antiquity of Lac and Superstitions Connected with It," *Current Science* 4, no. 6 (1935): 390.

92. Sreenivasaya, "Antiquity of Lac," 390.

93. Sreenivasaya, "Antiquity of Lac," 391.

94. On science's translation of nonscientific knowledge, see Isabelle Stengers, *Cosmopolitics* (Minneapolis: University of Minnesota Press, 2011), vol. 2, ch. 19.

95. See Melillo, "Global Entomologies."

96. Sreenivasaya, "Antiquity of Lac," 391.

97. Laurence Oliver, "Shellac," *Nash's Pall Mall Magazine*, December 1930, pp. 32–35, 107–12. Illustrations to the story were by D. Lloyd Wynne, a regular contributor to the women's illustrated press.

98. As previously mentioned, the Lac Research Institute was also located in

a village outside Ranchi. Yet this institute is never mentioned in the story: the unspecified town is instead presented as a rural idyll, unencumbered by connections with scientific bureaucracy.

99. The illustrations shown in figure 1.3 are found on pages 107–8.

100. Oliver, "Shellac," 110.

101. On the "misogynous recognition of distant labor," see Bruce Robbins, *The Beneficiary* (Durham, NC: Duke University Press, 2017), 56–57.

102. Ogilvie Mitchell, *The Talking Machine Industry* (London: Pitman, 1922), 70.

103. Berliner, the inventor of the gramophone, experimented with vulcanite before trying shellac. Berliner, "Development of the Talking Machine"; see also Jerrold Northrop Moore, *A Matter of Records* (New York: Taplinger, 1977), 18.

104. Indicator [pseud.], "The Ingenuous Amateur and the Sine Qua Non Opposite," *The Gramophone*, August 1924, p. 94.

105. Compton Mackenzie, "Good Singing," *The Gramophone*, April 1923, p. 9.

106. In addition to "Shellac," the story discussed above, the material featured in a number of journalistic and popular science accounts; see, for example, George R. Harrison, "From Shellac to Symphony: New Perfections in Storing and Re-Creating Sound," *Technology Review* 41, no. 1 (1938): 17–20.

107. Theodor Adorno, *Current of Music* (Malden, MA: Polity, 2009), 114. Here Adorno was writing in English, but the concept appears throughout his writings in German as the *Hörstreife* (acoustic stripe); see Richard Leppert's discussion of this word in Theodor Adorno, *Essays on Music,* ed. Richard Leppert (Berkeley: University of California Press, 2002), 218–19.

108. Smith, *Eco-Sonic Media*, 38.

109. Devine, *Decomposed*, 76, which acknowledges Tsing, *Friction.*

110. Adorno evoked the industrial secret of the gramophone record's material contents in the opening of a well-known article of 1934: "A black pane of composite mass which these days no longer has its honest name any more than automobile fuel is called benzine." Adorno, "The Form of the Phonograph Record," *October* 55 (1990): 56.

111. Michael B. Silvers, *Voices of Drought: The Politics of Music and Environment in Northeastern Brazil* (Chicago: University of Illinois Press, 2018), ch. 1.

112. See Jennifer Gabrys, Gay Hawkins, and Mike Michael, "Introduction: From Materiality to Plasticity," in Gabrys, Hawkins, and Michael, eds., *Accumulation: The Material Politics of Plastic* (London: Routledge, 2013), 1–14. See also Heather Davis, "Toxic Progeny: The Plastisphere and Other Queer Futures." *philoSOPHIA* 5, no. 1 (2015): 231–50.

113. Much more research could be undertaken to track a history of shellac as a musical plastic from Adivasi and other rural perspectives. The present chapter highlights the neglect and importance of these perspectives as it outlines the broad picture, while only scratching at the surface. The larger issue of rural and Adivasi relations with colonists in the forests of northern and central India has been much studied, however, making it plausible to imagine lac/shellac belonging to a long and ongoing history of "peasant insur-

gency" and resistance to imperial power. See Ranajit Guha, *Elementary Aspects of Peasant Insurgency in Colonial India* (Durham, NC: Duke University Press, 1999), 1–17; Ramachandra Guha, *The Unquiet Woods: Ecological Change and Peasant Resistance in the Himalaya* (Berkeley: University of California Press, 2000); Sarah Jewitt, *Environment, Knowledge and Gender: Local Development in India's Jharkhand* (Aldershot, UK: Ashgate, 2002); Alpa Shah, *In the Shadows of the State: Indigenous Politics, Environmentalism and Insurgency in Jharkhand, India* (Durham, NC: Duke University Press, 2010); and Alpa Shah, *Nightmarch: A Journey into the Naxal Heartlands* (Noida, India: HarperCollins, 2018), ch. 2.

114. In a celebrated account that prefigured the interdisciplinary field of sound studies, Jonathan Sterne argued that the "cultural origins of sound reproduction" lay in a twofold process: in techniques of the body that zoned in on the ear as the site for, and object of, sound; and in creating a larger network of machines, discs, and listeners that could elaborate technical possibilities into full-fledged media forms such as the telephone, the phonograph, and radio. Sterne's history began and ended in North America, the undeclared site of sound reproduction's "cultural origins," and tracked its development there as a social construction: as the heavily mythologized product of white-collar invention, naturalized through "social faith" in sprawling media infrastructures. Sterne, *Audible Past*, 1–30. More recently, Steingo and Sykes have urged sound scholars to "turn to the global south" and to broaden their notions of technology to include the "constitutive technicity" of all sounds: Steingo and Sykes, "Introduction: Remapping Sound Studies." But as this chapter suggests, this turn might also involve decentering "Western" technology. This is true not only for shellac but, as others have shown, for carnauba wax and mica, and perhaps many other materials. On wax see Silvers, *Voices of Drought*, ch. 1; and on mica see Alejandra Bronfman, *Isles of Noise: Sonic Media in the Caribbean* (Chapel Hill: University of North Carolina Press, 2016), 40–42.

CHAPTER 2

1. "Sale of Household Furniture," *Straits Times*, (11 June 1901), 2; the advert also appeared in *The Singapore Free Press and Mercantile Advertiser* (12 June 1901), 2. A cloth-of-gold is a type of crocus (angustifolius); the 'bridal rose' is perhaps another tree species designation in historical use.

2. *The Singapore and Straits Directory* (Singapore: Singapore and Straits Printing Office, 1896), 460.

3. Brenda S. A. Yeoh, *Contesting Space in Colonial Singapore: Power Relations and the Built Environment* (Singapore: Singapore University Press, 2003), 36.

4. Barbara Watson Andaya and Leonard Y Andaya, *A History of Malaysia*, Third Edition (London: Palgrave, 2017), 208–213.

5. John G. Butcher, *The British in Malaya: The Social History of a European Community in South-East Asia* (Oxford: Oxford University Press, 1979), 1–10.

6. *The Directory and Chronicle for China, Japan, Corea, Indo-China, Straits*

Settlement, Malay States, Siam, Netherlands, India, Borneo, The Philippines, &c. (Hong Kong: Hong Kong Daily Press, 1889), 694.

7. For example, in 1907, a piano tuner was fired from Robinson & Co. for mending a gramophone at his home, and went on to sue his employer. "Claim for Wages," *Eastern Daily Mail and Straits Morning Advertiser* (21 September 1907), 3.

8. Allan Sutton, "The American Zonophone Discography II: The Roots and Early History of American Zonophone Records, 1898–1905," Discography of American Historical Recordings, University of California, Santa Barbara Library <adp.library.ucsb.edu/index.php/resources/detail/403> (accessed 18 July 2021).

9. Geoffrey Jones, "The Gramophone Company: An Anglo-American Multinational," *The Business History Review* 59 No. 1 (1985), 76–100; Geoffrey Jones, *Multinationals and Global Capitalism: From the Nineteenth to the Twenty-First Century* (Oxford: Oxford University Press, 2005), 79–80.

10. The relationship between recorded sound and musical globalization was a pressing issue for music scholars during the 1990s, but has since been largely avoided (or more indirectly approached); see, for example, Steven Feld, "pygmy POP: A Genealogy of Schizophonic Mimesis," *Yearbook for Traditional Music* 28 (1996), 1–35; and Pekka Gronow and Ilpo Saunio, *An International History of the Recording Industry*, translated by Christopher Moseley (London: Cassell, 1999), 8–36. On the distributed emergence of technologies, musical and otherwise, see Gary Tomlinson, *A Million Years of Music: The Emergence of Human Modernity* (Cambridge, MA: Zone Books, 2015), 293–98.

11. Michael Denning, *Noise Uprising: The Audiopolitics of a World Musical Revolution* (London: Verso, 2015), 40–46.

12. See, for example, Andrew F. Jones, *Yellow Music: Media Culture and Colonial Modernity in the Chinese Jazz Age* (Durham, NC: Duke University Press, 2001), 53–72.

13. Tan Sooi Beng, "The 78 RPM Record Industry in Malaya Prior to World War II," *Asian Music* 28 No. 1 (1996–1997), 1–41; Tan Sooi Beng, "Negotiating 'His Master's Voice': Gramophone Music and Cosmopolitan Modernity in British Malaya in the 1930s and Early 1940s," *Bijdragen tot de Taal-, Land- en Volkenkunde: Journal of the Huamnities and Social Sciences of Southeast Asia* 169 (2013), 457–494.

14. As Tan Sooi Beng points out, the impact of sound-on-record was initially small: "The rich in urban areas, who could afford to buy a gramophone player and discs, included British officers, plantation and tin mine owners, Malay aristocrats, and well-to-do local born Chinese and Indian Muslims." Ibid., 466.

15. Parthasarthi, "Not Just Mad Englishmen and a Dog," 1–30; Vibodh Parthasarathi, "The Public Sphere of Marketed Sound: The Business of Early Recorded Music in India," in Tejaswini Niranjana, ed., *Music, Modernity and Publicness in India* (New Delhi: Oxford University Press, 2020).

16. For a history of the gramophone that disrupts assumptions of ownership

of machines, and which focuses on dancing rather than more passive forms of listening, see Ulrik Volgsten, "A Technology and Its Vicissitudes: Playing the Gramophone in Sweden, 1903–1945," *Popular Music* 38, no. 2 (2019): 219–36.

17. See Hugo Strötbaum, "William Barry Owen," http://www.recordingpioneers.com/RP_OWEN1.html (accessed 27 July 2021).

18. Peter Martland, *Recording History: The British Record Industry, 1888–1931* (Plymouth, UK: Scarecrow Press, 2013), 46–58.

19. https://victorrecords.com/edmund-trevor-lloyd-williams (accessed 29 March 2022).

20. Martland, *Recording History*, 48.

21. Frank Hoffman, *Encyclopedia of Recorded Sound* (Oxford, UK: Taylor and Francis, 2004), 55.

22. Jones, "The Gramophone Company," 85.

23. Martland, *Recording History*, 124–26.

24. Martland, *Recording History*, 137–38.

25. Vikram Sampath, *"My Name Is Gauhar Jaan!" The Life and Times of a Musician* (New Delhi: Rupa, 2010), 7–14.

26. In 1911, the recording experts employed by the Gramophone Company were Sinkler Darby, Frederick Gaisberg, Franz Georg Hampe, Arthur Clarke, Charles Anton Scheuplin, William Charles Hancox, and Hugh De Lacy O'Connor Murtagh, as well as Max Hampe and George Dillnutt. See letter from Sinkler Darby to the managing directors of the Gramophone Company, Ltd., Hayes (18 July 1911); contained in "George Walter Dillnutt" (brown file) at the Electrical Musical Industries Archive, Hayes, London.

27. Parthasarathi, "Not Just a Mad Englishman and a Dog," 4.

28. Parthasarathi, "Not Just a Mad Englishman and a Dog," 4.

29. For example, in 1908, Charles Anton Scheuplin was offered a five-year contract with a salary of £425, with annual expenses worth £2,500; See the letter to Mr. Broad, Great Winchester Street (29 January 1908), contained in "George Walter Dillnutt" (brown file) at the Electrical Musical Industries Archive, Hayes, London.

30. "Robinson & Co. of Raffles Place, Singapore, are our sole agents for the Straits Settlement and Federated Malay States for Gramophones and Typewriters as manufactured by our Company. They undertake not to deal in any other disc talking machine goods so long as they retain our agency. The arrangement was made with them to 30th of June 1903 subject to six months notice hereafter on either side. Goods are supplied at a discount of 33 1/3 % off regular Calcutta retail prices, subject to an undertaking to meet them regarding any reduction in prices that may be made by our London Company." See letter from Addis[?] in Calcutta to the Gramophone & Typewriter Company, London (14 July 1904), contained in "Chinese Box to 1915" at the Electrical Musical Industries Archive, Hayes, London. Similar arrangements with Mr. Kim Hoa Hen (in Siam) and Mr. Misquith & Co. of Rangoon are also discussed in this letter.

31. Before being sent out from the disc-pressing factories in Riga and

Hanover, the discs might be sent back to London, where board members could judge samples of their recording experts' latest work in the field—resulting in further delays. See the previously cited letter to Mr. Broad (29 January 1908).

32. The report goes on to emphasize the point: "What is absolutely necessary and what we must certainly have is a plating plant. The risks [of] the shipment of these masters is too great, and in the past we have lost hundreds of pounds on the masters arriving at Hanover or England with their surfaces mildewed and injured in other ways." See anonymous, "Report RE: Singapore and Java Records" (1909) contained in "Chinese Box to 1915" at the Electrical Musical Industries Archive, Hayes, London. See also Philip B. Yampolsky, "Music and Media in the Dutch East Indies: Gramophone Records and Radio in the Late Colonial Era, 1903–1942" (PhD dissertation, University of Washington, 2013), 92–93n122.

33. Emphasis added. "Report RE: Singapore and Java Records" (1909), previously cited.

34. Tan Sooi Beng, "The 78 RPM Record Industry in Malaya Prior to World War II," 1–2.

35. Robin Cherry, *Catalog: The Illustrated History of the Mail Order Shopping* (Princeton, NJ: Princeton Architectural Press, 2008), 11–31. From 1899, the Gramophone Company published annual catalogs of its entire disc collection. However, the London branch, in collaboration with the piano department at Harrods (the city's famous luxury department store), switched tack after 1905, printing monthly brochures focusing entirely on new releases.

36. *The Singapore and Straits Directory* (Singapore: Kelly & Walsh, 1909), inside front cover.

37. As a result, the recordings of individual singers, such as Miss Bhavani of Thiruvidaimaradur, were scattered throughout three different sections of the catalog: her songs appeared in the Tamil (female), Telegu (female) and Sanskrit (female) sections.

38. Yeoh, *Contesting Space in Colonial Singapore*, 28–35.

39. Tan Sooi Beng, "The 78 RPM Record Industry in Malaya Prior to World War II," 6.

40. By comparison, in 1909 UK catalogs of the Gramophone Company also began with selections for brass band; but for British audiences they listed fewer band recordings, almost all of them by the Coldstream Guards. See, for example, *New Gramophone Records: October 1909* (London: Harrods, 1909), 1–2.

41. Anonymous [Albert Whelan], "Football Match No. 1: Newcastle United v Manchester City," recorded 23 November 1905 (Zonophone, X-49265); Arthur Gilbert, Stanley Kirkby, Peter Dawson (as Johnnie Wakefield, Walter Miller, Percy Clifton), "The Lancashire Lad's Trip Round London," recorded 1908 (Zonophone, X-41029). See Allen Kelly, *Matrix Suffix–e: Ten Inch Wax Process Recordings made by W. C. Gaisberg et al., 1903–1921* (October 1994, published online), 84; kellydatabase.org/pdf/file C–Suf-e.pdf (accessed 5 August 2021; link no longer active).

42. Gilbert Girard and Peter Dawson, "Old Dog Sport, Descriptive," recorded

February 1908 (Zonophone X-41030); Peter Dawson, "The Auction Sale of a Piano" (Zonophone X-41028). Kelly, *Matrix Suffix–e*, 170.

43. Timothy D. Taylor, Mark Katz, and Tony Grajeda, eds., *Music, Sound and Technology in America: A Documentary History of Early Phonograph, Cinema, and Radio* (Durham, NC: Duke University Press, 2012), 48–51.

44. A total of 113 articles, letters, and illustrations mention a "gramophone" in the *Straits Times* and *Singapore Free Press and Mercantile Advertiser* during the first decade of the twentieth century (1900–1909); the comparable figure mentioning a "phonograph" is 101. Source: eresources.nlb.gov.sg/newspapers/ (accessed 10 August 2021).

45. "Malacca Notes," *Straits Times*, 13 April 1901, p. 8.

46. Bradley G. Shope, *American Popular Music in Britain's Raj* (Rochester, NY: University of Rochester Press, 2016), 25–52.

47. *Singapore and Straits Directory*, 515.

48. Edward Marsh Merewether, listed as a justice of the peace in Singapore, Malacca, and Penang as an inspector of prisons, was the tenth most important civil servant in the Straits Settlement in 1896; *Singapore and Straits Directory*, 33, 73, 481. Mrs. Merewether was a committee member of the Ladies' Lawn Tennis Club; ibid. 84.

49. "Malacca Notes," 8.

50. See Delia Casadei, *Risible: Laughter without Reason and the Reproduction of Sound* (Berkeley: University of California Press, 2024), ch. 3.

51. "Smoker at Pulo Brani," *Straits Times*, 15 August 1903, p. 5.

52. "Singapore Chinese Weekly Entertainment Club," *Straits Times*, 9 November 1908, p. 7.

53. "Singapore Chinese Weekly Entertainment Club," *Straits Times*, 9 November 1908, p. 7.

54. See, for example, "The Bioscope," *Straits Times*, 15 October 1902, p. 5; Jan Uhde and Yvonne Ng Uhde, *Latent Images: Film in Singapore,* second edition (Singapore: National University of Singapore Press, 2009), 188.

55. Uhde and Uhde, *Latent Images*, 16.

56. Patricia Matusky and Tan Sooi Beng, *The Music of Malaysia: The Classical, Folk and Syncretic Traditions*, second edition (Oxford, UK: Taylor and Francis, 2017), 81–89; Tong Soon Lee, *Chinese Street Opera in Singapore* (Chicago: University of Illinois Press, 2009), 15–41.

57. Eugene Dairianathan and Ming Yen Phan, *A Narrative History of Music in Singapore* (Singapore: National Arts Council, 2002), 260–64. See also Trevor Herbert and Helen Barlow, *Music & the British Military in the Long Nineteenth Century* (Oxford, UK: Oxford University Press, 2013), 240–68.

58. See, for example, "Moonlight Music," *Singapore Free Press and Mercantile Advertiser*, 17 May 1900, p. 11.

59. Of the roughly 220,000 people who lived in Singapore in 1900, fewer than 1 percent were British or of other European ethnicities. Yeoh, *Contesting Space in Colonial Singapore*, 318.

60. In the following decades, the monopoly of Western companies would be increasingly challenged, and dissolved from within. In the case of HMV in Malaya, the "dog label" (chap anjing) gave way to the "cat label" (chap kucing) and "lion label" (chap singa). On this topic, see Tan Sooi Beng, "Negotiating 'His Master's Voice,'" 457–94. See also Tan Sooi Beng, "Cosmopolitan Identities: Evolving Musical Cultures of the Straits-Born Chinese of Pre–World War II Malaya," *Ethnomusicology Forum* 26, no. 1 (2016): 35–57.

61. Radano and Olaniyan, eds., *Audible Empire*.

62. See, for example, Jairo Moreno, "Imperial Aurality: Jazz, the Archive, and U.S. Empire," in Radano and Olaniyan, eds., *Audible Empire*, 135–60.

63. Gavin Steingo, "Musical Economies of the Elusive Metropolis," in Radano and Olaniyan, eds., *Audible Empire*, 246. See also Gavin Steingo, *Kwaito's Promise: Music and the Aesthetics of Freedom in South Africa* (Chicago: University of Chicago Press, 2016).

64. Theater impresarios and local musical intermediaries were also crucial, but have not been much researched. See, for example, the oral history of Zubir bin Said, composer of Singapore's national anthem, who also worked as a recording manager for HMV during the 1930s. Zubir bin Said, "Oral History Interview," transcript of an oral history conducted 1984 by Liana Tan, Special Project, Oral History Department, National Archive of Singapore, Singapore (transcribed in 1987).

65. "Dear Sirs . . . you have deferred [Mr. Dillnutt's visit to Singapore] much too long and though we hope that he will be very successful with the new records we cannot see the same prospect of business resulting which there certainly would have been had his visit been made earlier." Letter from Robinson & Co. (Calcutta) to the Gramophone Company London (6 November 1908), contained in "George Walter Dillnutt" (brown file) at the Electrical Musical Industries Archive, Hayes, London.

66. To recall the phrasing of the corporate memo discussed above, Asians and Africans were "extremely musical and pleasure-loving" in "their own native way." Such was the company's view of the Global South: a view deeply inflected by nineteenth-century orientalist depictions of a decadent East. But now Asians and Africans become targets for the gramophone industry, as listeners and as potential consumers.

67. Jones, *Multinationals and Global Capitalism*, 5.

68. Jones, "The Gramophone Company," 77.

69. Goh Chor Boon, *Technology and Entrepot Colonialism in Singapore, 1819–1940* (Singapore: Institute of Southeast Asian Studies, 2013), 245.

70. In response to (and to prolong and amplify) protests against the World Trade Organization's 1999 meeting in Seattle, Philippe Pignarre and Isabelle Stengers discuss a formidable challenge presented to activists: simply to get a "hold" (*prise*) on contemporary capitalism in its multinational form. See Philippe Pignarre and Isabelle Stengers, *Capitalist Sorcery: Breaking the Spell*, trans. Andrew Goffey (New York: Palgrave Macmillan, 2011).

INTERLUDE

1. Abu Bakar Ali, oral history interview conducted by Stella Ng at the Oral History Centre, Singapore, 22–29 May 1996. *National Archives of Singapore*, accession number 001755, reel 1 (16 mins., 55 secs.), 12. Web 15 January 2020.

2. Patricia Oh Choo Neo, oral history interview conducted by Bonny Tan at the Oral History Center, 9 May 1995. *National Archives of Singapore,* accession no. 001631, reel 6 of 17 (2 mins., 20 secs.), transcript page 99. Web 15 January 2020.

3. Douglas Hiorns, oral history interviews at multiple locations; reel 1 recorded at Bukit Sembawang Estates, Singapore, conducted by interviewers Lim How Seng and Lim Guan Hock, 10 July 1987. *National Archives of Singapore*, accession no. 000799, reel 1 of 10 (29 mins., 40 secs.), transcript page 13. Web 15 January 2020.

4. Marie Ethel Bong, oral history interview conducted by Chua Chee Huan at Marie Bong's residence, 1 December 1992. *National Archives of Singapore*, accession no. 001390, reel 2 of 64 (3 mins., 25 secs.), 10. Web 15 January 2020.

5. Paul Abisheganaden, oral history interview conducted by Chua Chee Huan at the Oral History Centre, Singapore, 9 March–5 September 1993. *National Archives of Singapore*, accession no. 001415, reel 9 (10 mins., 20 secs.), transcript page 6. Web 15 January 2020.

6. Researchers beware: the results have changed since I first conducted this keyword search. Whereas 38 results have come up as of 30 March 2022, there were 160 back in January 2020, spread across interviews in English, Mandarin, Malay, and Tamil. Although I have not been able to confirm it, this discrepancy seems to be the result of a change in the search algorithm: to return only instances where a keyword is mentioned in the metadata, whereas before it also included keywords that appeared across entire transcripts.

7. Abu Bakar Ali, oral history interview, reel 1 (16 mins., 55 secs.).

8. Abu Bakar Ali, oral history interview, reel 1 (16 mins., 55 secs.).

9. Patricia Oh Choo Neo, oral history interview, reel 6 of 17 (40 seconds), [edited] transcript page 98.

10. Patricia Oh Choo Neo, oral history interview, reel 6 of 17 (40 seconds), [edited] transcript page 98.

11. "Gitar Berbunyi" comes from the Malay film *Do Re Mi,* released in 1966. "One Day When We Were Young" refers to the chorus of a duet by Nelson Eddy and Jeanette MacDonald, "Will You Still Remember?" from the 1936 film *Maytime*.

12. An earlier example occurs in a Chinese-language oral history interview with Ang Siew Ghim, 1985. *National Archive of Singapore,* accession no. 000536, reel 34. I am grateful to Min-Erh Wang for pointing this out to me.

13. Douglas Hiorns, oral history interview, reel 1 of 10 (29 mins., 40 secs.), transcript page 13.

14. Douglas Hiorns, oral history interview, reel 1 of 10 (29 mins., 40 secs.), transcript page 13.

15. Marie Ethel Bong, oral history interview, reel 2 of 64 (2 mins., 55 secs.), transcript page 10.

16. Christopher Robin, "When We Were Very Young," 78 rpm, BD 937 (His Master's Voice: Hayes, 1929).

17. Paul Abisheganaden, oral history interview, reel 9 (10 mins., 20 secs.), transcript page 6.

18. On policing the sonic environment in Singapore, see Jenny McCallum, "Conflict and Compromise over Processional Sound in 19th-Century Singapore," *Indonesia and the Malay World* 45 (2017): 315–33. See also Jim Sykes, "Towards a Malayan Indian Sonic Geography: Sound and Social Relations in Colonial Singapore," *Journal of Southeast Asian Studies* 46, no. 3 (2015): 485–513.

19. Cited in Nancy MacKay, "Memories and Reflections, the Singapore Experience: Documenting a Nation's History through Oral History" (review), *Oral History Review* 35, no. 2 (2008): 220–22.

20. I am grateful to Min-Erh Wang for summarizing several Chinese interviews relating to the gramophone. Some of these interviews recall musical connections between Singapore and mainland China through discs. See, for example, Teong Ah Chin, oral history interview conducted by Ang Siew Ghim, 1985, National Archive of Singapore, accession no. 000536, reel 34; and Tan Ngiang Kaw, oral history interview conducted by Loke Tai Tay, 2005, National Archive of Singapore, accession no. 002937, reel 1.

21. "Public Can Stream National Archives' Oral Interviews from Own Computers," *Straits Times*, 21 January 2014, https://www.straitstimes.com/singapore/public-can-stream-national-archives-oral-interviews-from-own-computers (accessed 30 March 2022).

22. Kimberly A. Christensen, "Does Information Really Want to Be Free? Indigenous Knowledge Systems and the Question of Openness," *International Journal of Communication* 6 (2012): 2870–93.

23. Of course, many historians have attempted to integrate oral history into larger accounts, including in Singapore. See, for example, L. K. Seng, "Voices of Survivors: Oral History and the Great Depression in Singapore," in Fiona Hu, ed., *Reflections and Interpretation: Oral History Centre, 25th Anniversary Publication* (Singapore: National Heritage Board, 2005), 212–26.

24. Nien Yuan Cheng, "'This Is My Doodle': Non-Participation, Performance, and the Singapore Memory Project," *Performance Paradigm* 14 (2018): 64–86.

25. Michel de Certeau, *The Writing of History*, trans. Tom Conley (New York: Columbia University Press, 1988), ch. 2.

26. Joanna Borat, "A Second Take: Revisiting Interviews with a Different Purpose," *Oral History* 31, no. 1 (2003): 47–53.

27. See Benjamin Walton, "Quirk Shame," *Representations* 132 no. 1 (2015), 121–129.

28. Tan Sooi Beng, "Negotiating 'His Master's Voice': Gramophone Music and Cosmopolitan Modernity in British Malaya in the 1930s and Early 1940s,"

Bijdragen tot de Taal-, Land- en Volkenkunde: Journal of the Huamnities and Social Sciences of Southeast Asia 169 (2013): 457–94; Tan Sooi Beng, "Cosmopolitan Identities: Evolving Musical Cultures of the Straits-Born Chinese of Pre–World War II Malaya," *Ethnomusicology Forum* 26, no. 1 (2016): 35–57.

CHAPTER 3

1. *Vanity Fair* nominated Caruso to its Hall of Fame alongside Eleftherios Venizelos, a leader of Greek national independence, "as the best-known singer of our time." See *Vanity Fair*, December 1916, p. 52.

2. Compton Mackenzie, "Gramophone Celebrities IV: Enrico Caruso," *The Gramophone* 2, no. 1 (July 1924): 45–47.

3. Robert Wallace, "First It Said 'Mary': The Phonograph Is Celebrating Its 75th Year," *Life*, 17 Nov 1952, pp. 87–102.

4. See, for example, Evan Eisenberg, *The Recording Angel: Music, Records and Culture from Aristotle to Zappa*, 2nd ed. (New Haven: Yale University Press, 2005 [1987]), 121.

5. See especially Karen Henson, "Au début de l'enregistrement sonore (1877–1906): Exotisme, opéra et science-fiction," in Nathalie Coutelet and Isabelle Moindroit, eds., *L'altérité en spectacle, 1789–1918* (Rennes, France: Presses universitaires de Rennes, 2015), 331–42.

6. David Suisman, *Selling Sounds: The Commercial Revolution in American Music* (Cambridge, MA: Harvard University Press, 2007), 125–50.

7. Suisman, *Selling Sounds*, 137–39.

8. Suisman has discussed Caruso's Italian identity elsewhere, but not in relation to sound reproduction technology. See David Suisman, "Welcome to the Monkey House: Enrico Caruso and the First Celebrity Trial of the Twentieth Century," *The Believer*, 1 June 2004, pp. 15–20.

9. Simona Frasca, *Italian Birds of Passage: The Diaspora of Neapolitan Musicians in New York* (New York: Palgrave, 2014), 39–76.

10. On the broader context of Neapolitan records in the United States, see Giuliana Fugazzotto, *Sta terra nun fa pi mia: I dischi a 78 giri e la vita in America degli emigranti italiani nel primo Novecento* (Udine, Italy: Nota, 2010).

11. See Davide Ceriani, "Opera as Social Agent: Fostering Italian Identity at the Metropolitan Opera House during the Early Years of Guilio Gatti-Casazza's Management, 1908–1910," in Magdalena Waligórska, ed., *Music, Longing, and Belonging: Articulations of the Self and the Other in the Musical Realm* (Newcastle upon Tyne, UK: Cambridge Scholars, 2013), 114–34. See also Anita Pesce, "The Neapolitan Sound Goes Around: Mechanical Music Instruments, Talking Machines, and Neapolitan Song, 1850–1925," in Goffredo Plastino and Joseph Sciorra, eds., *Neapolitan Postcards: The Canzone Napoletana as Transnational Subject* (London: Rowman and Littlefield, 2016), 45–72; and Paolo Prato, "The Good, the Bad and the Ugly: Transatlantic Stereotypes, 1880s–1950s," in ibid., 183–208.

12. Frasca, *Italian Birds of Passage*, 73–76.

13. On the forgetting and occluding of stories as a powerful force in music history, see Jairo Moreno, "Imperial Aurality: Jazz, The Archive, and U.S. Empire," in Radano and Olaniyan, eds., *Audible Empire*, 143–48.

14. Thomas Russell Ybarra, *Caruso: The Man of Naples and the Voice of Gold* (New York: Harcourt Brace, 1953).

15. These childhood memories were recalled during a series of interviews with Caruso's first biographer in the years before his death. See Pierre Van Rensselaer Key and Bruno Zirato, *Enrico Caruso: A Biography* (Boston: Little, Brown, 1922), 17.

16. Key and Zirato, *Enrico Caruso*, 47.

17. Enrico Caruso Jr. and Andrew Farkas, *Enrico Caruso: My Father and My Family* (Portland, OR: Amadeus, 1990), 32.

18. Caruso Jr. and Farkas, *Enrico Caruso*, 655–59.

19. Peter Martland, "Caruso's First Recordings: Myth and Reality," *Association for Recorded Sound Collections Journal* 25, no. 2 (1994): 192–201.

20. On a contemporary means of opera broadcast, see Melissa Van Drie, "Hearing through the Théâtrophone: Sonically Constructed Spaces and Embodied Listening in the late Nineteenth-Century French Theatre," *Sound Effects* 5, no. 1 (2016): 73–90.

21. Martland, "Caruso's First Recordings," 198–200.

22. Montrose J. Moses, *The Life of Heinrich Conried* (New York: Thomas Y. Crowell, 1916), 193; see also Key and Zirato, *Enrico Caruso*, 181.

23. Moses, *The Life of Heinrich Conried*, 193.

24. Key and Zirato, *Enrico Caruso*, 170–72.

25. The Simonelli medallion has resurfaced online in a blurry image. See https://en.wikipedia.org/wiki/Pasquale_Simonelli (accessed 13 February 2020).

26. On another commemorative medal presented to, rather than by, an opera singer, see Flora Willson, "Classic Staging: Pauline Viardot and the 1859 *Orphée* Revival," *Cambridge Opera Journal* 22, no. 3 (2010): 301–26.

27. Key and Zirato, *Enrico Caruso*, 289. These "little souvenirs" may have taken the form of a gold pendant measuring three centimeters across; one such object was so described on eBay in 2013.

28. Frasca, *Italian Birds of Passage*, 17–37. See also Larry Hamberlin, *Tin Pan Opera: Operatic Novelty Songs in the Ragtime Era* (Oxford, UK: Oxford University Press, 2011), 48; and Ceriani, "Opera as Social Agent," 114–34.

29. Ruth Baurle, "Caruso's Sin in the Fiendish Park: 'The Possible Was the Improbable and the Improbable the Inevitable,'" *James Joyce Quarterly* 38, no. 1–2 (2000): 125–42. See also Suisman, "Welcome to the Monkey House," 15–20.

30. One of the earliest reports of Caruso's arrest, appearing in the *New York Times* on 17 November, gave a contradictory account of where the arrest took place; "Signor Caruso, Tenor, Arrest in the Zoo," *New York Times*, 17 November 1906, p. 1.

31. "Police Add to Charges against Signor Caruso," *New York Times*, 18 No-

vember 1906, p. 1. Such slits were a common feature of gentlemen's overcoats at this time. See Baurle, "Caruso's Sin in the Fiendish Park," 129.

32. "Conried Aids Caruso," *Washington Post*, 20 November 1906, p. 3. For an even more elaborate account of Conried's reenactment, see "Caruso May Sue City if Case Is Not Approved," *New York Times*, 20 November 1906, p. 3.

33. "Caruso in Court; Case Not Ended," *New York Times*, 22 November 1906, p. 1; see also "Caruso on Stand," *Washington Post*, 22 November 1906, pp. 1 and 4.

34. "Caruso in Court; Case Not Ended," 1. The *New York Times* described onlookers present in court differently from *Washington Post*. The former reported there were "a few women," but that the crowd was "overwhelmingly" Italian and male; see ibid. *The Washington Post* estimated six hundred people had been squeezed into the two-hundred-seat courtroom, many of whom were female and regular operagoers, including a party of sixteen "girls" from the "Normal [i.e., Hunter] College," and several prominent women from outside New York, resident at local hotels. See "Caruso on Stand," 1 and 4.

35. Caruso's lawyer, the former judge A. J. Dittenhoeffer, wanted the new allegations ruled out; but the magistrate included the new plaintiffs, noting that the registered charge was for "annoying women," rather than one woman in particular. "Caruso in Court; Case Not Ended," 2.

36. Dittenhoeffer argued that the police routinely used women to ensnare wealthy men at the zoo, extorting money from them to avoid the scandal of arrest. See "Caruso Convicted but Will Appeal," *New York Times*, 24 November 1906, p. 1. However, Graham (not her real name) was tracked down by a journalist a week after the trial ended. Bauerle, "Caruso's Sin in the Fiendish Park," 134.

37. Kerry Segrave, *Beware the Masher: Sexual Harassment in American Public Places, 1880–1930* (Jefferson, NC, 2014), 156–72.

38. "Caruso Convicted but Will Appeal," 2.

39. "Caruso on Stand," 1; and "Caruso in Court; Case Not Ended," 1.

40. The partly legible handwritten caption below Caruso's self-caricature reads: "GUARDA CON [VISO?] TORVO UN CERTO CAVAGLIERE 'M'! MISTERO!" *La Follia di New York*, 17 February 1907, p. 1. Microform held at the New York Public Library, call no. ZAN-7336 1907.

41. "Il tenore Caruso, Caricaturista: Una lettera d'una signorina Americana," *La Follia di New York*, 1 June 1907, p. 1:

> Caro Signore, Ho ricevuto le tre copie della "Follia" richieste, sulle quali ho ammirato le splendide caricature di Caruso. Caruso è un uomo meraviglioso. Ho letto pochi giorni fa l'avviso del "Libro di Caruso" ma il prezzo ($50) mi ha impaurita. Se nel detto libro ci fosse QUALCHE SCHIZZO ORIGINALE ESEGUITO DALLA SUA PROPRIA MANO, allora sì che avrebbe avuto un gran valore. Io non conosco Enrico Caruso, né lo avevo mai udito cantare (imperdonabile errore) prima dell'ultima stagione; ma, dovendo giudicare dal pubblico che va al

> "Metropolitan Opera House" debbo arguire ch'egli ha molti ammiratori e che è popolarissimo, più popolare di quanto si crederebbe. A DISPETTO DI TUTTE LE DICERIE DIVULGATE SUL SUO CONTO NELLO SCORSO INVERNO ED ALLE QUALI—È INUTILE DIRLO—IO NON HO MAI CREDUTO. Con piacere vi mando i due dollari per un anno di abbonamento alla "Follia." NON C'È PREZZO SUFFICIENTE A PAGARE UN GIORNALE CHE HA L'ONORE DI PUBBLICARE DEGLI SCHIZZI ORIGINALI ESEGUITI DAL GRANDE TENORE ENRICO CARUSO. Vostra Dev.ma MISS HELEN WESTON.

42. "You might even say that the minor and unfounded accusation has increased the halo of admiration that already surrounded the name of the great tenor—admiration due to his unquestionable merits as a courageous and eminent artist." ("Si direbbe anzi che quella triviale quanto infondata accusa, abbia allargata intorno al nome del grande tenore l'aureola di ammirazione che già lo circondava per i suoi meriti indiscutibili di artista valoroso ed illustre.") "Il tenore Caruso, Caricaturista," 1.

43. Bauerle, "Caruso's Sin in the Fiendish Park," 137–40.

44. Hamberlin, *Tin Pan Opera*, 48.

45. Published as sheet music in 1908, "My Cousin Caruso" was also released as a gramophone record the following year. Hamberlin, *Tin Pan Opera*, 48.

46. Hamberlin, *Tin Pan Opera*, 48, 56.

47. Michael Rogin, *Blackface, White Noise: Jewish Immigrants in the Hollywood Melting Pot* (Berkeley: University of California Press, 1996), 45–72.

48. As Eric Lott has described, "The scarifying vision of human regression implicit, for whites, in 'blackness' was somewhat uneasily converted through laughter and humor into a beloved and reassuring fetish." Eric Lott, *Love and Theft: Blackface Minstrelsy and the American Working Class*, 20th anniversary edition (New York: Oxford University Press, 2013), 147.

49. On the "whitening" of Italians in the United Staes, see David R. Roediger's afterword in Jennifer Guglielmo and Salvatore Salerno, eds., *Are Italians White? How Race Is Made in America* (New York: Taylor & Francis, 2003), 259–64; and Peter G. Vellon, *A Great Conspiracy against Our Race: Italian Immigrant Newspapers and the Construction of Whiteness in the Early Twentieth Century* (New York: New York University Press, 2014), 1–14.

50. Jennifer Lynn Stoever, *The Sonic Color Line: Race and the Cultural Politics of Listening* (New York: New York University Press, 2016); Nina Sun Eidsheim, *The Race of Sound: Listening, Timbre and Vocality* (Durham, NC: Duke University Press, 2018), 1–38.

51. My interpretation of the vocality both enacted and elicited by Caruso's statuette draws on a forthcoming publication by Delia Casadei, presented as a talk in the University of California, Berkeley, 28 September 2018: "Contagion, Erasure, and Laughter as the Reproduction of Sound in Two 1890s Laughing Songs."

52. Turnbull had previously been involved in a film about a woman with multiple personality disorder (*The Case of Becky*; 1915). See Sarah Delahousse, "Margaret Turnbull," in Jane Gaines, Radha Vatsal, and Monica Dall'Asta, eds., *Women Film Pioneers Project* (New York, 2013), https://doi.org/10.7916/d8-5zao-x430 (accessed 13 Feb 2020).

53. Giuliana Muscio, *Napoli/New York/Hollywood: Film between Italy and the United States* (New York: Fordham University Press, 2019), 15–27. See also Ilaria Serra, *The Imagined Immigrant: Images of Italian Emigration to the United States between 1890 and 1924* (Madison, WI: Rosemont, 2009), 96–131.

54. However, sources that repeat this claim, such as the *Guinness Book of World Records*, avoid mentioning when the millionth copy was sold. There is in fact no evidence that Caruso's voice sold unusually well in 1904, at least in the United States. American corporate registers account for no more than a few thousand copies of any of Caruso's records, "Vesti la giubba" included. See John Bolig, *Caruso Records: A History and Discography* (Littleton, CO: Mainspring Press, 2002), 15. Pirated copies are of course hard to trace, but were probably widespread. In the most thorough survey of the British or any other record market to date, Peter Martland has shown that by the end of 1906 the Australian soprano Nellie Melba outsold Caruso, selling thirty-one thousand discs to his eleven thousand. In every year from 1907 to 1914, however, Caruso sold more records in the United Kingdom than any other singer; and from 1910 onward he sold more records annually than all other opera singers combined. By 1913 he had sold around 330,000 discs in the UK, one of the largest markets alongside the US and Russia at that point. See Peter Martland, *Recording History: The British Record Industry, 1888–1931* (Plymouth, UK: Scarecrow Press, 2013), 195.

55. "Trade Conditions in Philadelphia," *Talking Machine World*, 15 March 1907, p. 17.

56. Jonathan Sterne, *The Audible Past: Cultural Origins of Sound Reproduction* (Durham, NC: Duke University Press, 2003), 216.

57. Stephen M. Best, *The Fugitive's Properties: Law and the Poetics of Possession* (Chicago: University of Chicago Press, 2004), 29–100.

58. "Best Voices for Records: A Laboratory Expert Discants on the Making of Good Records," *Talking Machine World*, 15 November 1906, p. 9.

59. Gramophones and phonographs, the machines, could recall Italian organ grinders in the United States, and subsequently formed the basis for emerging Italian identities. See Siel Agugliaro, "From Grinder to Nipper: Home Phonographs and the Making of Italian American Musical Identity" (forthcoming).

60. Donna R. Gabaccia, *Foreign Relations: American Immigration in Global Perspective* (Princeton, NJ, 2012), 112–75. On geopolitical construction of Italian vocal excess, see Delia Casadei, "A Voice That Carries," in *Hearing the Crimean War: Wartime Sound and the Unmaking of Sense* (Oxford, UK: Oxford University Press, 2019), 150–74.

61. Fitzcarraldo's real-life counterpart Frederick Starr took Caruso records with him on anthropological expeditions to the Congo Free State. "Music of the Jungle," *Talking Machine World*, 15 April 1907, 16. See also Erik Mueggler, "Bodies Real and Virtual: Joseph Rock and Enrico Caruso in the Sino-Tibetan Borderlands," *Comparative Studies in History and Society* 53, no. 1 (2011): 6–37.

62. The following summary of his earnings was typical: "$2,500 a performance at the Metropolitan and his royalties from phonograph records and his wages as a motion picture actor." See "Career of Caruso a Long Crescendo," *New York Times*, 3 August 1921, p. 6.

63. "Caruso Immortalized" (1921) is reproduced in James N. Weber, *The Talking Machine: The Advertising History of the Berliner Gramophone and Victor Talking Machine* (New York: Adio Inc., 1997), 62. "Characteristic Photographs of Caruso: Caruso's Glorious Voice Kept for Posterity by Phonograph," *San Francisco Chronicle*, 3 August 1921, p. 7; "Caruso Records Are Imperishable," *New York Times*, 3 August 1921, p. 3.

64. Key and Zirato, *Enrico Caruso*, 6.

65. Another use of Caruso's records which became newly significant after his death was vocal pedagogy. See Salvatore Fucito and Barnet J. Beyer, *Caruso and the Art of Singing, Including Caruso's Vocal Exercises and His Practical Advice to Students and Teachers of Singing* (New York: Frederick A. Stokes, 1922), 209–10; and Marafioti, *Caruso's Method of Voice Production: The Scientific Culture of the Voice* (New York: Appleton, 1922), 22.

66. Edmund Wheeler Scripture, "The Curves of Caruso," *Musical Times* 65, no. 976 (1 June 1924): 517–19. For a more complete analysis, see Jean-Pierre Mouchon, "Particolarità fisiche e fonetiche della voce incisa di Caruso," in Riccardo Vaccaro, ed., *Caruso* (Naples: Edizioni Scientifiche Italiane, 1995), 36–47.

67. Scripture had a penchant for morbid excerpts; one of his first experiments examined "The Sad Story of the Death and Burial of Poor Cock Robin." See Edmund Wheeler Scripture, "How the Voice Looks," *Century Illustrated Monthly Magazine* 64 (May–Oct 1902): 148–54; and Edmund Wheeler Scripture, *Researches in Experimental Phonetics: The Study of Speech Curves* (Washington: Carnegie Institute of Washington, 1906), 48–59.

68. Emphasis added. Scripture, "The Curves of Caruso," 519. There was a tradition of championing Italian vowels, going back to Manuel García's laryngoscope; see James Q. Davies, *Romantic Anatomies of Performance* (Berkeley: University of California Press, 2014), 19.

69. Sterne, *The Audible Past*, 48.

70. Scripture, "The Curves of Caruso," 519.

71. Scripture, "The Curves of Caruso," 519.

72. Scripture does not say whether he isolated the voice from its orchestral accompaniment, nor does he address noises created through recording and playback. Scripture, "The Curves of Caruso," 519.

73. Here is a recent example from media theory: "Once Enrico Caruso's voice is articulated by replay from beyond the grave, it miraculously emanates

against the entropy of its technical embodiment in the shellac record." Wolfgang Ernst, *Sonic Time Machines: Explicit Sound, Sirenic Voices and Implicit Sonicity* (Amsterdam: Amsterdam University Press, 2016), 86.

74. See Benjamin Piekut and Jason Stanyek, "Deadness: Technologies of the Intermundane," *TDR: The Drama Review* 54 (2010): 14–38.

75. Thomas Stockham et al. "Blind Deconvolution through Digital Signal Processing," *Proceedings of the International Electrical and Electronics Engineers* 63, no. 4 (1975): 678–92.

76. On the voice as a body and as mouth missile, see Brandon LaBelle, *Lexicon of the Mouth: Poetics and Politics of Voice and the Oral Imaginary* (London: Bloomsbury, 2014), 1–5.

CHAPTER 4

1. Leonard F. Emms, "A Working Man's Choice of Records," *The Gramophone* 3, no. 5 (October 1925): 228.

2. In reference to the then-mandatory period of military service, Emms adds, "Those of us who have done a bit of route marching know the value of good tunes such as 'Colonel Bogey,' 'Old Comrades,' 'Preciosa,' and other old favourite marches."

3. Emms, "A Working Man's Choice of Records," 228. Further discographical information is supplied in Emms's article: "The Belle of New York" (HMV 915, 12 inches, 4s. 6d.), "The Beggar's Opera" (Columbia 927, 12 inches, 4 s. 6d.), "Folk Song Suite" (Vocalion, K. 05086, no price). All short quotations in the opening paragraph are from this article.

4. An irritated response to Emms's article, which argued for the need to represent the "average" male listener rather than the "working man," appeared a few months later. See Edward L. Murray, "The Average Man's Choice of Records," *The Gramophone* 3, no. 10 (March 1926): 473–74.

5. On this topic, see Colin Symes, *Setting the Record Straight: A Material History of Classical Recording* (Middletown, CT: Wesleyan University Press, 2004), ch. 6., 152–81. *The Gramophone* also published reviews of jazz and popular music.

6. Philip Styles, *A History of the County of Warwick: Volume 3, Barlichway Hundred* (London: Victoria County History, London, 1945), 234–44.

7. [Scrutator], "Where are the Ladies?" *The Gramophone* 3, no. 1 (June 1925): 39. See also [T. A. F.], "Ladies and the Gramophone," *The Gramophone* 3, no. 3 (August 1925): 147.

8. Gladys M. Collin, "Women and the Gramophone," *The Gramophone* 3, no. 5 (October 1925): 247. Anthologized in Timothy Taylor, Mark Katz, and Tony Grajeda, eds. *A Documentary History of Early Phonograph, Cinema and Radio* (Durham, NC: Duke University Press 2012), 75.

9. Emphasis in original. Collin, "Women and the Gramophone." See also Nick Morgan, "The National Gramophonic Society," PhD thesis, University of Sheffield, 2013.

10. Francis E. Terry, "Women and the Gramophone," *The Gramophone* 3, no. 5 (October 1925): 247.

11. Terry, "Women and the Gramophone."

12. A report titled "Average Weekly Wages," submitted to the House of Commons by the minister of labor in 1925, noted that, in the coal industry, for example, "The average earnings per man-shift worked in all districts [. . .] in the quarter ended 30th June, 1920, were 16s. 10½d. compared with 6s. 5¾d. in June, 1914, an increase of about 160 per cent. Those in May, 1925 (the latest date for which the figures are available) were about 10s. 7¾d or 64 per cent. higher than in June, 1914." See *Hansard* 187 (July 1925), columns 671–73, deb. 30.

13. In 1921 the *Musical Times* established a gramophone column which was perhaps the earliest regular column devoted to disc reviewing in the United Kingdom. See "Gramophone Notes," *Musical Times* 62, no. 935 (1921): 40–42.

14. Geoffrey Evans, "Jazz Bands of the South Wales Valleys," *Amgeuddfa Cwm Cynon / Cynon Valley Museum*, cynonvalleymuseum.wales/2021/02/10/jazz-bands-of-the-south-wales-valleys-1926/ (accessed 20 December 2021).

15. Sue Bruley, *The Women and Men of 1926: A Gender and Social History of the General Strike and Miners' Lockout in South Wales* (Cardiff: NBN International, 2010), 1–16.

16. "Labour Day: Carnival and Demonstration at Maesteg," *Glamorgan Advertiser*, 7 May 1926, p. 5.

17. "Troedyrhiw," *Merthyr Express*, 19 June 1926, p. 14.

18. Catherine Tackley, *The Evolution of Jazz in Britain*, 1880–1935 (London: Routledge, 2005), 35–80.

19. All short quotations in this paragraph are from "Bargoed Carnival: Town en Fete in Aid of Canteen Fund," *Merthyr Express*, 19 June 1926, p. 20.

20. Short quotations in this paragraph are from "The Maesteg Carnival: A Picturesque Procession," *Glamorgan Advertiser*, 23 July 1926, p. 6.

21. "The Maesteg Carnival," 6.

22. "Carnival at Abertillery: Successful Relief Fund Function," *South Wales Gazette*, 23 July 1926, p. 13.

23. "Carnival at Abertillery," 6.

24. "Carnival at Abertillery," 6.

25. "Carnival at Abertillery," 13.

26. Gweirydd [pseud.], "Colofn Y Cymro: Carnivaliaeth yn y Rhondda," *Pontypridd Observer*, 31 July 1926, p. 7.

27. "Jazz Procession," *Merthyr Express*, 29 May 1926, p. 17.

28. "Newtown Knights," *Merthyr Express*, 17 July 1926, p. 14.

29. "Tredegar Town Talk," *Merthyr Express*, 28 August 1926, p. 16.

30. Handouts from the SWMF were routinely referred to as "Russian money." See Hwyel Francis and David Smith, *The Fed: A History of the South Wales Miners in the Twentieth Century* (London: Lawrence and Wishart, 1980), 53.

31. It was also adapted for a collection of short stories. Gwyn Thomas, *Gazooka: A Short Novel and Twelve Stories in Which (for the Form Suits Him to Perfection) We Get the Guintessential Gwyn Thomas* (London: Victor Gollancz, 1957). All quotations from *Gazooka* below come from this source.

32. Thomas, *Gazooka*, 70.

33. A jazz band (the Victoria Prize Jazz Band of Hulme) hoisting a Britannia and playing gazookas can be seen and heard in Humphrey Jennings's documentary *Spare Time* (1939). The band's performance takes place in a field on an estate near Manchester, thus illustrating the spread of the kazoo jazz band phenomenon to other areas of heavy industry beyond South Wales.

34. Along with the word "voters," "elements" is used for "people" throughout Gwyn Thomas's writings. See, for example, Thomas, *Gazooka*, 72.

35. Thomas, *Gazooka*, 108.

36. Huntley Trevor [pseud. Raymond Wallace] and Tolchard Evans, *Barcelona: Indigo—Yes!—Indigo* (London: Cecil Lennox, 1926), 78 rpm.

37. Perhaps significantly, the reverse side of this disc features a matador-themed tango. See "Savoy Orpheans, Barcelona—Savoy Tango Orchestra, Matador" (London, HMV B5045), 78 rpm, released April 1926.

38. The melody took on a second life in the United States, where it was recorded by the house orchestra of the Victor Talking Machine Company, led by conductor Nat Shilkret, and with newly pared-down lyrics by Gus Kahn, one of the most successful American pop-music wordsmiths of the period. Kahn transformed "I'm One of the Nuts of Barcelona" into "I Married the Belle of Barcelona." These words appeared only briefly during the chorus (as was common in recorded dance music of the 1920s), and were sung by Bill Murray, a well-known gramophone artist. See Gus Kahn and Tolchard Evans, *Barcelona* (London and New York: Cecil Lennox and Leo Feist, 1926), 78 rpm; and "Nat Shrilket and the Victor Orchestra, Barcelona—Fox Trot / Nat Shrilket and the Victor Orchestra On the Riviera—Fox Trot" (Camden, NJ, Victor 20113), 78 rpm, released 1926.

39. Victory for the Matadors was not to be. On the day of the competition, they would be foiled by the surprise entry of the Aberclydach Sheiks, sporting veils and swaying deeply to the "The Sheik of Araby"—another song first released on disc in 1921, and revived in a string of recordings that came out following *The Son of the Sheik* (1926), a silent film starring Rudolph Valentino. Thomas, *Gazooka*, 116.

40. Thomas, *Gazooka*, 64.

41. Thomas, *Gazooka*, 64.

42. On riparian and passerine networks of early blackface performance, see W. T. Lahmon, *Raising Cain: Blackface Performance from Jim Crow to Hip Hop* (Cambridge, MA: Harvard University Press, 1998), 1–7.

43. Thomas, *Gazooka*, 64.

44. Bruley, *The Women and Men of 1926*, 8.

45. Thomas, *Gazooka*, 64.

46. Thomas, *Gazooka*, 109.

47. Michael Pickering, *Blackface Minstrelsy in Britain* (Aldershot, UK: Ashgate, 2008); Robert Nowatzki, *Representing African Americans in Transatlantic Abolitionism and Blackface Minstrelsy* (Baton Rouge: Louisiana State University Press, 2010).

48. Inspired by the words of the nineteenth-century US newspaper magnate Charles Anderson Dana, the *Advertiser* set out to report on "everything that occurs, everything that is of sufficient interest to arrest and absorb the attention of the public, or any part of it." The first issue of the newspaper anticipated that "the important interests of mining will demand their fair of attention, and local trade and industry, religious and philanthropic agencies, music and literature, recreation and sport, in short, all the many-sided activities of local life, will receive the publicity and support to which they are entitled." While of course striving toward journalistic objectivity, the *Advertiser* promoted "humane and democratic" movements that furthered the social progress of the working classes. Editorial, *Glamorgan Advertiser & Weekly News For the Llynfi, Ogmore, Garw and Avon Valleys*, 6 June 1919, p. 4.

49. Stylus [pseud.], "Gramophone Notes," *Glamorgan Advertiser*, 29 January 1926, p. 3.

50. Recorded by Arthur de Greef, Landon Roland, Royal Albert Hall Orchestra (HMV D 1237–40). Stylus [pseud.], "Gramophone Notes: Grieg's Piano Concerto," *Glamorgan Advertiser*, 8 July 1927, p. 3; Stylus [pseud.], "Gramophone Notes: The Complete 'Valkyrie,'" *Glamorgan Advertiser*, 17 February 1928, p. 2.

51. On this context, see Francis and Smith, *The Fed*, 1–26.

52. I take inspiration from Emanuele Senici's approach to reading the layout of newspaper pages and the place of music criticism within them. Senici shows how a shift in critical attention in opera from performance to work, ca. 1800, coincided with "policing borders" in French-occupied Milan. See Emanuele Senici, "Delirious Hopes: Napoleonic Milan and the Rise of Modern Italian Operatic Criticism," *Cambridge Opera Journal* 27, no. 2 (2015): 113–20.

53. Stylus [pseud.], "Gramophone Notes," *Glamorgan Advertiser*, 20 April 1928, p. 2.

54. Stylus, "Gramophone Notes," 2.

55. Under the Needle [pseud.], "Gramophone Notes," *Glamorgan Advertiser*, 23 January 1931, p. 3.

56. "Free Concert: Cardiff Instrumental Trio at Maesteg," *Glamorgan Advertiser*, 26 April 1929, p. 5.

57. "Free Concert: Cardiff Instrumental Trio at Maesteg," 5.

58. "Free Concert: Cardiff Instrumental Trio at Maesteg," 5.

59. Stylus [pseud.], "Gramophone Notes: Chamber Music For All," *Glamorgan Advertiser*, 10 May 1929, p. 7.

60. "Free Concert: Cardiff Instrumental Trio at Maesteg," 5.

61. Intriguingly, Stylus goes on to say, "Mr. Rees makes his own gramo-

phones and achieves remarkable results in this direction." Stylus [pseud.], "Nantyffyllon," *Glamorgan Advertiser*, 29 March 1929, p. 5.

62. A typical example, which frequently recurs: "On Wednesday evening the members were entertained to a gramophone concert, arranged by Mr. John Richards, John-street. Mr. Richards must be complimented upon his beautiful selection of records, *which was appreciated by all present*." Emphasis added. Such formulas, however clichéd, were virtually obligatory. See, for example, "Nantyffyllon," *Glamorgan Advertiser*, 1 Feb 1929, p. 5.

63. "Nantyffyllon Lounge Society: Enjoyable Gramophone Concert," *Glamorgan Advertiser*, 30 November 1928, p. 7.

64. N. Woodward, "Why Did South Wales Miners Have High Mortality? Evidence from the Mid Twentieth Century," *Welsh History Review / Cylchgrawn Hanes Cymru* 20, no. 1 (2000): 116–41.

65. Gwyn Thomas, *The Dark Philosophers* (Boston, MA: Little, Brown, 1946). It was translated into German as *Die Liebe des Reverend Emmanuel,* trans. L. Fankhauser (Zürich: Büchergilde Gutenberg, 1951). All quotations in the main text come from a more recent text: Gwyn Thomas, *The Alone to the Alone with The Dark Philosophers* (Carmarthen, UK: Golden Grove House, 1988).

66. Michael Denning, *The Cultural Front: The Laboring of American Culture in the Twentieth Century* (London and New York: Verso, 1997), 230–42.

67. Thomas, *The Dark Philosophers,* 173.

68. Jen Wilson explores the place of jazz in South Wales café culture between the wars. See Jen Wilson, *Freedom Music: Wales, Emancipation and Jazz, 1850 -1950* (Cardiff: University of Wales Press, 2019), 153–82.

69. Thomas, *The Dark Philosophers,* 173.

70. Thomas, *The Dark Philosophers*, 174.

71. Thomas, *The Dark Philosophers,* 174.

72. Thomas, *The Dark Philosophers*, 165–66.

73. Thomas, *The Dark Philosophers*, 176.

74. Thomas, *The Dark Philosophers*, 175.

75. Thomas, *The Dark Philosophers*, 209.

76. Thomas, *The Dark Philosophers*, 206.

77. Raymond Williams, *Culture and Society, 1780–1950* (London: Chatto and Windus, 1958).

78. Stuart Hall, "Encoding/Decoding," in Stuart Hall, Dorothy Hobson, and Andrew Lowe, eds., *Culture, Media, Language: Working Papers in Cultural Studies, 1972–79* (Birmingham, UK: Centre for Contemporary Cultural Studies 1980), 117–27.

79. Christopher Bayly makes a more general point about the proliferation of differences through the rise of global standards of dress, behavior and so on. See Bayly, *Birth of the Modern World*, 12–18.

80. Frederic Jameson, *The Political Unconscious: Narrative as Socially Symbolic Act* (Ithaca, NY: Cornell University Press, 1981), 1–88.

81. I quote from Gwyn Thomas's voiceover from a documentary *One Pair of*

Eyes (1969), which is widely available online. On the concept of "structures of feeling," see Raymond Williams, *Marxism and Literature* (Oxford, UK: Oxford University Press, 1977), 128–35.

CHAPTER 5

1. See, for example, "Some Record and Needle Wear Experiments (I) by Our Expert Committee," *The Gramophone* 6 no. 67 (1928), 317–21.

2. Jean-Paul Sartre, *La Nausée* (Paris: Gallimard, 1938). I take my quotations mainly from the first English translation: *Nausea*, trans. Lloyd Alexander ([1964] New York: New Directions, 2007).

3. Sartre, *Nausea*, 21.

4. "Un disque Pathé pour aiguille à saphir," *Nausea*, 21. For an overview of Pathé's international activities, see Howard Rye, "Pathé," in *Grove Music Online* (2003; accessed 4 August 2020); doi.org/10.1093/gmo/9781561592630.article.J347500.

5. Sartre, *Nausea*, 22.

6. Iris Murdoch, *Sartre: Romantic Rationalist* (New Haven, CT: Yale University Press, 1953), 13.

7. Mark Carroll, "'It Is': Reflections on the Role of Music in Sartre's 'La Nausée,'" *Music & Letters* 87, no. 3 (2006): 398–407.

8. On sound recording as a "songish formation," see Michael Denning and Gary Tomlinson, "Cantologies," *Representations* 154, no. 1 (2021): 127–28.

9. Dominick LaCapra, "Sartre and the Question of Biography," *French Review* 55, no. 7 (1982): 22–56; Eugenia Noik Zimmerman, "'Some of These Days': Sartre's *petite phrase*," *Contemporary Literature* 11, no. 3 (1970): 375–81.

10. Eileen Southern, *Biographical Dictionary of Afro-American and African Musicians* (Westport CT: Greenwood Press, 1982), 213.

11. Michael Garber, "'Some of These Days' and the Study of the Great American Songbook," *Journal of the Society for American Music* 4, no. 2 (2010): 175–214.

12. See, for example, hymn no. 22, "Some of These Days," in J. Lincoln Hall and Irvin H. Mack, *Boundless Love: For Sunday Schools and Gospel Meetings* (Philadelphia: Hall Mack, 1896).

13. Rev. F. J. Grimké, "The Signs of a Better Future for the American Negro: Extracts from His Sermon on the Race Problem," in Daniel Wallace Culp, *Twentieth Century Negro Literature: Or a Cyclopedia of Thought on Vital Topics Relating to the American Negro* (Toronto, Naperville, IL, and Atlanta: J. L Nichols, 1902), 427–33. For the complete sermon, "Sources from Which No Help May Be Expected: The General Government, Political Parties, etc.," dated 27 November 1900, see Francis James Grimké, *The Works of Francis J. Grimké*, ed. Carter G. Woodson, vol. 1 (Washington: Associated Publishers, 1942), 247–60.

14. Grimké, "The Signs of a Better Future for the American Negro," 432.

15. Theodor Parker, *The Works of Theodor Parker*, vol. 1 (London: Barker, 1863), 34–52.

16. Both lyrics ("'Cause some o' dese days you'll call me honey," etc.) and melody are very close to Frank Williams's song. See Graber, "'Some of These Days' and the Study," 175–214.

17. For another interpretation—which highlights the modernity and ruse of the contrast between its status as a self-consciously "old" song and its ongoing "emotional and stylistic validity"—see Graber, "'Some of These Days' and the Study," 207–8.

18. Hedges Brothers and Jacobson's stage performance likely inspired the inclusion of an arrangement for "male or mixed quartette" after the vocal score. Shelton Brooks, "Some of These Days," notated music (Chicago: Will Rossiter, 1910), www.loc.gov/item/ihas.100004309/ (accessed 4 August 2020).

19. American Quartet (vocal group, with orchestra), "Some of These Days," Shelton Brooks, composer and lyrcist (Camden NJ: Victor, 1910), catalog no. 16834-A; 10-inch disc; www.loc.gov/item/jukebox-254467/ (accessed 4 August 2020).

20. Elise Stevenson (with orchestra), "Some of These Days," Shelton Brooks, composer and lyricist (Columbia, 1 May 1911 and 29 May 1911), catalog nos. 19327 and 19393; 10-inch discs. See *Discography of American Historical Recordings*, adp.library.ucsb.edu (accessed 4 August 2020). Sophie Tucker (with orchestra), "Some of These Days," Shelton Brooks, composer and lyricist (Edison, 1911), catalog no. EDIS 35979, cylinder. See freemusicarchive.org (accessed 4 August 2020). On Tucker's blackface performances, see Lori Harrison-Kahan, *The White Negress: Literature, Minstrelsy, and the Black-Jewish Imaginary* (New Jersey: Rutgers University Press, 2011), 16–57; Maria de Simone, "Sophie Tucker, Racial Hybridity and Interracial Relations in American Vaudeville," *Theatre Research International* 44, no. 2 (2019): 153–70.

21. Sophie Tucker and Dorothy Giles, *Some of These Days: The Autobiography of Sophie Tucker* (New York: Country Life Press, 1945), 33.

22. Harrison-Kahan, *The White Negress*, 23.

23. Tucker voiced Elkins's intervention as follows: "See here, young lady, since when are you so important you can't hear a song by a colored writer?" Tucker and Giles, *Some of These Days*, 114.

24. Tucker and Giles, *Some of These Days*, 114.

25. At least one journalist assumed the book was dedicated to Brooks. Al Monroe, "Swinging the News," *Chicago Defender*, 28 May 1949, p.16.

26. Tucker and Giles, *Some of These Days*.

27. Tucker and Giles, *Some of These Days*, 257.

28. Tucker and Giles, *Some of These Days*, 35.

29. This issue of "belief" in blackface performance is complex. See Lott, *Love and Theft*, xii; W. T. Lhamon, *Raising Cain: Blackface Performance from Jim Crow to Hip Hop* (Cambridge, MA: Harvard University Press, 1998), 42.

30. "Defender Forum," *Chicago Defender*, 7 September 1929, p. A1.

31. "Defender Forum," *Chicago Defender*, 1 September 1934, p. 14.

32. "'I Thought You Were a Negro,'" *Chicago Defender*, 17 April 1937, p. 21.

33. "'I Thought You Were a Negro,'" p. 21. In drawing a firm distinction between Tucker and those in the "actual profession" of the blues, this last comment illustrates one strategy of resistance against white appropriation: by insisting on the Blackness of real blues singers. At the same time, this anonymous journalist for the *Defender*, the widest-circulating black newspaper in the United States, recognized Tucker's antiracist contributions as both performer and benefactor.

34. Andy Fry, *Paris Blues: African American music and French popular culture, 1920—1960* (Chicago: University of Chicago Press, 2014), 1–28.

35. See Elodie A. Roy, "Worn Grooves: Affective Connectivity, Mobility and Recorded Sound in the First World War," *Media History* 24, no. 1 (2016): 26–45. On the US context, see Joshua Villanueva, "American Music in World War I: How America Won the First World War with Song" (exhibition), United States World War One Centennial Commission, published online (accessed 6 August 2020).

36. Beauvoir mentions, among other records, "The Man I Love"—which also, though much more briefly, was featured in *Nausea*—and "Ol' Man River," along with unspecified "negro spirituals," "chants de travails," and "blues." Simone de Beauvoir, *La Force de l'âge* (Paris: Gallimard, 1960), 145. See also James Donald, *Some of These Days: Black Stars, Jazz Aesthetics, and Modernist Culture* (Oxford, UK: Oxford University Press, 2015), 1–2, 222–24. Sophie Tucker is briefly mentioned as gramophone artist, along with Al Jolson, in Sartre's short story "The Childhood of a Leader" (1938); Jean-Paul Sartre, *The Wall, and Other Stories,* trans. Lloyd Alexander (New York: New Directions, 1948), 194.

37. Joseph Murrell's compilation of discs perhaps unreliably reports the disc to have sold unusually well. See Joseph Murrells, *The Book of Golden Discs*, revised edition (London: Barrie and Jenkins, 1978), 15.

38. Sophie Tucker, *Some of These Days: The Autobiography of Sophie Tucker* (New York: Editions for the Armed Services, 1945).

39. Ross Laird, *Moanin' Low: A Discography of Female Popular Vocal Recordings, 1920–1933* (Westport, CT: Greenwood 1996), 131, 145, 390. See also Ethel Waters (voice), William Tyler (violin), Leonord Jeter (cello), and Pearl Wright (piano), "Some of These Days," Shelton Brooks, composer and lyricist (Columbia, 1927), catalog no. 14264-D, 10-inch disc, Discography of American Historical Recordings, adp.library.ucsb.edu (accessed 6 August 2020).

40. In the United States, "Some of These Days" was released by Pathé in the cover by Betty Morgan; but of course this does not necessarily mean that her recording was the version Sartre had in his collection.

41. Sartre, *Nausea*, 173.

42. Sartre, *Nausea*, 173.

43. Dan Zahavi, "Shame and the Exposed Self," in Jonathan Webber, ed., *Reading Sartre: On Phenomenology and Existentialism* (London: Routledge, 2011), 211–26.

44. Sartre, *Nausea*, 174–75.

45. James Wood, introduction to *Nausea*, trans. Lloyd Alexander, xv–xvii.

46. Emphasis added. Sartre, *Nausea*, 175–76.

47. Jean Paul Sartre, *Being and Nothingness: An Essay in Phenomenological Ontology*, translated by Sarah Richmond (New York: Washington Square Press, 2018), 41.

48. Sartre, *Being and Nothingness*, 41.

49. Sartre, *Being and Nothingness*, 42.

50. Sartre, *Being and Nothingness*, 170.

51. Sartre, *Being and Nothingness*, 170.

52. Sartre, *Being and Nothingness*, 176.

53. Sartre, *Being and Nothingness*, 176.

54. Sartre, *Being and Nothingness*, 177.

55. One critic argues torturously that the error was deliberate. See Jonathan Judaken, *Jean-Paul Sartre and the Jewish Question: Anti-Semitism and the Politics of the French Intellectual* (Lincoln: University of Nebraska Press, 2006), 44–45.

56. ". . . Ils penseraient à ma vie comme je pense à celle de cette Négresse: comme à quelque chose de précieux et d'à moité légendaire." Sartre, *La nausée* (Paris: Galliard, 1974), 248.

57. Edmund Husserl, *The Phenomenology of Internal Time-Consciousness*, ed. Martin Heidegger, trans. James S. Churchill (Bloomington: Indiana University Press, 2019), 22–26.

58. Sartre became enamored by the idea of nothingness, interposing it liberally through his most famous work—not only across the difference between present and past, but in the interstices between subjects and objects, selves and others. Sartre, *Being and Nothingness*, 121–28.

59. On philosophies of listening embodied in everyday experience, see Carolyn Abbate, "Sound Object Lessons," *Journal of the American Musicological Society* 69, no. 3 (2016): 793–829.

60. Emphasis added. René Bizet, "Musique: Disques," *L'Intransigeant*, 4 May 1927, p. 5. For a map and database of disc stores in Paris between 1890 and 1960, see Thomas Henry, disquairesdeparis.fr/ (accessed 7 August 2020).

61. See Louis Chude-Sokei, *The Last "Darky": Bert Williams, Black-on-Black Minstrelsy, and the African Diaspora* (Durham, NC: Duke University Press, 2006), 1–16; Nowatzki, *Representing African Americans*, ch. 2.

62. Jennifer Lynn Stoever, *The Sonic Color Line: Race and the Cultural Politics of Listening* (New York: New York University Press, 2016), 4.

63. Matthew D. Morrison, "Race, Blacksound and the Remaking of Musicological Discourse," *Journal of the American Musicological Society* 72, no. 3 (2019), 781–823; Matthew D. Morrison, "Blacksound," in Tomás McAuley, Nanette Nielsen, Jerrold Levinson, and Ariana Phillips-Hutton, eds., *The Oxford Handbook to Western Music and Philosophy* (Oxford, UK: Oxford University Press, 2020), 555–78.

64. On this topic, see Delia Casadei, *Risible: Laughter without Reason and the Reproduction of Sound* (Berkeley: University of California Press, 2024), ch. 3.

65. Jean-Paul Sartre, "Black Orpheus," *Massachusetts Review* 6, no. 1 (1964–65): 13–52. See also Jean-Paul Sartre, *Colonialism and Neo-Colonialism*, trans. Azzedine Haddour, Steve Brewer, and Terry McWilliams (London: Routledge, 2001).

66. My reading of the "/" draws loosely on Viveiros de Castro's notion of perspectivism, according to which objects and worlds change depending on who sees them. As he explains, this concept is closely related to Deleuze's idea of multiplicity, which can itself be tracked (via the writings of Claude Lévi-Strauss) to indigenous cosmologies of the Northwest Amazonian region. Eduardo Viveiros de Castro, *Cannibal Metaphysics: For a Post-Structural Anthropology*, trans. Peter Skafish (Minneapolis: Univocal, 2014), 69–73.

67. Ralph Ellison, *The Invisible Man* ([1952] Penguin: Milton Keynes, 2016), 3.

68. Ellison, *Invisible Man*, 8.

69. Ellison, *Invisible Man*, 8.

70. See, for example, Colin Symes, "From 'Tomorrow's Eve' to 'High Fidelity': Novel Responses to the Gramophone in Twentieth Century Literature," *Popular Music* 24, no. 2 (2005): 193–206; Zan Cammack, *Ireland's Gramophones: Material Culture, Memory, and Trauma in Irish Modernism* (Oxford, UK: Oxford University Press, 2021), 131–64.

71. Nicole Brittingham Furlonge, "'To Hear the Silence of Sound': Making Sense of Listening in Ralph Ellison's 'Invisible Man,'" *Interference Journal: A Journal of Auditory Cultures* 1 (2011): 1–12; published online at http://www.interferencejournal.org/to-hear-the-silence-of-sound/.

Bibliography

Abbate, Carolyn. "Sound Object Lessons." *Journal of the American Musicological Society* 69 no. 3 (2016): 793–829.

Abū al-Faẕl ibn Mubārak. *Āʾīn-i Akbarī*. Second Edition. Translated by Heinrich Blochmann. Revised and edited by D. C. Phillott. Lahore: Sang-e-Meel Publications, 2004.

Adarkar, Bhalchandra Pundlik. *Report on Labour Conditions in the Shellac Industry*. Labour Investigation Committee. Simla: Government of India, 1945.

Adorno, Theodor. *Current of Music*. Edited by Robert Hullot-Kentor. Malden, MA: Polity, 2009.

Adorno, Theodor. "The Form of the Phonograph Record." Translated by Thomas Y. Levin. *October* 55 (1990): 56–61.

Adorno, Theodor. *Writings on Music*. Edited by Richard Leppert. Berkeley: University of California Press, 2002.

Agugliaro, Siel. "From Grinder to Nipper: Home Phonographs and the Making of Italian American Musical Identity." Forthcoming.

Akay, Adnan. "Acoustics of Friction." *Journal of the Acoustical Society of America* 4, no. 111 (2002): 1525–48.

Allen, Aaron S., and Kevin Dawe, eds. *Current Directions in Ecomusicology: Music, Nature, Environment*. New York: Taylor and Francis, 2016.

Andaya, Barbara Watson, and Leonard Y. Andaya. *A History of Malaysia*. Third Edition. London: Palgrave, 2017.

Anonymous. *The Directory and Chronicle for China, Japan, Corea, Indo-China, Straits Settlement, Malay States, Siam, Netherlands, India, Borneo, The Philippines, &c.* Hong Kong: Hong Kong Daily Press, 1889.

Anonymous. *The Shellac Industry*. Namkum, Ranchi: Indian Lac Research Institute, 1936.

Anonymous. *The Singapore and Straits Directory*. Singapore: Singapore and Straits Printing Office, 1896.

Appadurai, Arjun, ed. *The Social Life of Things: Commodities in Cultural Perspective*. Cambridge, UK: Cambridge University Press, 1986.

Attali, Jacques. *Noise: The Political Economy of Music*. Translated by Brian Massumi. Minneapolis: University of Minnesota Press, 1985.

Babbage, Charles. *The Ninth Bridgewater Treatise: A Fragment*. London: John Murray, 1837.

Balsom, Erika. "Instant Failure: Polaroid's Polavision, 1977–1980." *Grey Room* 66 (2017): 6–31.

Bates, Eliot. "The Social Life of Musical Instruments." *Ethnomusicology* 56, no. 3 (2012): 363–95.

Baurle, Ruth. "Caruso's Sin in the Fiendish Park: 'The Possible Was the Improbable and the Improbable the Inevitable.'" *James Joyce Quarterly* 38, no. 1–2 (2000): 125–42.

Bayly, Christopher. *The Birth of the Modern World, 1780–1914: Global Connections and Comparisons*. Oxford, UK: Blackwell Publishing, 2004.

Beauvoir, Simone de. *La Force de l'âge.* Paris: Gallimard, 1960.

Bennett, Jane. *Vibrant Matter: A Political Ecology of Things.* Durham, NC: Duke University Press, 2010.

Berliner, Emile. "The Development of the Talking Machine." *Journal of the Franklin Institute* 176, no. 2 (1913): 189–200.

Berliner, Emile. *Three Addresses*. Washington: n.p., 1913.

Berninghaus, Oscar. *The Story of Barytes: Where and How It Was Found and Its Importance to the World's Industries*. St. Louis, MO: DeLore, 1920.

Best, Stephen M. *The Fugitive's Properties: Law and the Poetics of Possession*. Chicago: University of Chicago Press, 2004.

Bijker, Wiebe E., Thomas P. Hughes, and Trevor Pinch, eds. *The Social Construction of Technological Systems: New Directions in the Sociology and History of Science.* Cambridge, MA: MIT Press, 2012 [1987]. 155–182.

Bijsterveld, Karin, and Trevor Pinch, eds. *The Oxford Handbook to Sound Studies*. Oxford, UK: Oxford University Press, 2011.

Bohlman, Andrea, and Peter McMurray. "Tape; or, Rewinding the Phonographic Regime." *Twentieth-Century Music* 14, no. 1 (2017): 3–24.

Bolig, John. *Caruso Records: A History and Discography*. Littleton, CO: Mainspring Press, 2002.

Borat, Joanna. "A Second Take: Revisiting Interviews with a Different Purpose." *Oral History* 31, no. 1 (2003): 47–53.

Born, Georgina. "On Musical Mediation: Ontology, Technology and Creativity." *Twentieth-Century Music* 2, no. 1 (2005): 7–36.

Born, Georgina, ed. *Music and Digital Media: A Planetary Anthropology*. London: UCL Press, 2022.

Boudreault-Fournier, Alexandrine, and Kyle Devine, eds. *Audible Infrastructures: Music, Sound, Media*. Oxford, UK: Oxford University Press, 2021.

Brockington, John L. *The Sanskrit Epics*. Leiden, Netherlands: Brill, 1998.

Brockway, Lucile H. *Science and Colonial Expansion: The Role of the British Royal Botanic Gardens*. New Haven, CT: Yale University Press, 2002.

Bronfman, Alejandra. *Isles of Noise: Sonic Media in the Caribbean*. Chapel Hill: University of North Carolina Press, 2016.

Bruley, Sue. *The Women and Men of 1926: A Gender and Social History of the General Strike and Miners' Lockout in South Wales*. Cardiff: NBN International, 2010.

Burckhardt, Jacob. "Format und Bild." In *Jacob Burckhardt Werke: Kritische Geam-*

tausgabe, edited by Maurizio Ghelardi and Susanne Müller, vol. 13, pp. 506–16. Munich: C. H. Beck, 2003.

Butcher, John G. *The British in Malaya: The Social History of a European Community in South-East Asia.* Oxford, UK: Oxford University Press, 1979.

Campbell, Jeffrey Y. *Women's Role in Dynamic Forest-Based Small-Scale Enterprise: Case Studies on Uppage and Lacquerware from India.* Rome: Food and Agricultural Organization of the United Nations, 1991. http://www.fao.org/3/x5859e/x5859e00.htm#Contents. Accessed 2 April 2020.

Cammack, Zan. *Ireland's Gramophones: Material Culture, Memory, and Trauma in Irish Modernism.* Oxford, UK: Oxford University Press, 2021.

Carroll, Mark. "'It Is': Reflections on the Role of Music in Sartre's 'La Nausée.'" *Music & Letters* 87 no. 3 (2006): 398–407.

Caruso, Enrico, Jr., and Andrew Farkas. *Enrico Caruso: My Father and My Family.* Portland, OR: Amadeus, 1990.

Casadei, Delia. *Risible: Laughter without Reason and the Reproduction of Sound.* Berkeley: University of California Press, 2024.

Casadei, Delia. "A Voice That Carries." In *Hearing the Crimean War: Wartime Sound and the Unmaking of Sense*, edited by Gavin Williams, 150–74. Oxford, UK: Oxford University Press, 2019.

Ceriani, Davide. "Opera as Social Agent: Fostering Italian Identity at the Metropolitan Opera House during the Early Years of Guilio Gatti-Casazza's Management, 1908–1910." In *Music, Longing, and Belonging: Articulations of the Self and the Other in the Musical Realm*, edited by Magdalena Waligórska, 114–34. Newcastle upon Tyne, UK: Cambridge Scholars, 2013.

Certeau, Michel de. *The Writing of History*. Translated by Tom Conley. New York: Columbia University Press, 1988.

Chakravarthy, R. S. "Watt's Dictionary: A Landmark in the Study of the Economic Plants of India." *Economic Botany* 29, no. 1 (1975): 31–38.

Cherry, Robin. *Catalog: The Illustrated History of Mail Order Shopping.* Princeton, NJ: Princeton Architectural Press, 2008.

Christensen, Kimberly A. "Does Information Really Want to Be Free? Indigenous Knowledge Systems and the Question of Openness." *International Journal of Communication* 6 (2012): 2870–93.

Chude-Sokei, Louis. *The Last "Darky": Bert Williams, Black-on-Black Minstrelsy, and the African Diaspora*. Durham, NC: Duke University Press, 2006.

Cimini, Amy, and Jairo Moreno. "Inexhaustible Sound and Fiduciary Aurality." *Boundary 2* 43, no. 1 (2016): 5–41.

Clarence-Smith, William Gervase. *The Economics of the Indian Ocean Slave Trade in the Nineteenth Century*. London: Routledge, 2013.

Crandall, Elizabeth Brownell. *Shellac: A Story of Yesterday, Today and Tomorrow*. Chicago: Day, 1924.

Davies, James Q. "Elijah's Nature." *19th Century Music* 45, no. 1 (2021): 49–64.

Davies, James Q. *Romantic Anatomies of Performance*. Berkeley: University of California Press, 2014.

Davis, Heather. "Toxic Progeny: The Plastisphere and Other Queer Futures." *philoSOPHIA* 5, no. 1 (2015): 231–50.

Deborah Kapchan, ed. *Theorizing Sound Writing*. Middletown, CT: Wesleyan University Press, 2017.

Defoe, Daniel. *A New Voyage around the World by a Course Never Sailed Before; Being a Voyage Undertaken by Some Merchants, Who Afterwards Proposed the Setting Up an East-India Company in Flanders*. London: Bettesworth and Mears, 1725.

Deleuze, Gilles. *Différence et Répétition*. Paris: Presses Universitaires de France, 1968.

Denning, Michael, and Gary Tomlinson. "Cantologies," *Representations* 154, no. 1 (2021): 113–28.

Denning, Michael. *The Cultural Front: The Laboring of American Culture in the Twentieth Century*. London and New York: Verso, 1997.

Denning, Michael. *Noise Uprising: The Audiopolitics of a World Musical Revolution*. London and Brooklyn, NY: Verso, 2015.

Devine, Kyle. "Decomposed: The Political Ecology of Music." *Popular Music* 34, no. 3 (2015): 367–89.

Devine, Kyle. *Decomposed: The Political Ecology of Music*. Cambridge, MA: MIT Press, 2019.

Donald, James. *Some of These Days: Black Stars, Jazz Aesthetics, and Modernist Culture*. Oxford, UK: Oxford University Press, 2015.

Eastaugh, Nicholas, Valentine Walsh, and Tracey Chaplin. *Pigment Compendium: A Dictionary of Optical Microscopy of Historical Pigments*. Oxford, UK: Elsevier, 2008.

Eisenberg, Evan. *The Recording Angel: Music, Records and Culture from Aristotle to Zappa*. Second Edition. New Haven, CT: Yale University Press, 2005.

Ernst, Wolfgang. *Sonic Time Machines: Explicit Sound, Sirenic Voices and Implicit Sonicity*. Amsterdam: Amsterdam University Press, 2016.

Falletti, Franca, Renato Meucci, and Gabriele Rossi Rognoni. *Marvels of Sound and Beauty: Italian Baroque Musical Instruments*. Milan: Giunti, 2007.

Feld, Steven "Pygmy POP: A Genealogy of Schizophonic Mimesis," *Yearbook for Traditional Music* 28 (1996): 1–35.

Fisher, Daniel. *The Voice and Its Doubles: Music and Media in Northern Australia*. Durham, NC: Duke University Press, 2017.

Francis, Hwyel, and David Smith. *The Fed: A History of the South Wales Miners in the Twentieth Century*. London: Lawrence and Wishart, 1980.

Frasca, Simona. *Italian Birds of Passage: The Diaspora of Neapolitan Musicians in New York*. New York: Palgrave, 2014.

Friedel, Robert Douglas. *Pioneer Plastic: The Making and Selling of Celluloid*. Madison: University of Wisconsin Press, 1983.

Fry, Andy. *Paris Blues: African American Music and French Popular Culture, 1920–1960*. Chicago: University of Chicago Press, 2014.

Fucito, Salvatore, and Barnet J. Beyer. *Caruso and the Art of Singing, Including Caru-*

so's Vocal Exercises and His Practical Advice to Students and Teachers of Singing. New York: Frederick A. Stokes, 1922.

Fugazzotto, Giuliana. *Sta terra nun fa pi mia: I dischi a 78 giri e la vita in America degli emigranti italiani nel primo Novecento*. Udine, Italy: Nota, 2010.

Gabaccia, Donna R. *Foreign Relations: American Immigration in Global Perspective*. Princeton, NJ: Princeton Univeristy Press, 2012.

Gabrys, Jennifer, Gay Hawkins, and Mike Michael, eds. *Accumulation: The Material Politics of Plastic*. London: Routledge, 2013.

Gallope, Michael. *Deep Refrains: Music, Philosophy, and the Ineffable*. Chicago: University of Chicago Press, 2017.

Garber, Michael. "'Some of These Days' and the Study of the Great American Songbook." *Journal of the Society for American Music* 4, no. 2 (2010): 175–214.

Gelatt, Roland. *The Fabulous Phonograph: From Edison to Stereo*. New York: Appleton Century Crofts, 1966.

Gibson, A. J. "The Story of Lac." *Journal of the Royal Society of Arts* 90, no. 4611 (April 1942): 319–35.

Gitelman, Lisa. *Always Already New*. Cambridge, MA: MIT Press, 2008.

Goh Chor Boon. *Technology and Entrepot Colonialism in Singapore, 1819–1940*. Singapore: Institute of Southeast Asian Studies, 2013.

Gopal, Priyamvada. *Insurgent Empire: Anticolonial Resistance and British Dissent*. London: Verso, 2019.

Grimké, Francis James. "The Signs of a Better Future for the American Negro: Extracts from His Sermon on the Race Problem." In *Twentieth Century Negro Literature: Or a Cyclopedia of Thought on Vital Topics Relating to the American Negro*, edited by Daniel Wallace Culp, 427–33. Toronto, Naperville, IL, and Atlanta: J. L. Nichols, 1902.

Grimké, Francis James. *The Works of Francis J. Grimké*, vol. 1. Edited by Carter G. Woodson. Washington: Associated Publishers, 1942.

Gronow, Pekka, and Ilpo Saunio. *An International History of the Recording Industry*. Translated by Christopher Moseley. London: Cassell, 1999.

Guglielmo, Jennifer, and Salvatore Salerno, eds. *Are Italians White? How Race Is Made in America*. New York: Taylor & Francis, 2003.

Guha, Ramchandra. *The Unquiet Woods: Ecological Change and Peasant Resistance in the Himalaya*. Berkeley: University of California Press, 2000.

Guha, Ranajit. *Elementary Aspects of Peasant Insurgency in Colonial India*. Durham, NC: Duke University Press, 1999.

Gupta, Uma Das, ed. *Science and Modern India: An Institutional History, ca. 1784–1947*, vol. 15, pt. 4. Delhi: Pearson Longman, 2011.

Hall, J. Lincoln, and Irvin H. Mack. *Boundless Love: For Sunday Schools and Gospel Meetings*. Philadelphia: Hall Mack, 1896.

Hall, Stuart. "Encoding/Decoding." In *Culture, Media, Language: Working Papers in Cultural Studies, 1972–79*, edited by Stuart Hall, Dorothy Hobson, and Andrew Lowe. Birmingham, UK: Centre for Contemporary Cultural Studies, 1980.

Hamberlin, Larry. *Tin Pan Opera: Operatic Novelty Songs in the Ragtime Era*. Oxford, UK: Oxford University Press, 2011.

Harlow, C. M., and H. A. F. Lindsay. *The Indian Forest Records: Report on Lac and Shellac*. Allahabad, India: Pioneer Press, 1921.

Harrison, George R. "From Shellac to Symphony: New Perfections in Storing and Re-Creating Sound." *Technology Review* 41, no. 1 (1938): 17–20.

Harrison-Kahan, Lori. *The White Negress: Literature, Minstrelsy, and the Black-Jewish Imaginary*. New Brunswick, NJ: Rutgers University Press, 2011.

Hemming, Emile. *Molded Electrical Insulation and Plastics*. New York: Ward Clausen, 1914.

Hemming, Emile. *Plastics and Molded Electrical Insulation*. Chicago: Chemical Catalog Company, 1923.

Henson, Karen. "Au début de l'enregistrement sonore (1877–1906): Exotisme, opéra et science-fiction." In *L'altérité en spectacle, 1789–1918*, edited by Nathalie Coutelet and Isabelle Moindroit, 331–42. Rennes, France: Presses universitaires de Rennes, 2015.

Herbert, Trevor, and Helen Barlow. *Music & the British Military in the Long Nineteenth Century*. Oxford, UK: Oxford University Press, 2013.

Hicks, Edward. *Shellac: Its Uses and Applications*. New York: Chemical Publishing, 1961.

Hoffman, Frank. *Encyclopedia of Recorded Sound*. Oxford, UK: Taylor and Francis, 2004.

Horning, Susan Schmidt. *Chasing Sound: Technology, Culture, and the Art of Studio Recording from Edison to the LP*. Baltimore: Johns Hopkins University Press, 2013.

Husserl, Edmund. *The Phenomenology of Internal Time-Consciousness*. Edited by Martin Heidegger; translated by James S. Churchill. Bloomington: Indiana University Press, 2019.

Imms, A. D., and N. C. Chatterjee. *Indian Forest Memoirs: On the Structure and Biology of Tachardia lacca, Kerr., with Observations on Certain Insects Predaceous or Parasitic upon It*. Calcutta: Superintendent Government Printing, India, 1915.

Indicator (pseudonym). "The Ingenuous Amateur and the Sine Qua Non Opposite." *The Gramophone* 2, no. 3 (1924): 94.

Jameson, Frederic. *The Political Unconscious: Narrative as Socially Symbolic Act*. Ithaca, NY: Cornell University Press, 1981.

Jazeel, Tariq. "Singularity: A Manifesto for Incomparable Geographies." *Singapore Journal of Tropical Geography* 40, no. 1 (2019): 5–21.

Jewitt, Sarah. *Environment, Knowledge and Gender: Local Development in India's Jharkhand*. Aldershot, UK: Ashgate, 2002.

Jones, Andrew F. *Yellow Music: Media Culture and Colonial Modernity in the Chinese Jazz Age*. Durham, NC: Duke University Press, 2001.

Jones, Geoffrey. "The Gramophone Company: An Anglo-American Multinational." *Business History Review* 59, no. 1 (1985): 76–100.

Jones, Geoffrey. *Multinationals and Global Capitalism: From the Nineteenth to the Twenty-First Century*. Oxford, UK: Oxford University Press, 2005.

Joshi, G. N. "A Concise History of the Phonography Industry in India." *Popular Music* 7, no. 2 (1988): 147–56.

Judaken, Jonathan. *Jean-Paul Sartre and the Jewish Question: Anti-Semitism and the Politics of The French Intellectual.* Lincoln: University of Nebraska Press, 2006.

Jung, Uli, and Martin Loiperdinger, eds. *Geschichte des dokumentarischen Films in Deutschland: Kaiserreich 1895–1918*. Stuttgart, Germany: Reclam, 2005.

Kabra, Kamal Nayan. *Dependence and Dominance: Political Economy of a Tribal Commodity*. New Delhi: Indian Institute of Public Administration, 1983.

Key, Pierre Van Rensselaer, and Bruno Zirato. *Enrico Caruso: A Biography*. Boston: Little, Brown, 1922.

Kinnear, Michael S. *The Gramophone Company's First Indian Recordings, 1899–1908*. Bombay: Popular Prakashan, 1994.

Koenigsberg, Allen, ed. *The Patent History of the Phonograph, 1877–1912: A Source Book*. New York: APM Press, 1990.

Kozarski, Richard. *An Evening's Entertainment: The Age of the Silent Feature Picture, 1915–1928*. Berkeley: University of California Press, 1990.

LaBelle, Brandon. *Lexicon of the Mouth: Poetics and Politics of Voice and the Oral Imaginary*. London: Bloomsbury, 2014.

LaCapra, Dominick. "Sartre and the Question of Biography." *French Review* 55, no. 7 (1982): 22–56.

Lahmon, W. T. *Raising Cain: Blackface Performance from Jim Crow to Hip Hop*. Cambridge, MA: Harvard University Press, 1998.

Laird, Ross. *Moanin' Low: A Discography of Female Popular Vocal Recordings, 1920–1933*. Westport, CT: Greenwood, 1996.

Latour, Bruno. "Perspectivism: 'Type' or 'Bomb'?" *Anthropology Today* 25, no. 2 (2009): 21–22.

Lott, Eric. *Love and Theft: Blackface Minstrelsy and the American Working Class*. Second Edition. Oxford, UK: Oxford University Press, 2013.

MacKay, Nancy. "Memories and Reflections, the Singapore Experience: Documenting a Nation's History through Oral History" (review). *Oral History Review* 35, no. 2 (2008): 220–22.

Malabou, Catherine. "The End of Writing? Grammatology and Plasticity." *The European Legacy* 12, no. 4 (2007): 431–41.

Malabou, Catherine. *Ontology of the Accident: An Essay on Destructive Plasticity*. Translated by Carolyn Shread. London: Polity Press, 2012.

Marafioti, Pasqual Mario. *Caruso's Method of Voice Production: The Scientific Culture of the Voice*. New York: Appleton, 1922.

Martland, Peter. "Caruso's First Recordings: Myth and Reality." *Association for Recorded Sound Collections Journal* 25, no. 2 (1994): 192–201.

Martland, Peter. *Recording History: The British Record Industry, 1888–1931*. Plymouth, UK: Scarecrow Press, 2013.

Matusky, Patricia, and Tan Sooi Beng. *The Music of Malaysia: The Classical, Folk and Syncretic Traditions*. Second Edition. Oxford, UK: Taylor and Francis, 2017.

Mauss, Marcel. "Les techniques du corps." *Journal de psychologie normale et pathologique* (1935): 271–93.

Maxwell, Richard, ed. *The Routledge Companion to Labor and Media*. London: Routledge, 2015.

McCallum, Jenny. "Conflict and Compromise over Processional Sound in 19th-Century Singapore." *Indonesia and the Malay World* 45 (2017): 315–33.

McLane, Betsy A. *A New History of Documentary Film, Second Edition*, 73–78. London: Continuum, 2012.

Meikle, Jeffrey. *American Plastic: A Cultural History*. New Brunswick, NJ: Rutgers University Press, 1995.

Melillo, Edward. "Global Entomologies: Insects, Empires, and the 'Synthetic Age' in World History." *Past & Present* 223 (2014): 233–70.

Merrifield, Mrs. *Original Treatises Dating from the XIIth to XVIIIth Centuries on the Art of Painting, Oil, Miniature, Mosaic and on Glass [. . .]*, vol. 2. London: John Murray, 1849.

Miller, Toby, and Richard Maxwell. *Greening the Media*. Oxford, UK: Oxford University Press, 2012.

Mishra, Y. D., and P. Kumar. "Lac Culture." In Omkar, ed., *Industrial Entomology*, 109–11. Singapore: Springer, 2017.

Mitchell, Ogilvie. *The Talking Machine Industry*. London: Pitman, 1922.

Moore, Jerrold Northrop. *A Matter of Records*. New York: Taplinger, 1977.

Moreno, Jairo. "Imperial Aurality: Jazz, The Archive, and U.S. Empire." In *Audible Empire: Music, Global Politics, Critique*, edited by Ronald Radano and Tejumola Olaniyan, 135–60. Durham, NC: Duke University Press.

Morgan, Nick. "The National Gramophonic Society." PhD thesis, University of Sheffield, 2013.

Morrison, Matthew D. "Blacksound." In *The Oxford Handbook to Western Music and Philosophy*, edited by Tomás McAuley, Nanette Nielsen, Jerrold Levinson, and Ariana Phillips-Hutton, 555–78. Oxford, UK: Oxford University Press, 2020.

Morrison, Matthew D. "Race, Blacksound and the Remaking of Musicological Discourse." *Journal of the American Musicological Society* 72, no. 3 (2019): 781–823.

Moses, Montrose J. *The Life of Heinrich Conried*. New York: Thomas Y. Crowell, 1916.

Mouchon, Jean-Pierre. "Particolarità fisiche e fonetiche della voce incisa di Caruso." In *Caruso*, edited by Riccardo Vaccaro, 36–47. Naples: Edizioni Scientifiche Italiane, 1995.

Mueggler, Erik. "Bodies Real and Virtual: Joseph Rock and Enrico Caruso in the Sino-Tibetan Borderlands." *Comparative Studies in History and Society* 53, no. 1 (2011): 6–37.

Murdoch, Iris. *Sartre: Romantic Rationalist*. New Haven, CT: Yale University Press, 1953.

Murrells, Joseph. *The Book of Golden Discs*. Revised edition. London: Barrie and Jenkins, 1978.

Muscio, Giuliana. *Napoli / New York / Hollywood: Film between Italy and the United States*. New York: Fordham University Press, 2019.

Nien Yuan Cheng. "'This Is My Doodle': Non-Participation, Performance, and the Singapore Memory Project." *Performance Paradigm* 14 (2018): 64–86.

Norris, Dorothy. *Lac and the Indian Lac Research Institute*. Calcutta: Criterion, 1934.

Novak, David, and Matt Sakakeeney, eds. *Keywords in Sound*. Durham, NC: Duke University Press.

Nowatzki, Robert. *Representing African Americans in Transatlantic Abolitionism and Blackface Minstrelsy*. Baton Rouge: Louisiana State University Press, 2010.

Ochoa Gautier, Ana María. "Acoustic Multinaturalism, the Value of Nature, and the Nature of Music in Ecomusicology." *Boundary 2* 43, no. 1 (2016): 107–41.

Oliver, Laurence. "Shellac." *Nash's Pall Mall Magazine* 86, no. 451 (1930): 32–35, 107–12.

Page, Thomas Walker, et al. *Barytes, Barium Chemical, and Lithopone Industries*. Washington: Government Printing Office, 1920.

Parker, Theodor. *The Works of Theodor Parker*, vol. 1. London: Barker, 1863.

Parthasarathi, Vibodh. "Not Just Mad Englishmen and a Dog: The Colonial Tuning of 'Music on Record,' 1900–1908." Working paper, Centre for Culture, Media and Governance, Jamia Millia Islamia, New Delhi (July 2007), 1–30.

Parthasarathi, Vibodh. "The Public Sphere of Marketed Sound: The Business of Early Recorded Music in India." In *Music, Modernity and Publicness in India*, edited by Tejaswini Niranjana. New Delhi: Oxford University Press, 2020.

Peluso, Nancy Lee. "What's Nature Got to Do with It? A Situated Historical Perspective on Socio-Natural Commodities." *Development and Change* 43, no. 1 (2012): 79–104.

Pesce, Anita. "The Neapolitan Sound Goes Around: Mechanical Music Instruments, Talking Machines, and Neapolitan Song, 1850–1925." In *Neapolitan Postcards: The Canzone Napoletana as Transnational Subject*, edited by Goffredo Plastino and Joseph Sciorra, 45–72. London: Rowman and Littlefield, 2016.

Picker, John. *Victorian Soundscapes*. Oxford, UK: Oxford University Press, 2003.

Pickering, Michael. *Blackface Minstrelsy in Britain*. Aldershot, UK: Ashgate, 2008.

Piekut, Benjamin, and Jason Stanyek. "Deadness: Technologies of the Intermundane." *TDR / The Drama Review* 54, no. 1 (2010): 4–38.

Pignarre, Philippe, and Isabelle Stengers. *Capitalist Sorcery: Breaking the Spell*. Translated by Andrew Goffey. New York: Palgrave Macmillan, 2011.

Prato, Paolo. "The Good, the Bad and the Ugly: Transatlantic Stereotypes, 1880s–1950s." In *Neapolitan Postcards: The Canzone Napoletana as Transnational Subject:*, edited by Goffredo Plastino and Joseph Sciorra, 183–208. London: Rowman and Littlefield, 2016.

Radano, Ronald, and Tejumola Olaniyan, eds. *Audible Empire: Music, Global Politics, Critique*. Durham, NC: Duke University Press, 2016.

Raj, Kapil. "Beyond Postcolonialism . . . and Postpositivism: Circulation and the Global History of Science." *Isis* 104, no. 2 (2013): 337–46.

Raman, Anantanarayanan. "Discovery of *Kerria lacca* (Insecta: Hemiptera: Coccoidea), the Lac Insect, in India in the Late 18th Century." *Current Science* 106, no. 6 (2014): 886–90.

Robbins, Bruce. *The Beneficiary*. Durham, NC: Duke University Press, 2017.

Rodríguez, Eva Moreda, and Elodie A. Roy, eds. *Phonographic Encounters: Mapping Transnational Cultures of Sound, 1890–1945*. Oxford, UK: Routledge, 2022.

Rogin, Michael. *Blackface, White Noise: Jewish Immigrants in the Hollywood Melting Pot.* Berkeley: University of California Press, 1996.

Roy, Elodie A. "Another Side of Shellac: Cultural and Natural Cycles of the Gramophone Discs." In *Audible Infrastructures: Music, Sound, Media*, edited by Kyle Devine and Alexandrine Boudreault-Fournier, 209–28. Oxford, UK: Oxford University Press, 2021.

Roy, Elodie A. *Media, Materiality and Memory: Grounding the Groove*. Oxford, UK: Ashgate, 2015.

Roy, Elodie A. "The Sheen of Shellac: From Reflective Material to Self-Reflective Medium." In *Materials, Practices, and Politics of Shine in Modern Art and Popular Culture*, edited by Antje Krause-Wahl, Petra Löffler, and Änne Söll, 105–22. London: Bloomsbury, 2021.

Roy, Elodie A. "Worn Grooves: Affective Connectivity, Mobility and Recorded Sound in the First World War." *Media History* 24 no. 1 (2016): 26–45.

Sabin, Alvah Horton. *The Industrial and Artistic Technology of Paint and Varnish, Second Edition*. New York: Wiley and Sons, 1917.

Sampath, Vikram. *"My Name is Gauhar Jaan!" The Life and Times of a Musician*. New Delhi: Rupa, 2010.

Sartre, Jean-Paul. *Being and Nothingness: An Essay in Phenomenological Ontology*. Translated by Sarah Richmond. New York: Washington Square Press, 2018.

Sartre, Jean-Paul. "Black Orpheus." *Massachusetts Review* 6, no. 1 (1964–65): 13–52.

Sartre, Jean-Paul. *Colonialism and Neo-Colonialism*. Translated by Azzedine Haddour, Steve Brewer, and Terry McWilliams. London: Routledge, 2001.

Sartre, Jean-Paul. *Nausea*. Translated by Lloyd Alexander. New York: New Directions, 2007.

Sartre, Jean-Paul. *La Nausée*. Paris: Gallimard, 1938.

Sartre, Jean-Paul. *The Wall, and Other Stories*. Translated by Lloyd Alexander. New York: New Directions, 1948.

Schafer, R. Murray. *The New Soundscape: A Handbook for the Modern Music Teacher*. Scarborough, ON: Berandol Music, 1969.

Schiebinger, Londa, and Claudia Swan, eds. *Colonial Botany: Science, Commerce, and Politics in the Early Modern World*. Philadelphia: University of Pennsylvania Press, 2005.

Schneider, Alexandra, Axel Volmar, and Marek Jancovic, eds. *Format Matters: Standards, Practices, and Politics in Media Cultures*. Lüneburg, Germany: Meson Press, 2020.

Scripture, Edmund Wheeler. "The Curves of Caruso." *Musical Times* 65, no. 976 (1 June 1924): 517–19.

Scripture, Edmund Wheeler. "How the Voice Looks." *Century Illustrated Monthly Magazine* 64 (May–October 1902): 148–54.

Scripture, Edmund Wheeler. *Researches in Experimental Phonetics: The Study of Speech Curves*. Washington: Carnegie Institute of Washington, 1906.

Segrave, Kerry. *Beware the Masher: Sexual Harassment in American Public Places, 1880–1930*. Jefferson, NC: McFarland, 2014.

Sen, Sudipta. *Empire of Free Trade: The East India Company and the Making of the Colonial Marketplace*. Philadelphia: University of Pennsylvania Press, 1998.

Seng, L. K. "Voices of Survivors: Oral History and the Great Depression in Singapore." In *Reflections and Interpretation: Oral History Centre, 25th Anniversary Publication*, edited by Fiona Hu, 212–26. Singapore: National Heritage Board, 2005.

Senici, Emanuele. "Delirious Hopes: Napoleonic Milan and the Rise of Modern Italian Operatic Criticism," *Cambridge Opera Journal* 27, no. 2 (2015): 97–127.

Serra, Ilaria. *The Imagined Immigrant: Images of Italian Emigration to the United States between 1890 and 1924*. Madison, WI: Rosemont, 2009.

Shah, Alpa. *In the Shadows of the State: Indigenous Politics, Environmentalism and Insurgency in Jharkhand, India*. Durham, NC: Duke University Press, 2010.

Shah, Alpa. *Nightmarch: A Journey into the Naxal Heartlands*. Noida, India: HarperCollins, 2018.

Shope, Bradley G. *American Popular Music and Britain's Raj*. Rochester, NY: University of Rochester Press, 2016.

Silvers, Michael B. *Voices of Drought: The Politics of Music and Environment in Northeastern Brazil*. Chicago: University of Illinois Press, 2018.

Silverstein, Shayna. "Michael Denning, Noise Uprising: The Audiopolitics of a World Musical Revolution." *Twentieth-Century Music* 14, no. 1 (2017): 164–68.

Simone, Maria de. "Sophie Tucker, Racial Hybridity and Interracial Relations in American Vaudeville." *Theatre Research International* 44, no. 2 (2019): 153–70.

Sivasundaram, Sujit. "Sciences and the Global: On Methods, Questions and Theory." *Isis* 101, no. 1 (2010): 146–58.

Small, Christopher. *Musicking: The Meanings of Performing and Listening*. Middletown, CT: Wesleyan University Press, 1998.

Smith, Jacob. *Eco-Sonic Media*. Berkeley: University of California Press, 2015.

Southern, Eileen. *Biographical Dictionary of Afro-American and African Musicians*. Westport, CT: Greenwood Press, 1982.

Sreenivasaya, Motnahalli. "Antiquity of Lac and Superstitions Connected with It." *Current Science* 4, no. 6 (1935): 390–91.

Sreenivasaya, Motnahalli. "The Industrial Outlook: Crisis in the Lac Industry." *Current Science* 1, no. 4 (1932): 111–13.

Steingo, Gavin. *Kwaito's Promise: Music and the Aesthetics of Freedom in South Africa*. Chicago: University of Chicago Press, 2016.

Steingo, Gavin, and Jim Sykes, eds. *Remapping Sound Studies*. Durham, NC: Duke University Press, 2019.

Stengers, Isabelle. *Cosmopolitics*. Vol. 2. Translated by Robert Bononno. Minneapolis: University of Minnesota Press, 2011.

Sterne, Jonathan. *The Audible Past: Cultural Origins of Sound Reproduction*. Durham, NC: Duke University Press, 2003.

Sterne, Jonathan. *MP3: The Meaning of a Format*. Durham, NC: Duke University Press, 2012.

Sterne, Jonathan. "'What Do We Want?' 'Materiality!' 'When Do We Want It?' 'Now!'" In *Media Technologies: Essays on Communication, Materiality and Society*, edited by Tarleton Gillespie, Pablo J. Boczkowski, and Kirsten A. Foot, 119–28. Cambridge, MA: MIT Press, 2014.

Stockham, Thomas, et al. "Blind Deconvolution through Digital Signal Processing." *Proceedings of the International Electrical and Electronics Engineers* 63, no. 4 (1975): 678–92.

Stoever, Jennifer Lynn. *The Sonic Color Line: Race and the Cultural Politics of Listening*. New York: New York University Press, 2016.

Suisman, David. *Selling Sounds: The Commercial Revolution in American Popular Music*. Cambridge, MA: Harvard University Press, 2009.

Suzuki, Hideaki. *Slave Trade Profiteers in the Indian Ocean: Suppression and Resistance in the Nineteenth Century*. New York: Palgrave, 2017.

Sykes, Jim. "Towards a Malayan Indian Sonic Geography: Sound and Social Relations in Colonial Singapore." *Journal of Southeast Asian Studies* 46, no. 3 (2015): 485–513.

Symes, Colin. "From Tomorrow's Eve to High Fidelity: Novel Responses to the Gramophone in Twentieth Century Literature." *Popular Music* 24, no. 2 (2005): 193–206.

Symes, Colin. *Setting the Record Straight: A Material History of Classical Recording*. Middletown, CT: Wesleyan University Press, 2004.

Tackley, Catherine. *The Evolution of Jazz in Britain, 1880–1935*. London: Routledge, 2005.

Tan Sooi Beng. "Cosmopolitan Identities: Evolving Musical Cultures of the Straits-Born Chinese of Pre–World War II Malaya," *Ethnomusicology Forum* 26, no. 1 (2016): 35–57.

Tan Sooi Beng. "Negotiating 'His Master's Voice': Gramophone Music and Cosmopolitan Modernity in British Malaya in the 1930s and Early 1940s." *Bijdragen tot de Taal-, Land- en Volkenkunde: Journal of the Huamnities and Social Sciences of Southeast Asia* 169 (2013): 457–94.

Tan Sooi Beng. "The 78 RPM Record Industry in Malaya Prior to World War II." *Asian Music* 28, no. 1 (1996–97): 1–41.

Taussig, Michael. *Mimesis and Alterity: A Particular History of the Senses*. London and New York: Routledge, 1993.

Tavernier, Jean-Baptiste. *Travels in India.*, vol. 2. Translated by Valentine Ball. Cambridge, UK: Cambridge University Press, 2012.

Taylor, Timothy. "The Commodification of Music at the Dawn of 'Mechanical Music.'" *Ethnomusicology* 51, no. 2 (2007): 281–305.

Taylor, Timothy D., Mark Katz, and Tony Grajeda, eds. *Music, Sound and Technology in America: A Documentary History of Early Phonograph, Cinema, and Radio*. Durham, NC: Duke University Press, 2012.

Théberge, Paul. *Any Sound You Can Imagine: Making Music / Consuming Technology*. Hanover, NH: Wesleyan University Press, 1997.

Thomas, Gwyn. *The Alone to the Alone with The Dark Philosophers*. Carmarthen, UK: Golden Grove House, 1988.

Thomas, Gwyn. *The Dark Philosophers*. Boston: Little, Brown, 1946.

Thomas, Gwyn. *Die Liebe des Reverend Emmanuel*. Translated by L. Fankhauser. Zürich: Büchergilde Gutenberg, 1951.

Thomas, Gwyn. *Gazooka: A Short Novel and Twelve Stories in Which (for the Form Suits Him to Perfection) We Get the Quintessential Gwyn Thomas*. London: Victor Gollancz, 1957.

Thompson, Emily. *The Soundscape of Modernity: Architectural Acoustics and the Culture of Listening in America, 1900–1933*. Cambridge, MA: MIT Press, 2002.

Titsworth, William E. *The Story of Shellac*. New York: William Zinsser, 1928 [1913].

Tomlinson, Gary. *A Million Years of Music: The Emergence of Human Modernity*. Cambridge, MA: Zone Books, 2015.

Tong Soon Lee. *Chinese Street Opera in Singapore*. Chicago: University of Illinois Press, 2009.

Tsing, Anna Lowenhaupt. *Friction: An Ethnography of Global Connection*. Princeton, NJ: Princeton University Press, 2005.

Tucker, Sophie, and Dorothy Giles. *Some of These Days: The Autobiography of Sophie Tucker*. New York: Country Life Press, 1945.

Uhde, Jan, and Yvonne Ng Uhde. *Latent Images: Film in Singapore*. Second Edition. Singapore: National University of Singapore Press, 2009.

Vágnerová, Lucie. "'Nimble Fingers' in Electronic Music: Rethinking Sound through Neo-Colonial Labour." *Organized Sound* 22 (2017): 250–58.

Van Drie, Melissa. "Hearing through the Théâtrophone: Sonically Constructed Spaces and Embodied Listening in the Late Nineteenth-Century French Theatre." *Sound Effects* 5, no. 1 (2016): 73–90.

Vellon, Peter G. *A Great Conspiracy against Our Race: Italian Immigrant Newspapers and the Construction of Whiteness in the Early Twentieth Century*. New York: New York University Press, 2014.

Verman, Lal C. "The London Shellac Research Bureau." *Current Science* 5, no. 1 (1936): 41.

Viveiros de Castro, Eduardo. *Cannibal Metaphysics: For a Post-Structural Anthropology*. Translated by Peter Skafish. Minneapolis: Univocal, 2014.

Volgsten, Ulrik. "A Technology and Its Vicissitudes: Playing the Gramophone in Sweden, 1903–1945." *Popular Music* 38, no. 2 (2019): 219–36.

The Voyages and Travells of the Ambassadors sent by Frederick Duke of Holstein [. . .] Containing a Compleat History of Muscovy, Tartary, Persia. [. . .] Whereto Are Added the Travels of John Albert de Mandelslo (a Gentleman Belonging to the Embassy) from Persia into the East Indies. Second Edition. London: John Starkey and Thomas Bassett, 1669.

Walker, Percy H., and Lawrence L. Steele. *Shellac*. Washington: Bureau of Standards, US Department of Commerce, 1922.

Walton, Benjamin. "Quirk Shame." *Representations* 132, no. 1 (2015): 121–29.

Watt, George, ed. *The Commercial Products of India*. London: John Murray, 1908.

Watt, George, ed. *A Dictionary of the Economic Products of India*. Six vols. Calcutta: Superintendent of Government Printing, 1889–93.

Watt, George, ed. *Economic Products of India Exhibited at the Calcutta International Exhibition, 1883–84*. Vol. 1. Calcutta: Superintendent of Government Printing, 1883.

Webb, Marianne. *Lacquer: Technology and Conservation; A Comprehensive Guide to Technology and Conservation of Asian and European Lacquer*. Oxford, UK: Butterworth Heinemann, 2000.

Weber, James N. *The Talking Machine: The Advertising History of the Berliner Gramophone and Victor Talking Machine*. New York: Adio, 1997.

Williams, Raymond. *Culture and Society, 1780–1950*. London: Chatto and Windus, 1958.

Williams, Raymond. *Marxism and Literature*. Oxford, UK: Oxford University Press, 1977.

Willson, Flora. "Classic Staging: Pauline Viardot and the 1859 *Orphée* Revival." *Cambridge Opera Journal* 22, no. 3 (2010): 301–26.

Wilson, Jen. *Freedom Music: Wales, Emancipation and Jazz, 1850–1950*. Cardiff: University of Wales Press, 2019.

Woodward, N. "Why Did South Wales Miners Have High Mortality? Evidence from the Mid-Twentieth Century." *Welsh History Review / Cylchgrawn Hanes Cymru* 20, no. 1 (2000): 116–41.

Yampolsky, Philip B. "Music and Media in the Dutch East Indies: Gramophone Records and Radio in the Late Colonial Era, 1903–1942." PhD dissertation, University of Washington, 2013.

Ybarra, Thomas Russell. *Caruso: The Man of Naples and the Voice of Gold*. New York: Harcourt Brace, 1953.

Yeoh, Brenda S. A. *Contesting Space in Colonial Singapore: Power Relations and the Built Environment*. Singapore: Singapore University Press, 2003.

Zahavi, Dan. "Shame and the Exposed Self." In *Reading Sartre: On Phenomenology and Existentialism*, edited by Jonathan Webber. London: Routledge, 2011.

Zimmerman, Eugenia Noik. "'Some of These Days': Sartre's *Petite Phrase*." *Contemporary Literature* 11, no. 3 (1970): 375–81.

NEWSPAPERS AND MAGAZINES

"Bargoed Carnival: Town en Fete in Aid of Canteen Fund." *Merthyr Express*, 19 June 1926, p. 20.
"Best Voices for Records: A Laboratory Expert Discants on the Making of Good Records." *Talking Machine World*, 15 November 1906, p. 9.
"The Bioscope." *Straits Times*, 15 October 1902, p. 5.
Bizet, René. "Musique: Disques." *L'Intransigeant*, 4 May 1927, p. 5.
"Career of Caruso a Long Crescendo." *New York Times*, 3 August 1921, p. 6.
"Carnival at Abertillery: Successful Relief Fund Function," *South Wales Gazette*, 23 July 1926, p. 13.
"Caruso Convicted but Will Appeal." *New York Times*, 24 November 1906, p. 1.
"Caruso in Court; Case Not Ended." *New York Times*, 22 November 1906, p. 1.
"Caruso May Sue City if Case Is Not Approved." *New York Times*, 20 November 1906, p. 3.
"Caruso on Stand." *Washington Post*, 22 November 1906, pp. 1 and 4.
"Caruso Records Are Imperishable." *New York Times*, 3 August 1921, p. 3.
"Characteristic Photographs of Caruso: Caruso's Glorious Voice Kept for Posterity by Phonograph." *San Francisco Chronicle*, 3 August 1921, p. 7.
"Claim for Wages." *Eastern Daily Mail and Straits Morning Advertiser*, 21 September 1907, p. 3.
Collin, Gladys M. "Women and the Gramophone." *The Gramophone* 3, no. 5 (October 1925): 247.
"Conried Aids Caruso." *Washington Post*, 20 November 1906, p. 3.
"Defender Forum," *Chicago Defender*, 1 September 1934, p. 14.
"Defender Forum." *Chicago Defender*, 7 September 1929, p. A1.
"Editorial." *Glamorgan Advertiser & Weekly News for the Llynfi, Ogmore, Garw and Avon Valleys* (Maesteg), 6 June 1919, p. 4.
Emms, Leonard F. "A Working Man's Choice of Records." *The Gramophone* 3, no. 5 (October 1925): 228.
"Free Concert: Cardiff Instrumental Trio at Maesteg." *Glamorgan Advertiser*, 26 April 1929, p. 5.
"Gramophone Notes." *Musical Times* 62, no. 935 (1921): 40–42.
Gweirydd (pseudonym). "Colofn Y Cymro: Carnivaliaeth yn y Rhondda." *Pontypridd Observer*. 31 July 1926, p. 7.
"Hall of Fame." *Vanity Fair*, December 1916, p. 52.
"'I Thought You Were a Negro.'" *Chicago Defender*, 17 April 1937, p. 21.
"Jazz Procession." *Merthyr Express*, 29 May 1926, p. 17.
"Labour Day: Carnival and Demonstration at Maesteg." *Glamorgan Advertiser*, 7 May 1926, p. 5.
Mackenzie, Compton. "Good Singing." *The Gramophone* 1, no. 1 (1923): 9.
Mackenzie, Compton, "Gramophone Celebrities IV: Enrico Caruso." *The Gramophone* 2, no. 1 (1924): 45–47.

"The Maesteg Carnival: A Picturesque Procession." *Glamorgan Advertiser*, 23 July 1926, p. 6.

"Malacca Notes." *Straits Times*, 13 April 1901, p. 8.

"Market Reviews." *Paint, Oil and Drug Review* 51, no. 22 (1883): 34.

Monroe, Al. "Swinging the News," *Chicago Defender*, 28 May 1949, p. 16.

"Moonlight Music," *Singapore Free Press and Mercantile Advertiser*, 17 May 1900, p. 11.

Murray, Edward L. "The Average Man's Choice of Records." *The Gramophone* 3, no. 10 (March 1926): 473–74.

"Music of the Jungle," *Talking Machine World*, 15 April 1907, p. 16.

"Nantyffyllon Lounge Society: Enjoyable Gramophone Concert." *Glamorgan Advertiser*, 30 November 1928, p. 7.

"Nantyffyllon." *Glamorgan Advertiser*, 1 Feb 1929, p. 5.

"Nantyffyllon." *Glamorgan Advertiser*, 29 March 1929, p. 5.

"Newtown Knights." *Merthyr Express*, 17 July 1926, p. 14.

"Police Add to Charges against Signor Caruso." *New York Times*, 18 November 1906, p. 1.

"Sale of Household Furniture." *Straits Times*, 11 June 1901, p. 2.

Scrutator (pseudonym). "Where Are the Ladies?" *The Gramophone* 3, no. 1 (June 1925): 39.

"Signor Caruso, Tenor, Arrest in the Zoo." *New York Times*, 17 November 1906, p. 1.

"Singapore Chinese Weekly Entertainment Club." *Straits Times*, 9 November 1908, p. 7.

"Smoker at Pulo Brani." *Straits Times*, 15 August 1903, p. 5.

"Some Record and Needle Wear Experiments (I) by Our Expert Committee," *The Gramophone* 5, no. 8 (1928): 317–21.

Stylus (pseudonym). "Gramophone Notes." *Glamorgan Advertiser*, 29 January 1926, p. 3.

Stylus (pseudonym). "Gramophone Notes." *Glamorgan Advertiser*, 20 April 1928, p. 2.

Stylus (pseudonym). "Gramophone Notes: Chamber Music For All." *Glamorgan Advertiser*, 10 May 1929, p. 7.

Stylus (pseudonym). "Gramophone Notes: The Complete 'Valkyrie.'" *Glamorgan Advertiser*, 17 February 1928, p. 2.

Stylus (pseudonym). "Gramophone Notes: Grieg's Piano Concerto." *Glamorgan Advertiser*, 8 July 1927, p. 3.

Suisman, David. "Welcome to the Monkey House: Enrico Caruso and the First Celebrity Trial of the Twentieth Century." *The Believer*, 1 June 2004, pp. 15–20.

T. A. F. "Ladies and the Gramophone." *The Gramophone* 3, no. 3 (August 1925): 147.

Terry, Francis E. "Women and the Gramophone." *The Gramophone* 3, no. 5 (October 1925): 247.

"Trade Conditions in Philadelphia." *Talking Machine World* (15 March 1907): 17.

"Tredegar Town Talk." *Merthyr Express*, 28 August 1926, p. 16.

"Troedyrhiw." *Merthyr Express*, 19 June 1926, p. 14.

Under the Needle (pseudonym). "Gramophone Notes." *Glamorgan Advertiser*, 23 January 1931, p. 3.

Wallace, Robert. "First It Said 'Mary': The Phonograph Is Celebrating Its 75th Year." *Life*, 17 November 1952, pp. 87–102.

WEBSITES

"The Borough of Stratford-upon-Avon: Historical Account." *British History Online*. Originally published by Victoria County History, London, 1945, in *A History of the County of Warwick: Volume 3, Barlichway Hundred*, edited by Philip Styles. https://www.british-history.ac.uk/vch/warks/vol3/pp234-244. Accessed 3 May 2023.

British Library Sound Archive. "From Phonoautographs to MP3s: A History of Recording Formats." https://www.bl.uk/history-of-recorded-sound/articles/timeline-of-formats. Accessed 19 Feb 2022.

Gaines, Jane, Radha Vatsal, and Monica Dall'Asta. Women Film Pioneers Project. https://doi.org/10.7916/d8-5za0-x430. Accessed 13 Feb 2020.

The Great 78 Project. https://great78.archive.org/. Accessed 27 March 2022.

Henry, Thomas. "Disquaires de Paris: 120 ans d'enregistrement sonore." http://disquairesdeparis.fr/. Accessed 10 July 2020.

"Jazz Bands of the South Wales Valleys." Amgeuddfa Cyn Cynon / Cynon Valley Museum, cynonvalleymuseum.wales/2021/02/10/jazz-bands-of-the-south-wales-valleys-1926/. Accessed 20 December 2021.

Russian Records. https://www.russian-records.com/. Accessed 27 March 2022.

Strötbaum, Hugo. *Recording Pioneers*. http://www.recordingpioneers.com. Accessed 27 July 2021.

Sutton, Allan. "The American Zonophone Discography II: The Roots and Early History of American Zonophone Records, 1898–1905." Discography of American Historical Recordings, University of California, Santa Barbara Library. adp.library.ucsb.edu/index.php/resources/detail/403. Accessed 18 July 2021.

ORAL HISTORIES

Abisheganaden, Paul. Interview by Chua Chee Huan at the Oral History Centre, Singapore, 9 March–5 Sept 1993. National Archives of Singapore, accession no. 001415.

Ali, Abu Bakar. Interview by Stella Ng at the Oral History Centre, Singapore, 22–29 May 1996. National Archives of Singapore, accession no. 001755.

Bong, Marie Ethel. Interview by Chua Chee Huan at Marie Bong's residence, 1 December 1992. National Archives of Singapore, accession no. 001390.

Hiorns, Douglas. Multiple interviewers and locations. National Archives of Singapore, accession no. 000799.

Kaw, Tan Ngiang. Interview by Loke Tai Tay, 2005. National Archives of Singapore, accession no. 002937.

Oh Choo Neo, Patricia. Interview by Bonny Tan at the Oral History Center, 9 May 1995. National Archives of Singapore, accession no. 001631.

Said, Zubir bin. Interview by Liana Tan, 1984; transcribed 1987. Special project, Oral History Department, National Archives of Singapore.

Tan Tong Seng. Interview by Bonny Tan at the Oral History Centre, Singapore, 2004. National Archives of Singapore, accession no. 002826.

Teong Ah Chin, Interview by Ang Siew Ghim, 1985. National Archives of Singapore, accession no. 000536.

Index